Winifred Brown

Britain's Adventure Girl No.1

Geoff Meggitt

Pitchpole Books

Published 2013 by Pitchpole Books
Cheshire, England
pitchpole.co.uk

ISBN: 978-0-9575549-0-0

To Joyce, for almost everything

ACKNOWLEDGEMENTS

My thanks go first to Tony Adams for his help throughout. We have spent many hours talking about his mother and their life together and he has been the source of most of the photographs reproduced here. I particularly thank him for access to the *Yellow Waters* manuscript. There are many others to thank too. Hilary Date, Ron Adams's daughter, was a source of many of the photographs and was, of course , the main source on Ron later in life. I am grateful for the time she spent searching out photographs and for the time she spent talking to me. She was also kind enough to put me in touch with Laurence Roberts and Eric Evans, two Anglesey residents with clear memories of Win; Eric sailed with her as a young man and is the Eric mentioned in *No Distress Signals*. I am grateful to both of them for an afternoon spent in happy reminiscence. Jean Farrar, Margery Walsh's daughter and Win's goddaughter, was an enormous help in tracking people down and digging out newspaper cuttings as well with her own recollections of Win. She was also a source of several photographs. My thanks also go to to Marjorie Cussons's daughter, Natalie Shrigley-Feigl, and Natalie's son Henry. Natalie was the source of several illuminating stories about Win and they were kind enough to search Marjorie Cussons's rich and well-organised archive for me. Roy Godfrey, *Perula*'s current owner, was kind enough to give me a tour of her as she lay on a slip at Rye in Sussex and kept me up-to-date with his restoration plans — with which I wish him well.

My thanks also to the people who read the book from cover to cover: Tony Adams, my daughter Ann Campbell and my wife Joyce. My grand-daughter Claire made numerous helpful comments which were much appreciated. Without their help, the book would have been a poorer thing.

Contents

SKETCH MAPS

King's Cup course 1930
The Amazon
The Irish Sea
The Menai Straits
UK, Norway and Svalbard
Svalbard and Bear Island

PHOTOGRAPHS

Win and friends 1915
With the Lancia Lambda, Torquay
Sawley Brown
Elsie Brown
North Manchester Ladies Hockey picnic
The Touring Team 1927. Marjorie Cussons on the left
Win and Sammy Brown in G-EBVZ 9 February 1928
Ron with the King's Cup and Win with the Siddeley Trophy
Ron in the canoe
Waiting for the fish
Perula launched at Dickies; Seaway in the background
Perula in Ålesund
Ron, Sverdrup and Win at Spitsbergen
Win and Dunny Walker
Win and Tony at Green Edge
Win in the mid-50s
Win with Edith Evans, Peggy Ashcroft and Michael Redgrave.
Ron in his garden at Menai Bridge
Win and Tony about 1980

The photographs,with a few exceptions, come from Tony Adams's private collection or are reproduced from Winifred's books with his permission. The one of the North Manchester hockey picnic is from Jean Farrar and that of the Australian touring team from Marjorie Cusson's collection with permission of Natalie Shrigley-Feigl. Ron in the canoe and in his garden are reproduced with the permission of Hilary Date. The photograph of G-EBVZ comes from the Avro Heritage Centre collection and is reproduced with their permission. For some of the photographs from the private collections it has not been possible, even after reasonable research, to establish conclusively who owns the copyright. If there are errors then the Publishers will be pleased to correct matters for future printings.

PREFACE

This book originated in the chance discovery that the first female member of my sailing club, the Manchester Cruising Association, was someone called Winifred Brown, the daughter of the Commodore at the time, Sawley Brown. She had been made an Honorary Member in 1933.

Perhaps scenting nepotism, perhaps just intrigued, I searched the internet for Winifred and found a short note, written by someone from Salford Library, that said she had won the King's Cup for flying in 1930. I then found she had written a book and then that she had written two more. This was beginning to sound interesting so I bought one of the books, *Duffers on the Deep*, and read it. Something about its direct and honest prose led me to go back to the Salford reference, produced by Salford Library, where I noticed acknowledgement to someone called Tony Adams. A phone call to the Library revealed that he was Winifred's son, but that they knew no more about him. However, I quickly found that a Winifred Adams gave birth to Anthony Sawley Adams on Anglesey in 1940.

I had been working for about a year on a biography of an American scientist but, by now, I was becoming very interested in Winifred; there seemed to be no existing biography. Perhaps I should write one.

There were several Tony Adams's thrown up in internet searches but only one of them had "S" as a second initial — maybe it stood for "Sawley"? He was an actor with a long string of past roles including, most notably, in the TV soap *Crossroads*. I eventually found the name of his agents and sent them a hopeful email. The very next day I had a reply from Tony in his joyous giant purple font and I telephoned him on the day after his 70th birthday. It was the beginning of an interesting, fruitful, enjoyable and entertaining series of meetings, emails and long telephone conversations. He generously lent me *Perula's* logbooks, endless photographs and the unpublished manuscript of Win's Amazon adventure. At some point Dr Muller, the American scientist, was put in a drawer for a while.

The information about Win's life up to about 1950 comes from her three books[1], the Amazon manuscript and newspaper articles about her activities.

The account of what happened after that is based almost entirely on Tony's memories supplemented with my own research. I have checked Tony's recollections where I could and found them to be remarkably accurate.

Geoff Meggitt
Lymm
January 2013

THE YOUNG WIN

Winifred Brown was born on 26 November 1899 at "The Hollies", Harboro (or Harborough) Road in Sale, Greater Manchester. Her parents had married earlier that year; Sawley had been selected by Elsie Rowlinson and lured to matrimony by this strong-willed young woman with help from a rice pudding at a church bazaar. They settled in a large house in this well-off suburb on the southern fringe of the city.

That year had been one of change. Sawley's father, James Sawley Brown, was a butcher, like his father, Richard Brown, before him. His business, James S Brown and Sons, was successful with several shops around Manchester and Salford and a farm at Broughton Road near the Manchester Racecourse, all run from the premises in Cateaton Street near the Cathedral. James had other business interests too: he was, for example, a director of the Manchester Real Ice Skating and Supply Company. In June 1899 he died at Riversdale, 17 Edge Lane, Chorlton-cum-Hardy in the same road where Elsie's parents lived. He left £28,668 6s 8d (worth nearly £2M today) in his will, to be divided between his wife Ann, Sawley and Sawley's two sisters Minnie and Amy. There is here a mystery because there were several other siblings who were not mentioned in the will: Margaret, Richard, Wallace, William, and Harvey. The most significant absence was Sawley's elder brother Richard because he was with the business when Elsie gave birth to Win. Indeed he arranged for a horoscope to be cast for the unborn child by the Hull astrologer and psychic Richard Bland. The horoscope promised, among much else:

> Disposition: She will be somewhat self-willed, strong-minded, self-opinionated, given to rule, to command, disliking too much restraint, not liking to quarrel, but if she has to quarrel the other side will find they have a serious opponent.

> She will be kind of heart, sympathetic, disliking meanness, full of generosity, a jovial, gracious spirit.[1]

The horoscope was a generous gesture, although Sawley dismissed it as claptrap, and after the birth they went off together to celebrate at the Mitre Hotel, near Cateaton Street. But then Richard disappears from the record. Soon Sawley is running the business on his own. Richard, presumably disinherited, may have decided to go off and find his fortune elsewhere. It is tempting to think that he may have been the Richard Brown who sailed from Liverpool to New York in 1900 — he was the right age.

But whatever the story, the business came to Sawley and the Browns lived in Sale for a few years. In that time Elsie lost a baby, the boy that Sawley always wanted. In compensation, Win always thought, he took up the new pastime of motoring. His car was the sixth registered in the Manchester area, as N 6. Often, in goggles and gloves, they would set off for "The Bells" at Peover, 25 kilometres south in the Cheshire countryside, for lunch. Sometimes they would go as far as Chester and, in 1904, Sawley took part in the Salford to Llandudno run.

Their neighbour in Harboro Road, George, was also a motoring enthusiast but, while he helped Sawley tinker with his car, through financial constraints he owned nothing more than a motor-bike. Keen to attract young ladies in those times before a young woman could just jump on a pillion, they decided to build a decorous trailer for George's bike. This they did but on the return from the test run to "The Bells", with Sawley as the guinea pig in the trailer, George was surprised to find the trailer and Sawley were no longer attached. It was mid-night (the celebrations of the trailer at the pub had been prolonged) but the trailer was found empty in a ditch and Sawley was eventually recovered, bruised, from a nearby doctor's house where stitches had been inserted for some nasty cuts. Elsie decided that George was a poor influence and this was confirmed when one of George's discarded cigarettes set fire to the car while they were tinkering with it, destroying it and the garage. Elsie decided it was time to separate them.

Some time around 1905 they moved to "Claremont", at Scholes Lane in Prestwich, just off Bury New Road. It placed the city between Sawley and George and was anyway more convenient for the farm and the office. Here Win, now aged five, attended Mrs Georgina Bland's school for ladies just across the main road at The Tower, 231 Bury New Road, now a bank. Then (we cannot be sure quite when) they moved, not too far, to Waterpark Road, Broughton.

BROUGHTON

Waterpark Road is today a rather lived-in road with cars parked on either side, recycling bins on display, tree-lined still but rather narrow. It is now home to an Orthodox Jewish community and almost every man on the streets wears their characteristic hats, black clothes and ringlets. The houses look care-worn. Some have strong bars on the windows and one has elaborate sliding security gates inside the windows and doors. The pleasures are inside rather than out on display.

In 1910, when the Browns moved here, it was quite different. Lower Broughton had been part of the Clowes family estate until it was sold and it was already a mass of terraced housing, close to the factories around. Upper Broughton had been held back, reserved for superior dwellings for a better class of person, close to Broughton Hall, the family residence. There were some mansions already dotted around but, by about 1900, houses for professionals and successful trades people were being built. It was an aspirational new development with the recently-electrified tram line down the Bury New Road providing an excellent link into the heart of Manchester.

Waterpark Road was being developed from the long drive that swept from Broom Lane between entrance posts, past the Lodge on the left, up through parkland to the Hall. Through the trees to the left there was a large lake with a boathouse. By 1910 there were a dozen houses on the east side with views across the lake ("Holmleigh", "Spurstow", "Norton House", "Violea") but Sawley bought the house on the corner with Broom Lane, a substantial semi-detached; it was called "Corner House". Waterpark Road was still un-made.

Winifred, now ten years old, was enrolled at Broughton and Crumpsall High School for Girls on the corner of Broom Lane and Bury New Road, perhaps better known as "Bella Vista" after the large house it occupied. Set up as a limited company, it was originally "managed by a Council (consisting of parents and others) elected by the Shareholders and by an Educational Committee."[2] However, by the time Winifred arrived it was run by a trust with governors from the the local authorities, the University and parents. It was presided over by Miss Edith Mary Clarke — who lived on the premises — and there were eight Assistant Mistresses and eight Visiting Mistresses. It was just a short walk of about 200 metres from "Corner House" and may well have been the reason they moved from Prestwich — the persistent middle-class desire to be close to a good school.

> On the first day of term Winifred was dressed with care in her new uniform, a navy gym tunic and white blouse. The cricket cap (after a scene) had been replaced by a woollen 'pork pie' cap with the school badge, but the boy's boots had been stuck to. She looked like a sack of flour with a rope tied round the middle, for after being painfully thin in early childhood, she now weighed ten stone [64 kilograms] at the age of ten.[3]

Upset because Jean, the girl detailed to take her to school on her first day, had made off after taking one look at her, she was escorted by Elsie and "was promptly sick, in the middle of prayers and all over the hymn-book and polished floor."

Elsie blamed nerves and Miss Laurie, Win's form mistress, "hurried Winifred out and, having laid the child on a settee, produced a clean handkerchief liberally sprinkled with eau-de-cologne."[4]

In the months that followed Winifred walked up and down Broom Lane with Elsie or the maid. Sometimes she no doubt walked on her own, kicking at stones and scuffing her shoes, as she made her way home. Miss Laurie seems to have been an inspiration because at the first Speech Day, with all the girls sat in their white dresses and blue-and-yellow sashes, Miss Clarke announced that Winifred had won the prize for progress and good conduct: a book titled *The Child's Book of Saints*. It was the pinnacle of Win's school career; she was the naughtiest girl in the school after that.

In these school years, she focused on extra-curricular activities of which the first was as President of the Swearers' and Smokers' Club which met in a disused potting shed in the grounds of Broughton Hall. Win was elected President because she could swear and blow smoke rings. Other members fitted into a strict hierarchy with, at the bottom, those who could hardly suck a cigarette then those who could actually smoke without being sick up to those who could blow smoke down their nose and, at the pinnacle, Win who could make rings. She stole the cigarettes from her father but confessed after the maid was accused of the theft and Sawley then, in a move at first caring but then bizarre, provided her with a bag of cigarettes "pink ones with scarlet tips, blue ones, green, yellow and brown, and most of them were scented." They were supposed to put the smoker off for life but Win enjoyed them and smoked them all with relish. Sawley returned to the tobacconist not to complain but, to the man's astonishment, to order more for her. He seemed pleased with his daughter's achievement.

It was soon after this, perhaps in 1912, that Elsie took a seaside house in Kensington Road, a then-untamed spot between St Anne's and Blackpool with sand drifting into the garden. A wind from the east brought a stink from the nearby gas works; one from the west more sand. Elsie may have wanted to get Win away from Sawley — he didn't have a car at the time — but Sawley bought a large and powerful dark red "Indian" motor-bike (probably the twin-cylinder model manufactured in Springfield, Massachusetts, USA by the Hendee Manufacturing Company and a descendent of the model that held the world speed record for a while) and came to the seaside. He wore "breeches, leather leggings, a dust coat. His cap and goggles were pulled down, revealing little of his face save his Jimmy Edwards moustache."[5] Deciding to take the dunes in Kensington Road at speed, he careered along, legs flying, until he crashed at Elsie's feet. Proudly he pulled out a gold pocket-watch and announced that he had covered the 70 kilometres in 2½ hours.

The achievement, the entrance and perhaps Sawley's gallant appearance (it could a few years hence have been described as that of a World War One air ace) seems to have marked an upturn in the rather fractured relationship with Elsie and Sawley was welcomed once more to the marital bed. It was a brief return. The following day the family set off to the beach with Elsie's golf clubs for a little practice. This seemed to go well with Sawley teeing the balls and Winifred retrieving them but Sawley soon had an idea. He would take a club and knock the balls back directly to Elsie, saving Winifred a lot of scurrying around. It sounds simple and sensible enough but Elsie pointed out, in a light-hearted way, a difficulty at the heart of the scheme: Sawley had never hit a golf ball in his life. His first attempt was an air shot — he missed the ball completely — but the second was much better, much much better. Too good in fact. The impeccable contact with the ball sent it rocketing back towards Elsie to strike her on the nose. She fell bludgeoned to the sands, gushing blood.

Sawley threw Elsie over his shoulder (Elsie's weight remains a mystery) and started up the beach. Winifred followed as far as a bar of pebbles and then, having lost her shoes and with the stones hurting her feet, sat down and screamed. Sawley's encouragement and threats would not move her so he threw her over his other shoulder and took them home. This is essentially Winifred's account of the events but, with a retrospective eye, the early part seems plausible but the idea that Sawley could walk with two females (and Winifred we are told weighing 70 kilograms at the time) thrown over his shoulders seems some sort of heroic concoction. And then there is the question of the golf clubs. Did Sawley carry them too?

It was not just Elsie's nose that was damaged. That anyway recovered in just a few days (although it may never have been quite the same again). Elsie seemed to be more hurt by the effect the event — and Sawley's handling of it — had on Win. Marital favours were withdrawn once more although Sawley may not have been too concerned about this for a while as he recovered from humping 130 kilograms or more across the Blackpool sands and through the Kensington Road dunes.

It was after this episode that Sawley went to Fleetwood and bought his first yacht which he named *Elwin* after his daughter and, in hope presumably, his wife. She was a 14 ton auxiliary cruiser with length overall of 13 metres and beam 3.5 metres with a 15 horsepower 3-cylinder Gardiner engine[6] and had been built by Neakle and Watterson at Peel on the Isle of Man and was launched by Ada Kaigin on 13 May 1912. Having the boat named after Elsie seems to have won a response from her and marked another upturn in their relationship. *Elwin* was to be based at Fleetwood.

One of these sunnier periods in the relationship between Sawley and Elsie led to Elsie becoming pregnant again. It is difficult to be sure when this was. Win tells us that the St Anne's house was disposed of before World War One It could have been as early as 1910 (intriguingly there was a sick nurse at "Corner House" on the April night of the 1911 census) but it is more likely to have been between 1912 and 1914.[7] Winifred's account is simply not clear on the date. Elsie was 40 years old in 1912; Sawley four years younger.

Whenever it was, Winifred was taken off to St Anne's by her Auntie Madge Rowlinson while Elsie remained at home; it was their first separation. Winifred was already distressed by the alarming and mysterious bulge that Elsie had developed and being wrenched away from her mother simply added to the misery. No doubt Auntie Madge suffered for the misery but Winifred developed new interests at the seaside. First she became an assistant (unpaid) donkey boy on the beach and then she bought Johnson. Johnson was a damaged white rat bought for ninepence in Blackpool. He had a broken tail (hence the good price), pink eyes and, according to

Winifred, a malevolent gaze directed at Madge. Johnson followed Win around and took refuge in her clothes when tired. He appeared from time to time perched on her head and usually slept with her. Johnson later turned out to be a lady rat but she remained Winifred's confidante through the next troubled period before simply disappearing from the narrative.

A telegram came warning of Elsie's arrival but before she came Win managed to have her upper lip torn apart by a startled terrier and to be struck on the nose and forehead by a brick thrown by the boy who had startled the terrier. She thus met her mother bandaged and plastered with a black eye.

Elsie took so little interest in her daughter's injuries that it was clear to everyone that she was not well. Win was taken to stay with a lady living across the road who comforted her with an explanation for Elsie's alarming bulge. It was, it seemed, down to the stork and involved a cabbage patch. Winifred could expect a present: a little brother or sister in the form of something that Win had no liking for at all — a baby.

Sadly the baby didn't arrive. Quite what happened is not clear

In her account of the episode in *Under Six Planets* Win quotes a conversation between Madge and the nurse that she overheard during Elsie's long convalescence.

> "I'm afraid she'll never get over it, nurse."
>
> "Can you blame her, Miss Rowlinson?" Nurse's voice was hard and stern.
>
> "No-no one can blame her and yet—even though I am her sister I cannot help feeling pity for him."
>
> "It is more than I do!"
>
> "Yes, but—well, I saw it all happening, nurse. Her one thought was Winifred—she never had time for him and it drove him else- where."
>
> "He could have been more careful in his choice!"
>
> "Maybe, but might not that be the inexperience of a decent man? He has certainly paid for his folly."

> "He has paid! What about her—poor innocent dear that she is — can you expect her to forget what happened ?"[8]

The oblique conversation hardly helps us understand what happened. We could conclude that the loss of the baby, the result of rare intimacy between Elsie and Sawley, was through miscarriage or stillbirth as a consequence of some trauma when Elsie discovered that Sawley had been unfaithful to her — with someone apparently considered unsuitable. There is also the possibility that the baby was born with something seriously wrong with it and was allowed to die. Sawley could have been blamed for that.

Win was puzzled when she heard the nurse say she thought "it was better dead". Mulling it over later with Johnson (in the rodent's farewell performance in *Under Six Planets*) she suddenly realised that the woman was referring to the stork. Elsie had killed it.

Elsie and Winifred spent several months at the seaside before returning to Sawley and, according to the account in *Under Six Planets*, a new four bedroom detached house in Waterpark Road: "Lodore", number 44.

Presumably Elsie or Sawley chose the name (which is still carved on the gateposts). It was probably picked to recall Lodore Falls, a picturesque waterfall at Derwentwater in the English Lake District, which perhaps had some special significance for them. One could hope that it was named after the novel *Lodore* written by Mary Shelley in which story two heroines have to sort out the mess left to them by Lord Lodore after his death. But that would have implied extraordinary foresight given what was to happen after Sawley's death. There is some doubt about when it was bought. If the *Under Six Planets* account is correct and they returned from St Anne's to Lodore, then they moved there just before World War One but Kelly's Directory has Sawley at the Corner House until 1920 and the Manchester Cruising Association Handbook has him there in 1918. Perhaps Win was wrong that they did go there more or less directly after the loss of the baby. Maybe she was right and Sawley kept the Corner House as a refuge.

WINIFRED BROWN

It was further up Waterpark Road on the right and Sawley had bought some extra land behind, where a hard tennis court was built. With his usual enthusiasm, he also purchased another plot on the other side of the road for a grass court. Win's reunion with Papa did not go well. It seemed to be by appointment and Sawley arrived early. When Win rushed to meet him Elsie shouted at him not to touch her. Sawley's present of an air gun horrified Elsie who ripped it from Winifred's hands. Relations did not improve as a result and Sawley was banished to the back bedroom[9] Winifred, after a sleep-walking accident, was given the master bedroom.

EXPULSION

Sometime after this Winifred fell in love with Clarence, the projectionist at the local cinema in Broughton. It was a painful experience with Winifred 14 years old and conscious of her weight (which approached 95 kilograms) and general appearance. She started to grow her hair from the boyish cut she had sported for several years but seems to have stuck to her pork pie hat. Clarence, with oiled and perfumed hair, patent leather shoes and a waisted jacket, toyed with her, flirting with other girls while all Win could do was fantasise on the basis of the flickering images she saw so often in his cinema. The best it ever got was Clarence allowing her to crank his projector while she burned with a miserable and unrequited passion.

However, the passion was to have a lasting effect on Winifred's life. One day in the Latin class she so loved Miss Edith Mary Clarke decided to cover the Latin verb "to love": *amo, amas, amat* etc. Winifred, instructed to write it in her exercise book, covered a whole page with the phrase "Amo Clarentius" unaware the Miss Clarke was now standing behind her. Miss Clarke's bellowed question "Who is Clarentius?" startled her so much that she sent her pencil case flying. Now Winifred had been warned about this before, being suspected of flinging her pencil case to the floor so she could crawl around recovering the contents and thereby disrupting the class. Miss Clarke had clearly been headmistressing long enough to distinguish malevolent pencil case dispersal from the accidental variety.

This final straw saw Winifred removed from the school, either expelled or taken away by Elsie with expulsion imminent. Elsie was outraged but we can suspect that there was more to it than a pencil case. Either Win's general behaviour had her thrown out or Miss Clarke was infuriated by the use of her beloved Latin in an inappropriate, amatory, way.

The expulsion seems to have led to a review of Win's developing character by the Rowlinsons and Auntie Madge in particular. Sawley was excluded from the process of review as being part of the problem rather than part of any possible solution . We can assemble a list of Win's deficiencies from *Under Six Planets*. Winifred: never said please and thank you; called her aunts and uncles by their first names; called Elsie "Nin"; called Sawley "Aussi" (the French for "also"); had once attacked Elsie with a carving knife while being squeezed into a corset; had a violent temper and smoked and drank. Much of it was put down to Sawley's influence.

Elsie's family had a great influence in what happened next and they decided that boarding school would be a remedy, getting Winifred away from Sawley and injecting some discipline into her life. In spite of Winifred's protests, it was arranged that she would go to a convent in Switzerland in the autumn of 1914 so July was spent buying the clothing she would need. As a farewell treat Elsie took her to the Norbreck Hall Hydro north of Blackpool. The Hydro was later a castellated 260 bedroom resort hotel for the comfortably-off with a 500 metre sea frontage, twenty or more tennis courts, an 18-hole golf course, indoor swimming pool, solarium, ballroom and cinema, all decorated in the Art Deco style. However, in 1914 it was a smaller, more modest, place based on the original villa that stood on the site but even then it was intended for the well-heeled, with tennis and golf. Well away from the corrupting temptations of Blackpool — for at 14 Winifred's tastes had become more advanced than nine-penny rats — it was also unlicensed. Winifred must surely have joined in some of the more strenuous activities but all she records is dancing with the hotel manager who kindly explained that fat girls always danced well. She seems to have bought drink from an off-licence in a side street and smuggled it into the Hydro.

While they were there Elsie took Winifred and some friends for a sail from Fleetwood in Sawley's boat with its paid skipper, something she did quite often. They sailed round to Glasson Dock, a 15 or so mile trip. On arrival they were greeted by a man with a gun who demanded their papers: it was 4 August 1914 and war had broken out. It must have seemed unlikely that a 13 metre boat with a few middle class English people on board posed too much of a threat to the United Kingdom so the man put his weapon away (Win says it was a muzzle-loader) and they were admitted to the Dock. It meant that Switzerland for Winifred was off.

Sawley was put in charge of meat distribution for the north west of England at the beginning of the war . Winifred with a girl friend took some delight in teasing soldiers, enticing them to quiet grassy spots where the soldiers did "queer things which she didn't like" to this plump young woman. This seems not to have gone too far — or no doubt from the soldier's viewpoint far enough — but the activity upset Elsie sufficiently for her to take a country cottage in Thornton, near Blackpool, well away from soldiers.

A series of photographs shows Winifred and some friends at Thornton about this time (they are marked 1914). Winifred is plump and buttoned tightly into a warm coat, her long wild hair cascading from beneath what must be her pork pie hat. The party look well-wrapped up. Doris Whittle (an Ella Doris Whittle is living in Fylde in 1911 and was the same age as Win), Frank Galley and Harry Errington are named and may be the boys in one of the snaps rowing Win on a boating lake. Others have nicknames: "the Chadwick child" and "mouldy Millicent". Some are just forenames: a Dorothy and an Elsie appear in several snaps and one is taken by someone called Vi.

Thornton was well away from servicemen but then (it may have been a year or two later) Win took up briefly with a professional footballer playing for Blackpool. One day she took him into town in a horse and trap. The horse proved difficult to control and they eventually collided with a tram. Win, feisty and keen to impress her passenger, had an obscene exchange with the tram driver, accusing him of scaring the horse with his bell. When a policeman intervened the professional footballer, clearly recognising that he had bitten off rather more than he could chew, made off while Win was distracted and was never seen again.

DRAWING AND PAINTING

A return to Broughton followed and it was decided that, to keep Winifred out of trouble, she should attend drawing and painting classes with Miss Elizabeth Orme Colles in Blackfriars, Manchester. It was an activity Win had always enjoyed, although hardly one might think much of a distraction from soldiers and soccer players. Nonetheless it was tried.

Miss Colles, a well-known local artist in her mid-forties who had studied under Sir Hubert von Herkome RA and was a member of a group known as The Society of Modern Painters, had been advertising life classes ("Drawing and painting from life") in the *Manchester Guardian* for some years. At first her studio was in Upper Broughton (so she may have been well-known to Elsie) but by the beginning of the war she had moved to Orme Buildings, Parsonage on Blackfriars. It was to there Winifred made her way in the mornings, travelling alone on the tram down Bury New Road. The subjects were initially still lifes and exercises in perspective but later a real living model was introduced — Mrs R. Mrs R, no oil painting according to Win, was always primly dressed and decorated with the odd scrap of fabric arranged around her shoulders.

Soon it was time to move on to life drawing and for this the class of seven or eight men and women assembled in the evening and paid a supplement of two and sixpence for the model and refreshments. Mrs R was there in a blue kimono which was removed to leave her standing there completely naked. Win was shocked that Mrs R was exposing herself to men for just five shillings an evening — around £10 in today's money.[10] When Win came to see how Mrs R's family lived what made the biggest impression was that they ate from the table with no crockery or cutlery but she saw a nobility in Mrs R's sacrifice. Mrs R, of course, may just have thought it was an easy way to make some cash, better than doing Elsie's scrubbing for example.

Winifred seems to have shown some talent. She later told a newspaper that she had exhibited two portraits in 1916. One was displayed in the Manchester Art Gallery and the other in the Walker Art Gallery in Liverpool.[11]

Elsie, presumably having deflected Winifred from her war work with soldiers, decided she should be doing some kind of patriotic activity herself. So, perhaps moved by Winifred's experience with Mrs R's family, she started a soup kitchen with bones and scrag ends of meat supplied by Sawley. He, as usual, rather overdid things and sent four cartloads of bones to Lodore. Elsie, with her usual spirit (and fury at Sawley) boiled up the bones and made a large quantity of soup ready for the poor who would have seen her advert in the evening paper. Only two people turned up in Waterpark Road for the free soup and they, profoundly ungrateful, demanded their tram fares home as well. The Browns therefore ate the soup themselves and the gardener buried the bones. A second attempt at good works foundered too. The family of Belgian refugees Elsie took in were too sullen or too flamboyant for her tastes. She may have coped with this but one day the Belgian lady made a stew with the Brown's ginger tom and the family was kicked out to live in a guest-house at Sawley's expense. No doubt in Elsie's mind it was all his fault anyway.

Winifred's war work was more successful. Prompted by a cleric she met at the tram stop, who encouraged her to see Florence Nightingale rather than Miss Colles as her role model, she took classes in first aid and home nursing in a local church school and set out to become an Angel of Mercy. Passing the exams with flying colours by the simple expedient of answering all questions with the phrase "Treat for shock and call the doctor", she was posted to nearby Sedgley Hall Auxiliary Hospital as a VAD. The British Red Cross

Society had linked up just before the war with the order of St John of Jerusalem and formed the organisation known as the Voluntary Aid Detachment. The Auxiliary Nurses they trained were often called VADs and were drawn largely from the middle and upper classes.

SEDGLEY HALL

The Hall was just a kilometre north of Waterpark Road. On her first day, in 1917, Winifred found herself washing and drying bandages for re-use and sterilising instruments under the supervision of Sister Riley. It started badly when she fainted while watching a doctor probe a leg wound but she was soon replacing dressings, treating festering wounds in the process.

Sex raised its head from time to time. One particular patient pestered her, blocking her path with his wheelchair, so she gave him cigarettes to stop. When, after he was discharged, a mother and daughter turned up to accuse him of getting the sixteen year-old daughter pregnant, Winifred showed that she had progressed from the stork and cabbage patch model of conception. She now believed baby's were caused by the act of marriage itself and described the girl to Sister Riley as the ex-patient's wife. Finding he didn't have a wife she moved on to her third theory of procreation: it was all to do with kissing.

Something closer to the truth struck her shortly after. While tidying beds in a room with just one patient in it, the rest being in the garden, he suddenly leapt upon her, forced her onto an empty bed with his hand across her mouth and started writhing about on top of her, panting heavily. She bit his hand and screamed, bringing an orderly to drag him off. Winifred was very upset because she though he was trying to kill her but Sister Riley remarked that it wasn't her life that was in danger. Pondering on this Winifred suddenly realised, at least according to the account in *Under Six Planets*, that humans did what she knew animals did and it was horrible. At 17 years of age a penny had dropped.

WINIFRED BROWN

The announcement of the Armistice on 11 November 1918 found Winifred asleep but she was soon in Manchester enjoying the celebrations; her shift that night was spent putting drunken patients to bed. The hospital wound down, discharging patients over the next few months, with sadly the last patient, Gunner Henry Knight of the Royal Field Artillery, dying on 13 March 1919, the only death of her nursing career. Nursing had been perhaps her first real acknowledged success in life.

NEW LOVES

HUBERT

She met Hubert (she says she picked him up) at the Globe Cinema while the war was on. A little on the small side, he was a corporal in a regimental band where he played the trombone. She promptly took him round to Lodore and introduced him to the folks. Elsie was surprised but Sawley was quite stunned by his beloved daughter turning up with a lower ranker. Unaccountably Winifred lobbed a cushion at him and he, inexplicably, lobbed a steak-and-kidney pie back at her. An argument (how could it get worse?) ensued which ended with Sawley emptying a bottle of lime-juice cordial over her head. Hubert managed to avoid the worst of it by hiding behind the furniture and surprisingly agreed to meet Winifred again.[1] She asked him to bring his trombone next time and they had a relationship based on his status as an army musician and his virtuosity on the instrument. It was a relationship that survived his posting towards the end of the war to Rhyl in North Wales which Sawley, with the disdain of someone engaged in vital and possibly dangerous work in meat distribution in the Northwest of England, thought something of a disgrace.

When he was demobbed Hubert returned to Manchester and bought Winifred a rather disappointing ring which she wore in secret as part of their secret engagement. Hubert fairly quickly engaged her in the animal act that she had thought so horrible not so long ago. He explained that pre-empting marriage in this way was quite normal among poorer folk who regarded the church service as a mere formality. She "thought little of the proceedings" but was pleased for the Trombone Player.

Things, we can now see, began to sour when Hubert started talking about babies. One of Winifred's passages in *Under Six Planets* coming from this period deserves record:

> Hubert was getting annoyed now. "I mean our souls would be one — our minds and bodies joined together — oh dash it! You're not listening — don't believe you love me."
>
> "Oh, but I do, Hubert, I do. I'll always love you — you said so yourself."[2]

She painted pictures of children and even of Hubert in the pierrot costume he had worn to the fancy-dress Victory Ball in February at the Free Trade Hall (Win had gone as an Egyptian princess). She exhibited some in the Spring Exhibition at Manchester Art Gallery. Hubert was unemployed at the time and looked mournful in the fancy outfit with its ruffle and dunce's cap.

Win had pressed Hubert to let her meet his mother who lived in a tiny house in a cobbled Manchester back-street. They dined off the working-class luxury goods of the time (and much later): tinned salmon and tinned fruit. Win sat in silence afterwards; Hubert cried at the void between this and Waterpark Road.

Hubert (we have no idea who he was) may have been horribly aware of the social gulf between but he didn't lack chutzpah so when the tennis club needed money he offered to organise a Grand Fete to raise some. The outdoor aspects of this must have organised themselves because Hubert spent all his time organising the entertainment in the marquee. He quickly had a line-up in mind: singers, a turn on the trombone from himself, Win's friend Marjorie on the flute and a recitation of "The Green Eye of the Little Yellow God" from Freddie "Microbe", a friend from Prestwich days. It would be rounded off by a rendition of "The Road to Mandalay" by Mr Rudd, an older, tall and dark baritone who "always smelled of a pipe."

The rehearsals were a nightmare with the expected arguments over the costumes and programme and a scramble over the refreshments Elsie had laid on. Win's mind was anyway elsewhere much of the time because she had developed a crush on Mr Rudd.

The concert itself went well with Winifred delighted to be seated on Mr Rudd's knee for the opening ensemble piece "Whispering" and with the noticeably unnecessary extra squeeze he gave her. By now Hubert had resigned as organiser in the face of Freddie Microbe's taunts about his accent, but the sound work he had put in carried the troupe through the concert and the Tennis Club funds leapt by £100. Indeed, so good was the show that the Vicar invited them to repeat it in the Church Hall at Christmas.

Hubert returned, presumably triumphant, to manage this but somehow it didn't quite match up to the previous performance and the audience seemed quiet, a little restrained. However, Hubert had planned and rehearsed a sensational, surprise final turn.

The lights dimmed and, to "snaky" music, Winifred writhed onto the stage dressed in her Victory Ball outfit: the Egyptian princess in powder blue pantaloons, blue bodice and veil. After a full ration of this, a man appeared in little more than a loincloth, chocolate brown with a turban, pointy slippers and whiskers. It was Hubert minus his trombone.

Hubert danced about for a while in what later became known as the Egyptian sand dance (although he lacked sand), his figure taking the shapes of bas-reliefs on tomb walls. The audience was already noticeably more interested in what was going on than had been the case earlier but there was more, much more, to come as the music soared to an Eastern crescendo. Suddenly Winifred leapt into the air and landed squarely on the back of Hubert's neck. He staggered from the impact (remember Win was a big girl) but managed to execute a few turns of a much-practised spin with Win spread-eagled on his shoulders before tripping over his pointy slippers and collapsing onto the stage. Winifred's loud and furious admonishment "You bloody fool!" seemed somehow to complete the piece but disturbed the Vicar who ordered the curtain lowered on the scene, the waves of roaring laughter suggesting that the audience had finally had their two-and-sixpence worth.

19

Embarrassing as this finale was, organising the concert was the making of Hubert because one of the cast was in fact the daughter of a prominent pickle manufacturer and he was offered a job in the factory. Earning money for the first time since the end of the war, Hubert threw himself into pickles and produced a jar whenever potential customers were in the offing. In his spare time he organised the work's band and the company's ladies' hockey team. He later deserted the work's team to organise the county one.

By now the relationship between Win and Hubert seems to have been accepted by her family. It survived her 21st birthday ball at Manchester's smart Midland Hotel. Win choose a striking contemporary ensemble for the occasion: an "embossed terracotta gown with its short skirt of the day edged by some nine inches of eider-duck" and a large rust-coloured ostrich-feather fan. It became a rather drunken affair hitting a low point when a merry Sawley fell over on the dance floor, dragging Win down with him. She lay for some time with her legs in the air, cackling with laughter to Hubert's clear disapproval. In fact, after this Win took to wearing the secret ring quite openly. Disappointingly and perhaps wisely Elsie quite ignored it while Sawley simply and characteristically remarked that it looked as if it had come out of a cracker. Winifred had really expected some kind of scene and the anti-climax made her more determined to marry the trombone player. He might be a rather dull tee-totaller and the ring might not be the full diamond but he was hers.

TENNIS

Winifred's sport had been hockey but as she was strolling one day up Deansgate in Manchester in 1921 she saw a notice in the window of a sports shop offering free tennis lessons to the most promising young player. The lean professional offering this, Bill, soon had his arms round her waist showing her how to improve her previously untutored strokes. Winifred was soon flushing with excitement at his closeness and his flattery. Bill broke the news that she wasn't that promising but suggested that free lessons might be possible anyway and Win proposed that they might use the courts at Lodore.

Winifred improved very quickly under his expert guidance but, like all Win's relationships, it was a turbulent process. After one particular spat over her forehand drive the narrative in *Under Six Planets* indicates a new direction: she came out of the bathroom after a post-practice bathe to find Bill outside and he apologised for being so brutal and "With a little sob she was into his arms." Win's thoughts quickly turned to love and marriage and they started going out to dine and drink (Hubert, briefly, is not mentioned). The *affaire*, as Winifred calls it, came to an end when Bill turned out to have a daughter of a similar age to Win — and a wife. However, the tuition continued.

This, now once more on a professional basis, was so successful that Win quickly improved, particularly her forehand drive, so she rose through the ranks and was soon playing for the Cheshire County second team. Bill decided that more experience was necessary so suggested to her that she might accompany him when he went to exhibition matches and play the odd doubles. They were very successful at this and often, both of them elated and tipsy, the car journey home would end with sex. Remorseful — there was Hubert and Bill's wife to consider — Win refused him after he stopped the car returning from some particularly drunken outing. Bill rather bluntly offered the "No sex, No teach" deal and the relationship ended. Bill's tennis career was over. When they met a few years later, he had taken to drink. He died soon after that. Some said he drank himself to death.

ERNEST

Tennis led to another relationship when Win, now aged 22, fled to the Norbreck Hydro to escape further encounters with Bill. As a favour to the manager (the one who who had danced with her and flattered her on earlier visits and now plied a ready bottle of gin as a softener), she agreed to partner Ernest. Ernest was small, not attractive and played mediocre tennis but was wealthy and, the manager pointed out, had a weak heart. A gift from heaven for many young women, he said.

They won their first match and Win found flowers delivered to her room and champagne at the dinner table. Afterwards there was a spin in a sleek Rolls coupé, a warm rug and chocolates. Later, as their success in the tournament continued, the trips in the Rolls became more intimate; we must deduce what we can from Win's statement that "he was clever in his love-making" always leaving her wanting more. Ernest invited her to play with him in Torquay and then Bournemouth. He said Elsie could come too; he would send one of his other cars to collect her. The other Rolls or perhaps the Bentley.

Although near-mesmerised by this prospect of opulence (and maybe the moreishness of Ernest's love-making), she seems to have remembered Hubert, her fiancé. She reminded Ernest that she was engaged but Ernest, no doubt scenting a lingering opportunity, asked what Hubert did. When Win told him that Hubert sold pickles and played the trombone, he must have thought his instinct right and asked to meet him. Since Win was collecting Hubert from Blackpool station for him to spend the weekend at Norbreck, Ernest's wish was granted the next day.

When the time to get Hubert approached she brought her car, a green Talbot-Darracq donated by Sawley, from the garage and parked it in front of the hotel while she had something to eat and met Ernest. Ernest didn't turn up so she set off to collect Hubert on her own only to find that the car, which had performed perfectly just minutes before, now refused to start. Although it was raining and she had her best frock on, she climbed out and was just opening the bonnet when Ernest sauntered up and offered to run her to Blackpool in the Rolls.

This he did very slowly so they were late meeting a furious Hubert, who became even more annoyed at the sight of this shrivelled plutocrat who was clearly pretty intimate with his beloved. Ernest insisted that Hubert and his luggage sat in the outside dicky seat in the rain so when they got back to Norbreck he was soaked to the skin. He found the story of the immobile Talbot-Darracq a little difficult to swallow and suspected he had been humiliated by Ernest who had set the whole thing up by tampering with Win's car as it stood out front (he was right about this). In the row that followed Win gave him back his ring. This had happened before but this time, when morning came, Hubert was gone. Fearing that he might commit suicide, Win was tempted to chase back to Manchester and save him but in the end decided to go to Torquay with Ernest instead.

Win never saw Hubert again. The relationship with Ernest seemed a bit troubled after that too. He was never quite as generous as he had been when they first met and began criticising her tennis. Worse still, he began to seem something of a wimp to her, unwilling to risk his weak heart. It came abruptly to an end when he remarked on Win's nice big hips, perfect for child-bearing, as he watched her emerge from the Irish Sea after an impromptu dip. Ernest took his dismissal well, with a shrug and a grin, perhaps thinking that the *affaire* had lasted longer than he had expected anyway.

Hubert went on to woo the daughter of the pickle factory owner in the hope of taking control of the business but was unsuccessful. Exiled to another branch of the company, he married someone else and, according to Win, had an orchestra of little Huberts. And presumably he still had his trombone too.

TIM AND RON

Winifred kept up her tennis and gave Ron Adams a lift to Southport in the new car, a Lancia Lambda, Sawley had bought for her. Ron played tennis for the Chorltonville club and for Lancashire but had been born in Inverness. His father was a principal clerk in the Customs and Excise Department according to the 1911 census, when the family lived in Chorlton-cum-Hardy, a suburb of Manchester. Ron may have tried to follow in the family trade but failed the Civil Service exams and, when he and Win met, he was struggling in a small partnership his father had bought him into. A few years later, when he became well-known by association with Win, he was described as an insurance broker and this was what appeared in his passport. It may be that the partnership thrived. Whatever, the job allowed him plenty of time off for adventures.

According to Win, Ron was lazy as a tennis player and never reached his potential. He must have been good though because there were rumours that he had come close to beating Fred Perry, unaware that he was playing one of the greats. Someone warned him and he was able to ease off and lose, an act of generosity (and maybe self-effacement) that hinted at things to come.

Win liked him enough to start trying to impress him. When they arrived at Southport and found that the match had been called off because of rain, Win suggested a swim in the open-air baths as an alternative. Ron preferred the Palais de Danse, somewhere warm in- doors and dry, but before any negotiations could get going between them to resolve the matter, Tim, "a clean-cut Englishman with a fresh complexion and fair hair" turned up and offered to go swim- ming with Win. Now of course Tim may not have been Tim (in- deed there is a photograph of a young man called Tom who fits the description) but, whoever he was, he was a good swimmer and greatly impressed Win. They found they were both members of Manchester Swimming Club and arranged to meet there.

She drove Ron home and was thrilled when he suggested they go to the theatre. The Friday evening outing was a success and they met again on subsequent Friday nights. Ron was good company but a serious man and short of cash (which was why they met only on Fridays). At the same time she was seeing Tim, the swimmer, who seemed more fun. Unable to choose between them, she seems to have decided to give herself to Tim to decide the matter. However, although she managed to persuade him to spend the night in his car on the sands at Southport, he rejected her suggestion that they spend it on the same seat and made her sleep alone in the back. After a freezing night, a rather bad-tempered exchange about Ron ended in Tim proposing marriage to her. Win postponed an answer and met Ron the following day but found herself unable to break the news. Instead, she decided to spend the night with him too. It would somehow help her decide.

So, sometime in 1925 and with Tim waiting for an answer, Ron was taken on a trip to a Derbyshire hockey match. On the way back and in spite of Ron's reservations, they spent the night in a dingy room at a remote hotel with a suspicious proprietor. It was another cold and disappointing night spent with a reluctant man. The "wedding ring" Win had brought, being thorough as well as enthusiastic, turned green overnight. They left cold, tired and with Ron soaking wet; Win had poured a jug of cold water over him because she thought he was dying when he was really just sobbing into a pillow. On the way home they went to see one of Ron's friends, a flying instructor. At this point Tim suddenly disappears from the narrative of *Under Six Planets* and presumably from her life. From now on Ron was shared with a new love.

Ron had already mentioned his interest in flying and indeed his preference for stunting over rather tediously flying in a straight line. Win had some experience of flying too — she had had (with her eyes tightly shut much of the time) a £5 joyride around Blackpool Tower with Paul Moxon when she was nineteen — but not of stunting.

FLYING START

The Lancashire Aero Club started, like so many good things, in a garage. In this case John Leeming's garage in Hale, Cheshire. Leeming had been an enthusiast for aviation since before the war and made model gliders — without it seems much success in flying them. In 1922, perhaps inspired by stories of German glider pilots, he approached Avro, the Manchester aircraft maker, and acquired enough spare parts to make a full-size glider himself. This, with the aid of a few friends, he did, first in his garage and later in the greenhouse. Within the year the enthusiasts grew to ten and the Lancashire Aero Club was founded. The glider was moved to the aerodrome at Alexandra Park in South Manchester in 1923 where it became airborne being towed by a car at the end of a long rope. There were various problems to overcome: the tow-rope broke, the glider's wheels came off and it frequently pitched forwards, scrunching alarmingly into the ground. A persistent challenge was posed by the long grass of the aerodrome which became wrapped around the wheels of "Bold Alfred", the tow car, slowing it to below the speed needed for take-off. The first proper gliding flight was made in 1924 when the glider flew about one hundred metres at a height of some two metres with, presumably, Leeming in it. Modest enough maybe but the LAC now had a plane.

It was a good year to fly because the Government, pressed by the newspapers to do something about this exciting and strategic new industry, had just decided to push civilian flying. The first part of their plan, announced in August 1924, was to be a prize of £2000 for the small trainer aircraft that performed best at trials to be held in ympne in Kent in September. The second part of the plan envisaged 10 light aeroplane clubs being provided with a grant to buy and maintain the prize-winning trainer. There were to be continued payments for each pilot trained by the clubs.[3]

The first trials at Lympne had been held the year before as a competition for economical aircraft, effectively motorised gliders. They reflected activity along the same lines in Germany where gliders were being used to train pilots, thus avoiding the restrictions placed on aviation there after World War One. Among the prizes was one offered by the *Daily Mail* newspaper for a flight of over 80 kilometres with an engine of capacity less than 750 millilitres. Bert Hinkler won the prize by flying 1600 kilometres in an Avro 560.

However, these under-powered planes could fly only in calm conditions so, in 1924, the emphasis shifted away from economy to practical two-seater dual-control trainers and it was then that the support came from the Air Ministry. The results showed how challenging the requirement was: there were 19 entrants, only eight aircraft made it to the trials in a state to fly and only two survived the flying tests. One of the features of the trials was a pre-flight test that involved folding or removing the wings and manhandling the aircraft along a course and into a small hangar.

The trials were repeated, with fewer entrants, in 1926 but by then the Air Ministry had lost interest, having in the meantime chosen the plane, the de Havilland Moth, to be supplied to aero clubs.

The Air Ministry thus went ahead with the second part of their plan. While some places had to be encouraged to set the clubs up, Lancashire was already there and maybe had been part of the inspiration for the idea of clubs anyway. They already had a machine that could briefly glide and it had by now been rebuilt after its first serious crash.

The first five clubs chosen by the Air Ministry were each offered two de Havilland Moths and promised one hundred pounds for each pilot trained. The LAC moved to Woodford in Cheshire when Alexandra Park was closed down (it is now playing fields) and their two planes were delivered there late in 1925. It was now that Win entered the story.

Ron's friend took them to the Woodford Aerodrome where the LAC had its headquarters in the loft of a dilapidated farmhouse. The club had no chairs but it did have the DH60 Moth aeroplane G-EBLV, newly delivered by the famous pilot Alan Cobham on 29 August, and Winifred thought it was the most beautiful thing she had ever seen.

It was a two-seater open cockpit biplane fitted with a Cirrus engine, derived from a World War One Renault engine. Later models had more powerful Cirrus engines (G-EBLV was re-engined in 1937) but, the engine supplies not being reliable, de Havilland developed its own engine, the Gipsy, leading to the series of Gipsy Moths. The line subsequently developed into the Tiger Moth. G-EBLV is the only remaining Cirrus Moth and is in the Shuttleworth Collection and still flying.

Win was soon kitted out and climbed into the back-seat of the plane. Before she realised it, she was flying and the instructor quickly gave her the controls. After an initial lurching stall, which the instructor sorted out, she found she could fly the plane straight and level. Back on the ground she realised she was hooked. The instructor suggested she joined the aero club, to be its first woman member. Win and Ron left, Win excited at the prospect of being a proper pilot.

Elsie was distraught: Winifred, always troublesome, was now involved in a truly dangerous activity. Sawley, who had tried to get her interested in sailing was delighted. Elsie seemed to have a reprieve when the LAC decided they did not actually want a woman member but Sawley and the instructor persuaded them they did and Win joined in June 1926.[4] Her first outing as a club member was the following week to the Yorkshire Air Pageant at Sherburn where LV (as the plane was known in the Club) was to show off its paces. Unfortunately, as the club planes were taxi-ing for the start of the race, Mrs Elliott-Lynn, an invited participant, flew in — and flew into LV putting it out of commission for the race. LAC members were outraged and anti-woman sentiment surged but Win was smitten with Mary Elliott-Lynn and flattered when she invited her to take a flying trip to Scotland with her. As far as we know it never came off.

Win had started her instruction in LV some months earlier, if *Under Six Planets* is to be believed, on 3 March 1926. The part-time unpaid instructor (unnamed but probably Joe Scholes[5]) had first to be found by trawling local pubs and then Win had a rather casual series of half-hour lessons (at £1 per hour) until a permanent instructor, Sam (or Sammy) Brown, was appointed in the autumn. Sammy was to become a good friend.

Captain Harry Albert "Sam" Brown (1896–1953) had fought in World War One and joined the Royal Naval Air Service to learn to fly but the war was over before he flew operationally. After the war he ran a joy-riding business from the beach at Blackpool and later Rhyl but, when this flagged, in 1920 he went to Spain to train naval pilots. He returned to Lancashire in 1926 to become the LAC instructor, at the same time testing production planes for A V Roe at Woodford. He was to survive a bad crash in an Avro Trainer in 1929 and become first test pilot for the Lancaster and the pilot for the first trial of the famous bouncing bomb.

By now the LAC had two more machines and it was in one of these that she went solo on 31 December 1926, a faultless episode except that no one had taught her how to taxi the plane so she went round and round in circles when she tried.

There were a few tests and more solo hours before she could get a licence. One of the tests was to fly to 3000 metres, cut the engine and glide in to land. There was a temporary hitch when a doctor refused to certify that she could safely fly to the required height without blacking out — she was after all a woman. But Sawley, who was very supportive of Win's flying ambitions, came to the rescue by getting his doctor to certify her fit for altitude and she successfully finished the tests. She was issued with her Private Pilot's Licence 1061 on 13 April 1927. By the time the Royal Aero Club awarded her an aviator's certificate[6] on 11 May, she was off on another adventure altogether.

GOALKEEPER

Win had played hockey at school where she was always picked as the goalkeeper. Her theory was that it was because of her volume rather than any particular talent for hockey; her bulk filled the goal. While at school she had played some games for the local Broughton Ladies and, after being ejected from "Bella Vista", she carried on playing regularly in goal for them. We can imagine she was an enthusiastic and physical player and she found herself in goal for Lancashire Ladies in the 1920s. Her first mention in the *Manchester Guardian* is in December 1924 when, now playing for the North Manchester Club, she went on the annual southern tour of the Lancashire Ladies. The team's 7–0 defeat by Kent could have been much worse: Miss Brown "saved more than that number by accurate kicking and timely coming out." She toured as a reserve the following season; her friend Marjorie Cussons was also a reserve. She sometimes played for the County second eleven, maybe because the first team was dominated by players from Manchester University. Whatever her exact hockey career (it's difficult to follow it at this distance) she was clearly at least a competent goalkeeper because in 1927 she was asked to join the England Ladies Team on their tour of Australia. It was her first opportunity to play for England and she realised it might be her only one. However, it meant leaving Ron, Sammy and flying for several months so, while Elsie pressed her to go, she was reluctant. Eventually Elsie proposed that Ron go to Australia too but with herself as chaperone. And they would travel first class while the team went second. And it was best to keep the fact that Ron was going a secret from the hockey people and from Sawley — until it was too late for them to do anything about it.

Frocks and tickets were bought. Elsie and Win were to share a de luxe cabin with beds, windows, dressing table and en suite bathroom; Ron, while travelling first also, had an ordinary four-berth one with bunks and portholes rather than beds and windows, but, with only fifteen first class passengers travelling, it turned out he at least had it to himself.

They travelled down to London on the train with Sammy flying above the train as far as Birmingham. Ron is recorded as looking gloomy during the trip and while this may have been his response to the deception of Sawley it may also have been a consequence of his girl-friend being followed half-way across the country by her flying instructor in a tender gesture of farewell. He may well have glanced up, out of the window, at the persistent tiny plane and wondered what was really going on. While in London, on 19 April, Winifred had a studio photograph taken by Lafayette. The negative held by the National Portrait Gallery[1] is not in good condition but it shows Win as a remarkably glamorous young lady wearing her flying helmet, with her goggles pushed back on her forehead. Looking at it, you can still almost hear Elsie's voice insisting that they make the girl look elegant for once.

They were travelling on P&O's *RMS Chitral*. The *Chitral* had been built (with her sister ships the *Cathay* and *Comorin)* specifically for the fortnightly UK-Australia mail service. Launched just two years earlier by her Glasgow builders, at 170 metres long she must have looked magnificent in her P&O mail-boat livery of black hull and funnels with light-ochre superstructure (sometimes called "black-and-stone") moored by the quay at Tilbury. She was designed with accommodation for 203 first-class and 103 second-class passengers. Not, at 16 knots, the fastest of mail-steamers, she was a comfortable, even luxurious, berth for the journey to come — even for Ron.

The team was led by Miss Edith Thompson CBE, the President of the All England Women's Hockey Association (AEWHA). Miss Thompson, born in 1879 was an early female graduate of King's College, University of London. In the First World War she was, like Winifred, a VAD but was also Controller of Inspection of Queen Mary's Auxiliary Nursing Corps. For her role in this and for her continued involvement with the service afterwards she was awarded the OBE in 1919 and the CBE the following year. Her interests included hockey and she was President of the AEWHA from 1925 to 1929. She wrote *Hockey as a Game for Women* in 1905. Her Times obituary in 1961 described her as "a woman of vivacious personality" with a natural organising ability. A tall, white-haired commanding lady, Win calls her "Madam" in *Under Six Planets*. Elsie and she didn't get on with each other. When Miss Thompson discovered that Ron was not Win's brother, as had been implied, but her boyfriend, she must have been outraged but concealed it rather well; her natural organising ability recognised instantly that she had no reserve goalkeeper in the party. The same ability led to her making a new rule for the AEWHA, when she got back, that touring team members could not take companions.

Sawley learned of Ron's presence after they had left Tilbury on 22 April and wrote indignant letters to Elsie, which she ignored. The ship headed through the Straits of Gibraltar, paused at Algiers (where Win was rescued from a street brawl by the police), went through the Suez Canal and into the Red Sea. An excursion with Ron, when they paused at Port Sudan on its western shore, nearly lost the team its goalkeeper when the car broke down (surely Miss Thompson had some plan for this contingency?). A stop at Aden was "disappointingly uneventful", but Colombo, Sri Lanka was reached on 14 May and the cooler weather and the greenery promised a more comfortable time.

Colombo was to be the first place that Win played hockey for England. It was rather less satisfying than it might have been because just before they ran onto the field Madam demanded that Win give her regulation sports knickers to the centre forward and wear her normal pink ones. This under protest she did. If the choice arose between saving a goal and exposing her non-standard underwear Madam told her she should let the ball go into the net. Since England won 12–0 it seems that the opponents were quite outclassed or Win defied instructions.

The next stop was Fremantle in Western Australia and here the team disembarked on 24 May for Perth where the Mayor and Mayoress gave a reception for them the following day. The first match was several days away so Win was soon at the Perth aerodrome hiring a plane — the first woman pilot they had seen. They insisted that she took a rather nervous man with her on the spin.

The team played Western Australia on 28 May at Perth's Subiaco Oval and won 13–1, Win making a couple of good saves according to the press. At the return match on 30 May the English trounced another West Australia XI 19–0. The visit seems to have been a social success (with a Hockey Ball, tours of the surrounding countryside and an enthusiastic press) and they set off on the three-day train journey to Adelaide on 31 May. The train crossed the Nullabor Plain on what is still, at some 700 kilometres, the longest straight stretch of railway track in the world. It was then that the most notable event of the journey occurred when the train stopped briefly and the team, stretching their legs, saw an aborigine selling boomerangs. The centre forward thought the things would not work and to prove it threw one. Inevitably the boomerang did return, striking her on the forehead and flattening her on the sand. Since this was the pretty dark girl who had had benefit of her hijacked knickers in Colombo, Win's emotions may have been mixed. In Adelaide the event was reported by the newspaper but here the injury was described as "a very severe blow on the jaw" to the pretty girl who was "very cheerful over it."[2]

A little further on she heard the story of Daisy M Bates (Win calls her Bate in *Under Six Planets*). Daisy was an immigrant from Ireland in 1882 and after three marriages, two of them bigamous, and a brief return to Britain, devoted herself to researching and recording the life of the Australian aboriginal people. She worked for their welfare and, from 1912, lived much of her life in tents with them. She was appointed Protector of Aborigines by the government and, in 1934, was awarded the OBE. She spent some time in Canberra and Adelaide advising government and writing for newspapers but returned to the outback, notably the tiny town of

Ooldea, until her health failed in 1945. She then returned to Adelaide and died there in 1951. She always dressed in a Victorian style and usually wore a veil. Her attitudes to the Aborigines would now be seen a paternalistic, indeed she was described as "an imperialist, an awful snob … a grand old lady" by someone who worked with her. Her 1938 book *The Passing of the Aborigines*[3] caused controversy. She had long been well known as a opponent of inter-marriage (she said it would destroy the native folk) but in *The Passing of the Aborigines* she claimed that cannibalism was part of Aborigine culture, a notion many felt untrue and repulsive. In 1927 Win learned why Daisy was not around when the train stopped at Ooldea:

> Daisy Bate had been tenderly keeping watch on two young lubras [now a racially offensive term for a young Aborigine woman] who were about to become mothers. One day she missed them, but finally tracked them down just in time to catch them enjoying a juicy feast. The horror of the sight so appalled Mrs Bate that she became really ill, for the two women were calmly eating their newly-born babies![4]

Quite where this story (so graphically told by Win) came from is not clear but baby cannibalism is described in Bates's book. Win accepted the explanation for Daisy's absence without comment.

The team arrived in Adelaide on the 3 June and there were receptions and motor tours and decisive victories over South Australia and over the Australian team in a first test match. The morning tea at the Town Hall went well, as the social column of *The Register* recorded with a lyricism long dead in newspapers:

> The room looked delightfully cosy in that cold, grey morning, the flowers were pink — roses, chrysanthemums and penstemons, and the lights pink shaded. The pianola joyed out strains of 'Red, red robin' and involuntarily those guests who were standing shuffled the Charleston! Most of them charmingly demonstrated the fact that no woman in the

world can wear a tailor-made coat and skirt as an English-woman can. [5]

In Melbourne they took part in a hockey festival in which they thrashed Victoria and Melbourne teams but had a hard match against a Tasmanian XI, winning by just 4–2. There were receptions too. At the one given by the Victorian Women's Hockey Association the English girls performed their speciality.

> It included a song describing their experiences since they left England by the Chitral on May 24, and a mock hockey match enacted by dancing.[6]

No *spontaneous* dancing in Melbourne it seems. It was here that Win and Ron managed to get away from the team, Madam and Elsie for a spot of dancing in the evening. The pub opening hours (6 am to 6 pm) seemed particularly unsociable — but were eased by the flask of brandy they carried around. On the hockey field they swept aside all opposition, beating the Australia side 8–2 in a second test.

Win's pilot's licence was mentioned by at least one newspaper when it remarked how brainy the English lasses were.[7] She also managed to impress in the air when she performed an aerobatic display at Essendon Aerodrome for the Australian Aero Club. Just under a year before Alan Cobham had landed his float-plane (given wheels for the purpose) in front of a large crowd at Essendon after flying from England. A year before that Cobham had, of course delivered the plane Win learned to fly in to the Lancashire Aero Club.

On 24 June the team sailed for Tasmania. Instead of the close-run affair of Melbourne, the English girls won their two matches: 17–0 against North Tasmania on 26 June in Hobart and and 19–0 against them in Launceston on 2 July. Miss Thompson had earlier told the press that the Tasmanian side was the best one they had seen in Australia so far, so there must have been some disappointment on the island. The failure was put down by the Press partly to the English being taught a skilful game by their female coaches while the Australians played the much more physical game promoted by their male coaches.

There were, as usual, receptions but these were now supplemented by demonstrations of sheep shearing and wool treatment. They travelled in three motor cars and saw many of the sites. In Launceston they visited the Cataract Gorge and the Alexandra Suspension Bridge where Win managed to get stuck in the turnstile on the bridge. They left for the mainland on 4 July.

Back in Melbourne they took the overnight express train to Sydney. Their success continued: on 9 July they outclassed by 9–0 a New South Wales team, on the 13th they beat Barmedan, a good country team, 16–0. On the 15th they closed a hockey carnival by winning the third test match 11–0. Someone calculated that by now in the tour they had scored 197 goals to their opponents' six.

While the team went off sightseeing in the Blue Mountains, Win was taken to Mascot Aerodrome — what is now Sydney (Kingsford Smith) Airport — by Harry Broadsmith, whom she had met in Sydney, and after a short practice took one of the club Moths for a solo flight — surprised only by the insistence that she abide by a club rule and wear gym shoes.

On the 17th they swept on towards Brisbane.

They stayed in Tenterfield, 350 kilometres south west of Brisbane, to beat the local team, perhaps the best in New South Wales, 8–0 on the 19th.

The game was fast and interesting but the English "combination and science were superior"; Tenterfield were pleased they had done better than the national side. A reception one evening was followed by a Grand Ball: "in a kind of barn, the men were roped off and when the music started the rope was lowered, and the men grabbed." The following day they took the train for Brisbane.

In Brisbane they played the last game of the tour against Queensland and won 15–2. This was in front of a crowd of 35,000 at the Exhibition Oval prior to an interstate rugby game. The aggregate score for the tour finally stood at England 228 – Australian sides 9. The team returned to Sydney and on the 25th they broke up to make their various ways back to England.

Four of the party were to stay behind for a few weeks to coach and one of them was Marjorie Cussons who was to stay in Brisbane. Marjorie had not played in many games but she had been picked out by some newspapers as one of the remarkable women on the team. She was the daughter of Tom Cussons, the well-known soap and perfume manufacturer, and had a hand in design of advertisements for the company. She took a great interest in the welfare of the women who worked in the Salford factory and had started four hockey teams for them.

She and Win were to be friends for life in spite of the fact that she was a tee-totaller — while Win was not. The difference was illustrated by an event that took place just before or just after the Australian tour.

Marjorie took a job as a masseuse and swimming instructor for Cunard cruises and travelled the world. This was a world of gritty glamour (she met Al Capone!) and hard drinking and it meant she had experience of staying sober while those around her were not. Before one voyage there was a send-off celebration for her in the elegant Adelphi Hotel in Liverpool which naturally enough developed into a drinking session — for everyone but Marjorie. There was a call at some point for food for the revellers — and it was declined by the Hotel. Presumably they had had enough.

Undismayed and resourceful, Win went outside and found a man selling hot chestnuts from a barrow, bought his entire stock and the barrow and wheeled it into the hotel foyer crying "Hot Chestnuts!" Marjorie went to bed and let them get on with it.

HOMEWARD

Win, Ron and Elsie were to go home round-the-world and on 28 July they boarded Union Steamship Company's SS *Niagara*[8] bound for New Zealand and Fiji.

New Zealand was apparently a brief blur because Win and Ron had an extended alcoholic celebration with an American with the name of Manchester — a good enough excuse for a few glasses. It would have been interesting to know what Elsie was up to while this was going on.

In Suva, the capital of Fiji, they stayed at the "Royal Pacific Hotel", built on the seafront by the Union Steamship Company to give staging passengers the impression that they were still at sea on a luxury liner. Win and Ron bathed on the reef admiring the coral and fish for so long that they were sun-burned. All Win's exposed skin peeled off.

They were intrigued by the notion that Fiji was a refuge for those who had failed or faltered in England. It produced, they found, a tight-knit community where nobody asked many questions. A former Guards officer had formed a local band but no-one knew why he had left England because no-one had asked — at least, that's what they said. They spent their time wandering around, being entertained by the apparently happy-go-lucky Fijians and swimming in fresh water pools for fear of sharks.

They persuaded Elsie to chaperone them on a trip on a small trading steamer, the SS *Makatea*[9], that carried people around the islands collecting copra, the dried kernels of coconuts and an important source of oil. Elsie had a cabin but could not face eating while looking at the feet of sleeping passengers, the doors being left open for the heat. The mate explained about the smell: part of it was from the copra they collected on passage and part from the collection of passengers. The Chinese and Fijians smelled different from the Indians and they all smelled different from Europeans. More alarmingly he explained that the different nationalities had to be kept apart otherwise they murdered each other. The Indians given the chance chopped the Chinese into eight pieces he told them. It was a "matter of religion."

Ron and Win went ashore at all the islands the vessel called at, fearful at times of reported head hunters. At one particularly remote one they were invited to drink karva (more usually spelled "kava" today), later discovering its devastating and famed effect on the legs. Ron thought it tasted like Gregory-powder, a laxative mixture devised by James Gregory (1753–1821) and composed of pulverised rhubarb, magnesia and ginger which was widely used in the first half of the twentieth century and particularly recommended for children. Its taste was apparently so awful that many potential recipients would conceal the problem rather than face the medicine

Later still they found out that it was made by a girl chewing the root of the kava plant and spitting the result into a bowl where it was left to ferment into the numbing brew.

On another island they lingered so long at a pig-eating feast that they returned to the ship to find it gone. Enduring a storm with a torrential downpour, alarmed by the wild drumming and shouting now coming from the feast and frightened by a startled pig in the dark, they had to wait until dawn for its return. It had steamed round to the other side of the island to shelter from the storm.

While these adventures were going on it seems that Elsie was not enjoying herself. Even the captain noticed. After explaining about the kava process he remarked on it:

This was the first time the captain had taken much notice of them, and over oyster cocktails in his cabin he explained why.

> "I was furious when they told me you were coming—two white women! On this ship!"
>
> "But I love it!" cried the girl.
>
> "I'm afraid your mother doesn't."
>
> "She is being a little difficult, but she likes her Indian steward. She says he is a very nice man, brings her milk and is the only person who has any thought for her."
>
> "Then you'd better not tell her he has cut a Chinaman into eight pieces," said the captain chuckling.[10]

One of the saddest tales Win tells in all her writing is of the white girl carried onto the ship at a tiny island stop. Born paralysed from the waist down, she had been rejected by her parents and banished to a hut at the bottom of their garden, where she was looked after by a local boy. Eventually he carried her to his canoe and paddled away, to a better life together. This was not allowed: "You can't have natives stealing white girls" Win was told. The pair were eventually tracked down and brought aboard the *Makatea*, the girl to be taken back to wherever she had come from and the boy, as a prisoner, to be tried and ("a foregone conclusion") hanged. The girl, understanding what would inevitably happen to the boy, was either mute and dazed or sobbing and weeping whenever Win saw her. The boy was kept locked away, out of sight.

As the *Makatea* returned to Suva, Ron asked if he could take a photograph of the captain and the mate. At the appointed time the two of them turned out in splendid white uniforms, the captain particularly with festoons of gold braid. It seemed so out of keeping with the modest *Makatea* that Win would have liked to ask about the magnificent uniforms but she was stopped from doing so by the mate. Questions like that were not asked of white men in the South Seas.

They left Suva on the *Aorangi* built just three years before in Glasgow. It was, unusually for its time, a motor ship powered by diesel engines. Indeed it was, at nearly 18,000 tons, the largest motor vessel at sea. It carried them to Honolulu, which they did not much like after the beauty of Fiji. The American customs almost undressed Ron and searched Win's bathing cap. Elsie, gazing on the population, commented on its large Chinese component: "a peaceful invasion."

Waikiki seemed to even then have lived up to its tacky reputation. Ron did like the Hawaiian guitars — although one night was enough. The next morning the *Aorangi* left for Vancouver.

THE ROCKIES

Vancouver seems not to have made much impression on Winifred because they are soon, in the narrative, on the Canadian Pacific Railway train steaming through the Rockies. The intriguing names slipped by: Ruskin, Dewdney, Suzzum, Cisco, Kamloops, as did the awe-inspiring scenery of snow-capped, jagged mountains and endless forests. The bell on the train clanged and the whistle moaned as the cow-catcher, led by a bright searchlight, carved its way through the dark. They broke the journey at Lake Louise where Winifred was entranced by the turquoise water stretching away between the mountains to the distant glaciers.

They went by coach to Banff and, at one of the frequent stops for a man who was either travel or altitude sick, a large brown bear came out of the woods, no doubt, in those far-off, less responsible days, being used to a good supply of biscuits and cakes from tourists. Win, armed with a fruity pastille sweet, decided she should befriend the creature and climbed out of the coach, approaching it with soothing words and the sweet held out in her hand. She managed to place the sweet-free hand on its head and was turning towards the bus to give Ron a better camera angle when the bear snarled and lunged towards her. She shut her eyes, felt the animals hot breath on her face and heard the snap of its jaws. When she opened her eyes again, expecting to find part of a limb missing, all that had gone were the bear and the sweet. Ron's photograph of the drama was a disappointment showing just Win's sleeve and her hand on the bear's head.

At Banff they rejoined the train and went on to Calgary, Moose-jaw, Winnipeg and Port Arthur.

One of the mysteries of the rail trip is where Ron slept. Elsie had booked a "drawing room" for three on the train but was outraged when she discovered that this meant that the three of them were expected to sleep on bunks in it. The whole thing was immoral Elsie complained and demanded that Ron slept in the guard's van. So maybe he did, spending the nights on a swaying, roughly-made bed far from Win and closer to the squealing wheels. We will never know.

ACROSS THE LAKES

At Port Arthur (now part of Thunder Bay city) on Lake Superior they boarded one of the steamers that ran via Lake Huron to Port McNicholl on Georgian Bay to join up with the next leg of the train route. Two steamers ran the 2 ½ day trip: the SS *Keewatin* and the SS *Assiniboia*[11] both 3800 tons and 100 metres long. They were near

41

enough identical with white hulls and superstructure and a tall funnel well set back. The funnel poured out copious black smoke from the coal-fired boilers as the vessels made a steady 14 knots across the lakes. They carried 288 passengers in considerable luxury; there were 105 staterooms on two decks. The spacious lobby led to a grand staircase and the dining rooms served the fine food for which the Canadian Pacific was famous. The main events on the journey were lifeboat drill as they approached the Sleeping Giant, an island off Port Arthur, and the passage through the lock at Sault St Marie.

It should have been entirely to Elsie's taste: a stylish, relaxing lake cruise with time to recline in the sun and read a book — without fraught sleeping arrangements. Alas, the boat was almost empty (making the advertised fine dining a rather dismal affair one imagines), the lake was rough and the rain poured down. The crossing ended at the neat and pretty town of Port McNicholl and they must then, with some relief, have taken the train to Toronto.

They visited Niagara Falls and wandered in the tunnels underneath as the water thundered outside and then travelled on to Montreal where they took a liner for home. We are not told which one it was but it was almost certainly Cunard's *Ausonia*, which sailed on 30 September 1927. The 14,000 ton *Ausonia* was launched in 1922 as an intermediate liner specifically for the UK-Canada emigrant trade and for the passage through the St Lawrence River. Built with two classes, cabin and third, it was converted to cabin, tourist and third in June 1927. Win, Ron and Elsie travelled cabin class.

It was a rough crossing. Elsie seems to have spent most of her time in their cabin, the trunks being thrown around as the ship lurched violently. Ron dodged a grand piano as it crashed across the lounge and walking on deck was forbidden but Win enjoyed a meal of roast pork and chocolate eclairs, the waiter weaving back and forth across the empty dining salon to deliver it. Some relief came from encounters with an inebriated animal impersonator, Mr Flinn, and his canary called Dickie.

The *Ausonia* arrived at Tilbury on 10 October, after stops at Plymouth and Cherbourg. A final embarrassment was that Ron had run out of money. It led to a revelation that Sawley, still annoyed by the deception of so many months ago, had refused to send any to Elsie during the trip. They went ashore to face him.

BACK IN THE AIR

Win had flown in Australia but she must have been looking forward to using the pilot's licence she had been awarded only days before leaving England several months before. There was such promise in this rapidly developing technology that was already, for the thrill-seeking well-off, an exciting new pastime. She would still be a pioneer, following close in the footsteps of some remarkable men and women.

EARLY FLIERS AND PLANES

The Wright brothers' first powered flight was on 17 December 1903 (three weeks after Win's third birthday); the first flight in Europe was a 60 metre hop at 2 metres height by the Brazilian Alberto Santos-Dumont at Bagatelle airfield near Paris on 23 October 1906 by which time the Wright brothers had managed to fly more than 39 kilometres. Real control of the aircraft remained a difficult problem but on 13 January 1908 Henry Farman managed to fly a Voisin machine for 1 kilometre with a 180 degree turn halfway at Issy-Les-Moulineaux, near Paris. On 25 July 1909 Louis Bleriot flew across the English Channel.

Women flew as passengers in 1908 but the first woman to pilot a heavier-than-air craft was probably the singer ("artiste lyrique") and aviation enthusiast Elise Raymonde Deroche (usually referred to by her stage name Raymonde de Laroche) who made a short solo flight in a Voisin plane on 22 October 1909. She is often styled "Baroness" from the title "baronne" given to her by Tsar Nicholas II[1] when he met her in St Petersburg in May 1910. She was in fact a plumber's daughter. She was awarded pilot's licence number 36 by the AéroClub de France on 8 March 1910.

The first woman to fly the English Channel was the American Harriet Quimby on 16 April 1912. This was the day before the *Ti-*

tanic sank so her achievement did not receive much attention. Quimby, a screenwriter and journalist with film-star looks, was the first woman to get a US pilot's licence (in 1911). Her clothing always attracted attention and for the Channel flight she wore a mauve satin flying suit with knickerbockers ending just below the tops of calf-clinging laced boots. With her head swathed in the hood that formed part of the suit, a blue silk motor veil thrown over her shoulder to stream in the wind as she flew, and goggles pushed up on her forehead she looked like a flying Sophia Loren. The crossing went without incident (she did don several more layers of warm clothing before setting off) but poor Harriet died just a few months later when she and her passenger were thrown from their plane during a demonstration flight in the USA.

The early aeroplanes were flimsy structures that flew quite slowly and were difficult to manoeuvre. There were numerous configurations of the wings and control surfaces: the pilots sat entirely in the open (and sometimes stood). By the beginning of World War One a pattern had become established and most aeroplanes had the wings towards the front and the tailplane with its control surfaces at the back. Cockpits were enclosed and the biplane or triplane were the dominant design types. The British BE2, a general purpose plane of 1914, could reach a top speed of around 110 km/h and had a duration of about 3 hours.

During World War One planes became more diverse and specialised with faster more manoeuvrable fighters and larger bombers with greater endurance appearing. By the end of the war the top speed of fighters was twice what it had been four years earlier and the large twin-engined bombers like the Handley-Page O/400 could carry nearly a ton and fly for ten hours at 160 km/h at altitude up to 8000 metres. This was due as much to the improvements in engines as in airframes; they were lighter, more reliable and had something like twice the power of their pre-war ancestors.

It was a modified Vickers Vimy bomber that was used by John Alcock and Arthur Whitten Brown in their momentous non-stop flight in June 1919 — just under ten years after Bleriot had crossed the English Channel. They left St Johns, Newfoundland on the afternoon of 14 June and crashed into a bog in Ireland the following morning. In the 16 hour flight they travelled almost 3200 kilometres, surviving continual icing up of the engine intakes (which required Brown to keep climbing out onto the wings to clear them) and poor weather. Both were knighted a few days later. Alcock had been born in Seymour Grove, just four kilometres from where Win was born, in 1892 and he and Alcock were given a civic reception in Manchester on 17 July 1917. Sadly, Alcock died before the year was out, crashing in a plane he was taking to the December Paris air show. It is difficult to believe that Win was not aware of and perhaps inspired by her distinguished fellow Mancunian.

People flew right around the world with many stops. Flying to distant parts of the Empire was the British endurance challenge. In 1924/5 there was a flight from London to Rangoon and in 1925/6 Alan Cobham flew from London to Cape Town and back — and then to Australia and back. Neville Stack flew from Croydon to Karachi in 1926/7. In 1928 Bert Hinkler flew his Avro Avian solo from England to Australia while Lady Heath (aka Mary Elliott-Lynn) flew hers back from Cape Town to England. In the same year Lady Mary Bailey flew her DH Moth to Cape Town and back in a round trip of some 30,000 kilometres. The first woman to be flown from England to Australia was Jessie "Chubbie" Miller who was a passenger with Bill Lancaster when he flew his Avro Avian *Red Rose* from Lympne in Kent, leaving on 14 October 1927 and taking five months.[2]

Chubbie (who acquired the nickname because she weighed less than 45 kilograms) went on to become a notable aviator herself. Lancaster, the pilot, escaped a murder conviction after he (almost certainly) shot Chubbie's lover, Haden Clarke, while they were living in Florida. He died in 1933 after crashing into the Sahara on a desperate bid to revive his fortunes by beating the record for a flight from England to Cape Town. He lived for seven days after the crash and kept a diary which was found with his mummified remains by French soldiers in 1962. The last words were "I have no water. No wind. I am waiting patiently."

But the flight that captured the world was that of Charles Lindbergh crossing the Atlantic from New York to Paris, covering the 5600 kilometres in his single-seater, single-engined monoplane *Spirit of St Louis*. Taking off from Roosevelt Field on Long Island early on the morning of 20 May 1927 he landed 33 hours later, at dusk the following day.

The Atlantic continued to claim the lives of daring and remarkable people. The prize of being the first woman across was to be a costly one.

MISSING

After a blessing by the RC Bishop of Cardiff, on 31 August 1927 *St Raphael*, a Fokker VII single-engined monoplane took off from Upavon aerodrome piloted by Captain Leslie Hamilton and Colonel F F (Dan) Minchin. In the back, in a wicker chair, sat 62-year old Princess Anne of Lowenstein-Wertheim-Freudenberg realising her dream to be the first woman to fly the Atlantic. She was dressed for flying in purple leather knee-breeches with matching jacket, a black crush hat, black silk stockings and high-heeled, fur-lined boots. Born Lady Anne Savile, the daughter of the 4th Earl of Mexborough, she had married Prince Ludwig Lowenstein-Wertheim-Freudenberg in about 1897. Sadly, after just a few months of marriage, Ludwig disappeared having failed to pay the man who had arranged for him, the impecunious prince, to meet the well-heeled British lady. Ludwig turned up in the Philippines some months later. He seems to have become involved in an insurrection against the US administration of the islands and was shot by US forces in an engagement with rebels in March 1899. Anne became very interested in flying — a problematical hobby for someone with a distinctly Germanic name who tried to buy an aeroplane in England during World War One — so she often went by the name of "Evelyn Ellis".

The flight was intended to finish in Ottawa but they were last seen some 1200 kilometres out above the ocean by a US ship. They either became lost in bad weather or suffered an engine failure.

A similar fate befell the Honorable Elsie Mackay, the daughter of Lord Inchcape of Glenapp, Chairman of P&O, who also wanted to be the first woman to be flown across the Atlantic. She bought a Stinson Detroiter, had it shipped from the USA and set off, with Capt Walter Hinchliffe DFC, a greatly-experienced pilot who had lost an eye in World War One, from Cranwell on 13 March 1928. They left in secret, Elsie having promised her father not to make the attempt. They were seen over Crookhaven, Ireland and then by a ship but never arrived in North America. A piece of undercarriage from the Detroiter was washed up on the Irish coast eight months later, suggesting that they had not got very far.

The prize of being the first woman across went to Win's heroine Amelia Earhart in June 1928, who been chosen by the aircraft's owner as a suitably well-brought-up young woman to carry off the honour. On this crossing she did little of the flying but four years later did all of it when she flew across solo, the first woman and only the second person to do so.

Of course there were adventures, if slightly more modest, in flying around Manchester and John Leeming, founder of the Lancashire Aero Club, was having some of them around the time Win went solo, before the hockey tour.

HELVELLYN

As part of the enthusiasm to promote flying with the public Leeming tried to land on Helvellyn mountain in the Lake District in December 1926. With Bert Hinkler in an accompanying plane with a press photographer, he took off from Woodford, just south of Manchester, in an Avro Gosport on the 15th. While the weather was fine when he took off, on the way to the mountain he encountered cloud, ground fog and finally hailstorms so he turned back to Woodford. The following week he tried again but was this time thwarted by gales. Retreating to Lancaster, on the following day, the

22 December, he and Bert, now a passenger in the Gosport, finally managed to land on the mountain. According to *Flight* they were "greeted by a Greek professor and left again almost immediately." Leeming had inspected the site on foot some time earlier and Win reported dark rumours that men had cleared the summit with picks and shovels. Presumably it was considered unsporting to do that.

Leeming made the newspapers again on 5 February 1927 when on a flight back from lunch in Chester to Woodford he landed in a field next to a garage at Bucklow Hill, taxied up to the pump and filled up. The plane was then wheeled back to the field and Leeming took off again. The plane was the one used for the Helvellyn landing. The *Manchester Guardian*'s account of the garage incident was titled "Mr Leeming Startles Garage".

AIRCRAFT

The two companies providing the majority of planes for recreational flying in the later 20s were de Havilland and A V Roe. The de Havilland Company was founded in 1920 by Geoffrey de Havilland when, Airco, where he had been chief designer, was sold. It set up business at Stag Lane, Edgeware, London. He had designed planes designated DH while at Airco and he continued this with the new company. His Moth series (DH60s) were successful trainers and recreational planes built from 1925, first with an ex-Renault Cirrus engine and then with others, notably the Gipsy engine produced by de Havilland itself. The DH60s given to clubs by the Air Ministry in their efforts to kick-start civil aviation in 1925 gave de Havilland a chance to further develop the series, producing the Tiger Moth, and to establish themselves as the predominant supplier in the market for years to come. It has been estimated that 85 out of every 100 small planes in the UK in 1929 were Moths — and these were mainly Gipsy Moths.[3]

Alliott Verdon Roe set up his aircraft factory in Manchester in 1910 and built over 8000 examples of its Avro 504 biplane during World War One. The company moved from its base at Alexandra Park (where Leeming had tested his glider) to Woodford in

Cheshire in 1924. Its most successful aeroplane for recreation and training was the Avro Avian introduced in 1926/7. It was produced with modifications and different engines for several years but, although used in several aviation adventures (as we have seen), it never sold as well as the DH Moths — probably because of the boost given to de Havilland by the Air Ministry order of 1925.

VZ

It was this environment that Win rejoined once she returned to Manchester and the Lancashire Aero Club, keen, no doubt, to get into the skies in one of the club planes. However Sawley had a surprise for her.

His anger at the way he had been kept ignorant of the plan to take Ron on the Australian hockey tour, sustained over the months of their absence, seems to have quickly faltered on seeing a happy healthy Win when she arrived back from Australia. He was also put on the back foot by accusations from Elsie that he had neglected Win by leaving her short of money. He must have realised long before that his months of freedom were all too limited; perhaps he thought that things might be different. Quickly he knew that they would be much the same. Whether during the long separation he had wondered what surprise he could give to the daughter he doted on we will never know. Maybe it was a response to meeting her again and being made to feel ungenerous by Elsie but, whatever, out of the blue, he asked her whether she would like a plane of her own. He had spoken to Roy Dobson (Dobbie as he was known to many), the Works Manager of Avro, and he thought that their new Avian with the 100 horsepower Cirrus engine would be just right. It was the model Bert Hinkler was planning to fly early in 1928 to Australia.

Win was given a registration mark G-EBVZ and flew her new plane, in the smart red and silver livery she had chosen, for the first time at Woodford on 14 February 1928, a week after Bert Hinkler left for Australia in his. A photographer from the *Manchester Guardian* was in a plane beside G-EBVZ and a photograph appeared in the paper the next day with the caption "A Manchester Woman Pilot".[4] A photograph in the Avro collection shows her being flown as a passenger in VZ by Sammy Brown just a few days before.[5]

Once she had her own wings things moved fast. She was soon invited to represent the Lancs Aero Club at an aviation display for King Amanullah of Afghanistan at Croydon on 21 March. The light aircraft clubs were seen as an important element in growing civil aviation and increasing public support for it, so pilots were invited from several clubs.

Win's flight down from Woodford was not without incident. Led by Sammy in a club plane, she and Ron found their way by the usual method of following the railway lines — it was called "Bradshawing" after the celebrated railway timetable. The first staging point was Crewe, a massive railway junction, which posed the particular problem that, even if you found it, there were so many lines that you could easily follow the wrong one from it. Sammy had come along exactly for this reason: Win had done little more than fly around Woodford up to now.

They soon became separated from Sammy and not long after that were completely lost. Win debated landing in a field to ask where they were — a standard practice of the time. But then they spotted a small plane and followed it to an airfield where it landed and they followed. They were surprised when Sammy landed just moments later and he was clearly impressed that they had managed to navigate to an airfield. They refuelled, found the airfield's name on the petrol bill, located it on the map and set off once more for Croydon.

At the aviation display there were many demonstrations for the King's benefit. Neville Stack dropped mail (picture postcards to King Amanullah from the Air Council) by parachute to land in front of the royal party. Win was presented standing in front of G-EBVZ and the King seems to have been impressed with the idea of a woman pilot. The murky photograph in the *Manchester Guardian* seems to show her enjoying a joke with him and the royal party (which included Sir Francis Humphreys, Sir Samuel Hoare, Sir Phillip Sassoon and Sir Sefton Brancker)[6] while a figure, who may be Ron, hovers a few paces back. The King was torn away for a flight in an Argosy airliner over London that lasted 25 minutes and he returned for another demonstration by Stack who, single-handedly, wheeled an Avro Avian with folded wings out of a hangar, spread its wings, started the engine with a flick of the prop and quickly flew up into the blue.

Later in the day the King travelled to Swindon on a special train from Paddington to inspect the railway works. He returned that night, disappointed that he had not been able to drive the engine himself; it had been too wet. A few days later the royal party spent a few days in Manchester, staying at the Midland Hotel. Win returned much sooner; the flight back took a mere 2½ hours.

On 25 April Win was at Woodford when she was asked to deliver a film, "What Price Glory", urgently to a cinema, the New Prince's Kinema in Stalybridge, a few kilometres east of Manchester; she was told it would be good publicity for aviation. The advertised plan had been for the film to be delivered by Capt Cantrill "the famous air ace" who would then do some aerobatics simulating an air battle. The publicity for this had attracted an enormous number of people to the landing ground. One estimate put the crowd at 12,000.[7]

Why Cantrill did not appear we do not know but Win gallantly stepped in. She was to land in a handy field rather than at an aerodrome but was told that the man who would carry the film had experience of flying (he was in fact a Pilot Lt Browning) and had previously measured the field. They found the field but Win was concerned that it was not big enough and full of people and circled, inclined to abandon the landing. The man with the film was furious: there were crowds waiting below. Win — by now she was a bundle of nerves — swooped down, side-slipped and landed safely in front of the cheering masses but quickly realised that she would not stop before the field ran out. She did the only thing she could: opened the throttle and tried to take off. It was too late. The undercarriage struck the wall around the field and worse, much worse, the spinning propeller decapitated a ten year-old boy, Jackie Hood, who had been sitting on it.

Win was briefly unconscious and when she came round she was concerned about the damage to VZ and her engine. She wanted to go round to the front of the plane to see but was prevented from doing so by a policeman who took her from the scene to a local pub where he broke the news that she had killed the boy and injured five other people. The subsequent inquest, perhaps surprisingly, cleared her of all responsibility for the accident and the death. It emerged that she had been duped into making the flight: the can had no film in it. It was all just a publicity stunt. This seemed to carry some weight with the coroner.

Quite what effect the trauma had on Win it is impossible to say; there is no record of her thoughts. But what we do know is that she carried on flying with her characteristic determination.

In July Win took part in the Air Pageant at Blackpool and won the main race. The prize should have been a cup but, when the donator withdrew, it was replaced, to Win's delight, by a gold cigarette case. She and Ron watched a demonstration of the new Avro Avenger by F Lt Waghorn which terminated early when the plane's engine cut out at low level. Waghorn simply landed on a fairway of the adjoining Blackpool Golf Club course.

OSTENDE

In August she and Ron flew to Ostende. They followed the railway lines to London but then, confused by the web of tracks below them, became lost until they struck upon Croydon and landed. It was here that they confessed to another pilot that once they reached the coast they did not know how to get across the Channel: there were no railway lines to follow. The pilot suggested that they fly to Folkstone and once they got there they would see a jetty pointing out into the Channel. They should fly out along the jetty, note the compass reading and keep to this until they made landfall in France. This proved successful until haze obscured the horizon. Then they

53

became disoriented, the compass whirled and they found them-selves upside down for a while. Luckily they soon spotted land, which Ron decided was France because there were no white cliffs to be seen, and turned left. Following the coast (perhaps not having bought a continental railway map), they landed safely at Ostende.

Here they ran into what could have been a big problem: they had no papers for the trip. This could have meant confiscation of VZ but, with a generosity that somehow fitted the spirit of early flying, the officials offered to look after the plane while they had a short holiday. So a few days later they flew back, this time making sure they could see England before they left the French coast.

The trip persuaded Win that she should learn a bit more about the compass and flying by it. She made a flight from Woodford to Hamble in Hampshire by sticking to a compass course worked out by someone else and ignoring the railway lines and was so im-pressed that she decided to learn how to do the calculations herself.

This she did by attending (at Sawley's suggestion that aerial and marine navigation had a great deal in common) Captain Austin Dobson's Nautical Academy in Brook Street, Manchester. Dob-son's ambition exceeded even Win's: he wanted to fly to the moon. He was convinced that this would be possible with the energy re-leased once someone split the atom, something he thought might happen quite soon. For a man with such aspirations and knowledge he had a surprisingly down-to-earth way of teaching trigonometry, or at least that necessary for marine navigation. Win, regretting not taking more notice at school, seems to have learned enough for fly-ing and sailing too. Now she could navigate but an incident led her to realise how little she knew about that other important element of flying: keeping the propeller turning.

She was flying VZ, following Sammy in a plane he was delivering to Northampton, planning to give him a lift back to Woodford when the engine started to splutter and then stopped. She managed, terrified and elated, to make her first forced landing in a field. Sammy did come back and picked her up, leaving VZ there awaiting mechanics to be sent to repair the engine. The incident prompted

Win to ask the engine manufacturers, Cirrus Aero Engines, if she could spend some time at their workshops in Croydon. They agreed and she spent three weeks stripping down engines and learning how to maintain them.

Then, on 6 July 1929 she went to see the competitors in the King's Cup Air Race land at Blackpool for an overnight stop.

THE KING'S CUP AIR RACE

In 1922 King George V offered a cup for an air race to promote the development of light aircraft and their engines. It was open to planes designed in Britain and the Commonwealth (from 1961 this restriction was dropped) and to British and Commonwealth pilots. The race has been run ever since (apart from a gap from 1939 to 1948) over a variety of courses with several handicapping systems. Until the wartime break the courses were 800 to 2800 kilometres long, running around the UK; after it the pilots lapped a much shorter course a few times for a total distance of under 200 kilometres.

The 1922 race started at Croydon on 8 September with five turning points around the mainland UK, where a compulsory stop of one hour was required, ending at Croydon the following day. At Glasgow there was an overnight rest. Twenty two planes started (one entered by Winston Churchill) and the winner was Frank L Barnard in an Airco DH4A with an average speed of 200 km/h. The following year a Siskin won but a remarkable entrant, that showed how fashionable air racing had become, was from the comedian George Robey whose DH9 was piloted by Alan Cobham. The 1924 race was notable for being completed in just one day and, for one pilot was probably memorable for his plane's propeller "working itself loose and flying off on its own" somewhere near Newcastle. The next year's race was run in terrible weather and only three out of the 15 entries survived the two days. In 1926 five planes of the 16 entrants finished a double triangle course run twice over two days (2400 kilometres in total) and a DH Moth flown by H S Broad won.

The following year was something of an organisational disaster because the handicapping system adopted penalised the faster planes excessively. This was not realised until the day of the race

56

when several competitors withdrew in protest. Two women had entered. Mary Elliott-Lynn did not start but Lady Mary Bailey did, retiring with engine trouble near Doncaster. Frank Barnard, winner in 1922 and 1925, was killed when his plane stalled after an engine failure while testing two days before the race.

The 1928 race saw the highest proportion of finishers so far when twenty three crossed the finishing line. Winifred Spooner made history by coming third and winning the Siddeley Trophy as the first aero club member home. Guy Warwick became the first fatality in the history of the race when his ANC Missel Thrush G-EBPI crashed on a hillside in the Scottish Borders near Peebles, probably because he became disoriented in bad visibility.

The 1929 race was run on 6 and 7 July with a leg from Heston to Blackpool on the first day and back to Heston on the second. There were 41 starters (18 of them were Gipsy Moths) and 12 finished. The finishers included the three ladies who entered: Lady Bailey came 12th, Winifred Spooner 5th and Mrs A S Butler 14th.

Winifred Spooner became the sixteenth woman to hold a pilot's licence in the UK when it was awarded in September 1927; she went on to obtain a B (commercial) licence. She started an air taxi service in Kent and was awarded the Harmon Trophy as the out-standing female pilot in the world in 1929. She won or was placed in many other events after the King's Cup success in 1928. In December 1930 she set out with Flying Officer E C T Edwards to fly to South Africa in five days. Edwards was at the controls and she was sleeping when the plane crashed into the Mediterranean off the toe of Italy. Leaving Edwards, who could not swim, sitting on the wreckage, she swam nearly four kilometres to the shore and raised the alarm. One feels that, in the same circumstances it is exactly what Win would have done. Miss Spooner died in January 1933 after a seemingly-normal cold turned into pneumonia.

Lois Reid Butler was the Canadian wife of Alan Butler (also a pi-lot in the Race). He had become Chairman of De Havilland after in-vesting in the company when it needed it in 1924. She was awarded her aviator's certificate on 26 June 1929, just two weeks before the race. She entered many air races and flew a Gloster AS31 with her husband from Hatfield to Cape Town in 1931 with a flying time of just 72 hours. She was a skier of some note, captaining the Canadian team at the 1936 Olympics when she was 38, and she was an early member of the wartime Air Transport Auxiliary ferrying all types of aircraft around the country. She died of a heart attack while on holiday in Greece in 1970.

In *Under Six Planets* Win summed up the hazards of the race:

> As usual, the King's Cup was taking its toll, and before the race was over aeroplanes would be stranded all over Britain, and men might be lying killed or injured. But it was all in the luck of the game. The casualties were surprisingly few considering the strain this race put on man and machine, for not only was the course long and arduous for the slow machines of that time, but the pilots often flew in appalling weather without the present-day [the mid-fifties when Win wrote the book] instruments and navigational aids.
>
> Then they nearly always flew low, climbing wasted valuable time, and when machines were only capable of a top speed of about 100 m.p.h. [160 km/h] a head-wind played hell with them. As wind usually increases with height, pilots would fly against it just above the treetops, where air currents caused the planes to bump and generally made conditions tiring. If anything went wrong with the engine, the pilot was not high enough to pick a suitable forced-landing ground and had to come down more or less straight ahead, no matter whether it was a ploughed field or a graveyard. Engines were always run flat out, quite regardless of a notice on the instrument board saying that a maximum number of revolutions must not be exceeded for more than ten minutes. Some pilots of a more nervous temperament had been known to stick a piece of blank paper over the notice before starting a race, but the majority merely pushed the throttle fully open and thereafter prayed.[1]

Win's visit to Blackpool for the 1929 King's Cup left her intoxicated by the challenge it presented and by the wildness of the pilots (who draped Blackpool in toilet rolls). She wondered whether she could dream of taking part. Ron said why not and Roy Dobson, the Avro Manager and a consistent supporter of Win's adventures in his plane, said much the same. No hope of winning the King's Cup, of course, but taking part, why not? It was decided she should get a little more experience anyway. She had already flown to Ostende and later to Antwerp for a pageant and Berlin for an air show but now she entered for the International Light Plane Competition held in Rotterdam 27–30 June 1929. Here there were take-off tests, landing tests, speed trials, altitude tests and a cross-country run of nearly 300 kilometres as a reliability trial — a rather tame affair with a Dutch plane as guide and stops for tea. We have a photograph in *Flight* of Win landing in the landing test — where the aim was to stop in the shortest distance after landing over a stretched tape. Win, in *Under Six Planets*, says she won the maximum load test but this presumably refers to the handicapping system which required each plane to carry a minimum load for some of the tests: most planes needed some extra ballast but, for Win, this was not needed. Another *Flight* photo shows the British team, 16 strong, with Win looking distinctly unfashionable (compared to Lady Bailey for example) and standing beside Sir Sefton Brancker. The competitors and officials were all accommodated at the "Weimar Hotel" in some luxury with plentiful alcohol for themselves and there was free oil, petrol and spare parts for the planes. The more serious events were lightened by others that sound rather alarming: "bombing the baby" and a balloon strafing competition.

At home she took part in the Newcastle Air Pageant in October 1929, watched by 20,000 spectators. and entered the Grosvenor Challenge Cup. She did not win but, in the roistering that followed the events, she experienced the exuberance that seemed an essential part of the aviation scene. During the speeches at the pageant dinner someone discovered that if you struck a fellow diner firmly on the head with one of the chrysanthemums that decorated the room, it exploded with a bang, scattering petals as benign and colourful shrapnel. One imagines the dismay of the proud burghers of the city as the sharp cracks and plumes of colour spread like contagion around the room in a kind of floral firework display. Later an official of the Royal Aero Club was forcibly weighed naked in the hotel lobby and a fire was started when someone soaked some curtains with whisky and ignited them. The night ended with Win riding on the step of the "Black Maria" police van that was conveying her "love of the moment" to the police station.

THE 1930 KING'S CUP

The Lancs Aero Club had grown since Win joined and the atmosphere seems to have changed from the time when Win was celebrated in a little poem in the club newsletter:

> We love our little Win 'cos she's mischievous and bonny
>
> We'd get a word in edgeways if it wasn't for our Ronnie,
>
> And we'd tell her how in Asia little girls are often hanged
>
> From climbing in through windows when the Uke is being twanged.[2]

Women were no longer welcome at events like the regular Lancashire hot-pot suppers and a notice appeared on the bar door: "Women Not Admitted". In protest, when Win entered for the 1930 King's Cup Air Race, she did so in the name of Hanworth Aero Club rather than Lancs. Lancs seemed not to be bothered (her entry for such a prestigious event was seen as something of a joke anyway) and she was hardly welcomed by Hanworth, who refused her a room in their clubhouse for the night before the race.

The 1930 race was to be run in just one day, 5 July, on a 1200 kilometre course. It started at Hanworth in West London with a first stop at Bristol, after rounding a turning point at Hamble, near Southampton. After Bristol the next stop was Barton at Manchester after turning points at Birmingham and Liverpool. From Barton the course took competitors to Cramlington, north of Newcastle turning at Woodford (home of the Lancs Aero Club) and Sherburn, east of Leeds. The next leg was a straight 200 kilometres to Hull and the final one took them back to Hanworth, with a turn at Leicester. At each of the stops there was time to top up with petrol, check the engine, get a new weather forecast, update the plan for the next leg and maybe munch a sandwich.

THE ENTRANTS

There was a record entry of 101 planes and 88 of them actually started the race; almost half the entries were DH Moths of one kind or another. One quarter were eligible for the Siddeley Challenge Trophy for best performance by a club aviator.

The pilots included many big names. Sqdr Leader Augustus Henry Orlebar had shot down seven enemy aircraft as a fighter pilot in World War One and in 1927 became the Officer Commanding the RAF High Speed Flight team set up to recover the Schneider Trophy, the prestigious international trophy for high-speed seaplanes racing around a small circuit, won by the Italians in 1926. This the team did when on 26 September 1927 Supermarine S5s claimed first and second place at Venice. Two weeks earlier Orlebar himself had flown the winning plane to claim the world airspeed record of over 560 km/h. He had led the RAF team to win the 1929 Trophy and it was to win it again in 1931, so retaining it in perpetuity. Now, in the King's Cup and the fastest man on earth, he was flying a Blackburn Bluebird. Also in the race was Fl Lt Richard Waghorn, the pilot of the winning Schneider Trophy plane in 1929 who Win had seen land so cleverly on the golf course at the Blackpool Pageant, also flying a Blackburn Bluebird. Fl Lt Richard Atcherley, in the Segrave Meteor, was another high speed flier, a member of the 1929 Schneider Trophy Team and the winner of the King's Cup that year.

There were other vastly experienced pilots. Fl Lt Sydney Pope had shot down six planes in World War One and won the Military

Cross. Now an RAF test pilot, he had had a lucky escape in February 1930 when the fin and rudder of the Parnall Pipit he was flying broke off. The plane turned over. Pope managed to get out and deploy his parachute at less than 300 metres and landed without injury. Geoffrey de Havilland and his son Geoffrey Jr were flying Moths. Neville Stack was in an Avro Avian monoplane. Previous winners of the Cup were flying too: Captain H S Broad (1926), W L Hope (1927, 1928 and later in 1932) and, of course, Atcherley. The great and the good had entries: Prince George, the Prince of Wales, the Rt Hon Sir Philip Sassoon Bt, PC, GBE, CMG, MP, Lord Trenchard, Marshal of the Royal Air Force, Lord and Lady Wakefield, Lord Wavertree and Lord M A Douglas Hamilton had all entered planes; Douglas Hamilton was to fly his own as was Lt Caspar John, son of the artist Augustus John and a future First Sea Lord. Colonel the Master of Sempill, otherwise William Francis Forbes-Sempill and soon to be the 19th Lord Sempill and Baronet of Craigevar, also flew his own plane.

Business was represented too with entries from Robert McAlpine the construction magnate (the Blackburn Bluebird flown by Waghorn); William Rootes, the car maker; Lord Rothermere the newspaper owner and, naturally, several key figures from aviation including the plane makers A M DeSoutter, the Blackburn family, de Havilland and the founder of the company that made cars and engines, J D Siddeley. Loel Guinness entered a plane but later withdrew. He was the heir to the Guinness banking fortune and had recently taken to flying; he is best remembered as an international socialite and for his three celebrated marriages. Altogether, in flying experience, speed, engineering resources and social standing the competitors were a daunting prospect for the butcher's daughter from Salford. The unprecedented size of the field just made it worse.

Six other women entered for the race: Lady Mary Bailey, Mrs C M Young, Winifred Spooner, Lois Butler (flying her husband's Puss Moth while he flew her Moth), Miss D C Guest (daughter of Captain the Hon F E Guest, also competing), and Miss F M Wood, who dropped out before the start.

Christina Mitchell Young had obtained her aviator's certificate in October 1929 as a member of the Suffolk and Eastern Counties Aeroplane Club and bought her Gipsy Moth G-ABAE at the end of May 1930. A few months after the King's Cup, on 4 October 1930, it was named *Chrysalis* by the Mayoress of Ipswich in the presence of Sir Sefton Brancker. When the ceremony was over Brancker must have travelled to Cardington in Bedfordshire to board the R101 airship for Karachi. He was killed with 47 others when the airship crashed during the night near Beauvais in France.

The day dawned beautifully bright and sunny with light winds, perfect for racing for the less powerful and rather slower entrants. Hanworth aerodrome itself looked charming: the magnificent clubhouse with the flight of steps up to its colonnaded portico, the lawns with the deck-chairs spread out under the shady trees to later welcome spectators seeking refuge from the hot sun. With the elegant setting, the large field and the public interest, *Flight* could speculate on air racing rivalling Henley as a summer spectacle.

Win started the day in some despair. Refused accommodation at the Hanworth club, she and Ron had booked into a pub some way from the airfield. Now, a lumpy mattress and a restless night worrying she might die had her peering out of the curtains at 5:30. The mist that blanketed the countryside was clearing with the sunrise and it looked as if it might be a fine day. She put on her flying suit and packed her other things in a suitcase to leave at Hanworth, tying a label to it with her name and address in case she didn't get back to collect it — for any reason. Ron was already toying with sausages at breakfast: he looked pale and had cut himself shaving. He pushed the sausages aside, Win went to the toilet again and they left for the airfield.

The handicapping system rated planes by their maximum speed and gave them take-off times so that, all other things being equal, they would arrive at the finishing line simultaneously. The first plane off would be W H Sutcliffe in his DH Moth with a Cirrus I engine at 7 o'clock and the last the massive Vickers Vellore at 10:41. Win was to start at 8:16 just after a group of five Blackburn Blue-birds, including the three piloted by Sempill, Waghorn and Orlebar.

VZ was parked, serviced and ready to go, in one of the neat lines of planes. Win started the engine — which sounded a little rough to her nervous ear — and cut it. There were final checks and she made adjustments to her planned course for the forecast wind. It seemed an age to wait after Sutcliffe's take-off. But soon the time came and she taxied VZ to the start line. When the starter's flag fell, she was away, rocketing up. As the ground fell away so did Win's nerves. The race was on.

Win flew her compass course for the Hamble turn with Ron monitoring progress as best he could from the rear cockpit to make sure that they were flying on the direct track from Hanworth to Hamble, Win's calculated course having allowed for being blown off it by the wind by pointing VZ just slightly into it. Just before 9:00 they sighted Hamble and made the turn for Bristol. Ron thought he saw them overtake another plane soon after (they saw hardly any other competitors during the race except on the ground) and in another half hour they landed at Bristol, to find that they had passed not just one plane but seven, including Waghorn and Orle-bar. The forty minute stop was just long enough to fuel up VZ and check the oil level and plugs and then, at 10:08, they were off again with Waghorn just one minute behind. Turning at Birmingham and then Liverpool they landed before a vast crowd at Barton, Manchester at 11:55 where an excited Sawley told her she was now third and two minutes ahead of Waghorn. She was steadily creeping up through the field in what had so far been an incident-free race simply keeping to her planned courses and keeping the throttle open. But now there was some bad news.

There was thick cloud reported over the Pennines and the advice was to climb to 2000 metres to clear it. This would be a slow pro-cess and carried with it the risk that they would lose sight of land-marks "in the smoke of Yorkshire"[3] and be disoriented: the margin over Waghorn was slim and would be easily lost. Win decided on a strategy that gave a prospect of stealing a march on the other competitors — but it was much riskier. Getting it wrong would put her out of the race altogether — and maybe result in much worse.

THE SHORT CUT

After making the turn at Woodford, her home port, she headed for the Woodhead Pass that went directly through the Pennines along the route now followed by the A628. At its highest point it was 500 metres high with hills on either side, now smothered in cloud. The tiny biplane raced up the valley in a corridor of clear air, Win not knowing if it might not close ahead of them at any time making them turn back. If they did turn back it was quite possible that the clouds had shut off their escape route and then they could be flying blind with hilltops all around them, an extremely dangerous situation. As they approached the summit of the pass they could see the clouds were blocking their path but they pressed on and, at the last moment the cloud thinned and they were through. Elated but very shaken, she made the turn at Sherburn and headed for the aerodrome at Cramlington, near Newcastle. She learned that the gamble had paid off. Waghorn was now 9 minutes behind after being lost over Yorkshire and she was in the lead.

Disaster almost struck again, this time on the ground. As she took off another plane taxied across in front of VZ. Rather than aborting and losing minutes she opened the throttle and, as soon as she could, heaved back the stick to skim over the plane with just inches to spare.

At Hull they were 12 minutes up on Waghorn but now Alan Butler was catching up so the last leg back to Hanworth was a nervous affair with Ron scanning the skies for overtaking planes. He did see one machine. Win dived towards the finishing line, VZ touching 240 km/h with everything straining and shuddering, but the plane overtook them and they thought the dream was over — and then they realised it was not in the race but just a spectator. They finished at 18:15:27. Win landed and found people racing towards her. Two, in white overalls, steadied the wings, and she was guided to a standstill. The crowds around the aerodrome seemed to be waving and cheering and then they were surrounded by officials, policemen and the press. With all this excitement they must have done well Win thought. When Joe Taylor from BP told her they had won she hardly took it in.

Alan Butler had overtaken Waghorn to come in second, twelve minutes after Win. Waghorn was third close behind and fourth was Butler's wife. The rest straggled in until I R Parker landed at 19:30.

The three other women who finished came in 14th (Winifred Spooner), 30th (Mrs Young) and 53rd Lady Bailey. Mrs Guest, re-tired. There were some bad luck stories. McKenna, who was third at Hull, ran out of petrol within sight of Hanworth. In spite of filling up at a local garage, he ended well down the order. Percival could also have been in the top few but got lost towards the end. One of the first to drop out had been the Segrave Meteor. After a start that nearly scythed down part of the pressing crowd, it quickly returned to Hanworth with a fuel problem.

THE CUP

Most of this news had yet to come in as Ron clambered rather stiffly out from the rear cockpit. Win climbed up and posed, sitting on the cockpit rim, acclaimed by the excited and growing group around her, to be photographed and filmed for Pathé News. She was helped down and almost frogmarched from VZ by Harold Per-rin, the Secretary of the Royal Aero Club known as "Harold the Hearty", in plus fours with a cigarette in the corner of his mouth throughout. Perrin supported her from one side and a very excited Roy Chadwick, the designer of the Avro Avian, from the other. A film cameraman retreated before them, men in cloth caps looked on and policemen stood by as Win was led off with Ron trailing some-where well behind, rather lost in the following crowd. As soon as they could Win and Ron headed to the bar with Chadwick, Joe Taylor and no doubt others for a calming beer.

She was of course still dressed in her flying gear with her face blackened a little by the emissions from the modified exhaust of

VZ. A titled lady (Win does not tell us who but there were plenty around) had been nominated to make Win respectable enough to receive the trophies from Sir Philip Sassoon. She suggested a pretty dress.

Win did the best she could. In her red suitcase she had a dress. It was potentially glamorous in a sheer fabric called ninon, made from either rayon or silk. Black and patterned with yellow flowers and green leaves it hung down, shapelessly, nearly to her ankles. The matching jacket had sleeves "that were neither full nor fitted" and gave the ensemble an unflattering square neck. Whether or not it looked good when she bought it, Win now felt uncomfortable as she was led "like a shy baby elephant" to the presentation. In fact, if the dress was not quite the thing, Win looks fresh, young and quite composed in the Pathé film.

The presentation took place under the portico of the clubhouse — still there and rather grand but derelict with grass growing in the masonry — where the more privileged sat or stood on the steps while the main crowd looked on from the lawns. Sir Philip was informal but as neatly dressed as always (was he wearing spats or were his shoes two-tone?) and surprisingly nervous-looking, fiddling constantly with his tie, as he made a short speech. Win stood, slightly round-shouldered, waiting and smiling. In some little ritual incomprehensible in the silent news film, after seeming about to hand the cup to Win, he calls up Harold Perrin and another official and they step up to the trophy table and appear to bow slightly to Win and gesture towards the Cup as Win touches it. Whatever is going on, the Siddeley Trophy is then presented and Win is invited to say a few words.

This she does. The content is unrecorded; the film is silent. She is nervous, looking at her fingernails and laughing rather more than her audience. The grand crowd on the steps displays amusement, indulgent puzzlement and, at moments, what looks like a degree of embarrassment; what the unseen crowd on the lawns thought we cannot even guess. But, although nervous and silent, Win looks like a determined performer, doing what she knows she has to do, and really rather enjoying the attention. The "shy baby elephant" was flying.

There was a congratulatory telegram from King George and an apology from a Hanworth official that she had been refused accommodation. It had all been a regrettable mistake. He had not been aware of the request and of course there was always a room for her. In fact, he said, the very best one, large and with a balcony at the front of the clubhouse was available for her right now. Win took some pleasure in refusing; the room that had been good enough before she won was certainly good enough now she had.

So after celebration, talking and laughter and, no doubt, much drinking Win and Ron returned in the early hours to the little inn they were staying at. The couple who ran it insisted on opening the bottle of wine they had set aside for a special event. In these quieter rather touching moments, just what the butcher's daughter had achieved must have begun to sink in.

Why did she win? She flew at the maximum speed she could throughout and perhaps was treated generously by the handicapper. VZ and the Cirrus engine performed faultlessly — but reliability of the aeroplanes was one of the remarkable features of the race. The flying conditions generally helped the lower-powered machines; more wind would have given an advantage to the planes with more power. The navigation was spot on but how much of this was down to Win's masterly planning with her wind vectors and how much to Ron looking over the side we can't know. The short-cut through the Pennines must have helped. The *Times* was not overly generous, pointing out that the hard flying was all between Newcastle and London, where many competitors raced through the field, and

> Miss Brown's flying had none of these hard flying qualities. What gave her success was consistently good work from a fairly good start.[4]

A mite unfair you may think given that she was already leading by Newcastle so had no-one to overtake — and that was because of some opportunistic and courageous flying through the hills. Anyway, the bonny lass from Salford had won the Royal Aero Club's King's Cup, a famous, large and shiny trophy — and it was hers to keep.

TRANUM

The next day the main event was a Reception given for Win by Henleys of Piccadilly, purveyors of cars and, in those days, aeroplanes. It was here that "a famous parachutist" arrived with a parachute for Win. This was surely the Dane John Tranum who had given a parachuting display on the day of the race. He worked for the British Russell Parachute Company and had acquired a parachute as a gift for Win as she had not worn one in the race. He decided that they should try it out and, since Win refused to jump, they borrowed a plane (the parachute was, unhelpfully, too big to fit in VZ) and she took him up to let him jump. After some flirtation and even a tender kiss, with Win struggling to keep the plane level, Tranum disappeared leaving Win suddenly very alone, the wind whistling through a strange plane. When she landed the was no sign of Tranum, and search parties were sent out. He was eventually located, according to Win, in a sewage farm. This part of the story sounds suspicious because Tranum did land in a sewage farm near Brooklands in a demonstration in March 1930. To do it twice in a few months maybe stretches credibility.

Tranum lived to parachute and would often hitch a ride, stepping off the plane, sometimes with bowler hat and briefcase, when he was over his destination. His exploits included jumping off bridges, riding a motorcycle off a 300 metre cliff and parachuting down, wing-walking, jumping from a plane over Southport beach at just 30 metres and record free-fall jumps. One of the more extreme adventures he planned was being a human bomb in 1932. He was to be fitted inside an aluminium casing shaped like a bomb with a window in the nose. Dropped from an aircraft at 7000 metres above Salisbury Plain, he would watch the earth rush towards him and at about 1000 metres flip open the nose, climb out and drift down on his parachute. It was not simply madness but, according to *Popular Sci-*

ence[5], a demonstration of a way to land passengers from futuristic pressurised planes anticipated to fly 15,000 metres up. The passengers could simply be bundled into something like Tranum's bomb and literally dropped off as the plane passed over their destination. There is no record that he performed the jump although he did set a new world record by free-falling for nearly 6000 metres over Netheravon the following year. He died in 1935, collapsing at 10,000 metres in an aeroplane taking him up for another free-fall record attempt. He was dead before the plane managed to land.

In this world of risk-takers, in which Win was now suddenly and unexpectedly a celebrated winner, there were, it seems, degrees of madness.

CELEBRITY

It was soon clear that Win had become a celebrity. Letters and telegrams flooded in, people recognised her on the street. The day after the reception they were back in Manchester for the Brooklands Open Tennis competition. Win had her photograph taken for the *Manchester Evening News* in her tennis kit ("Trying for Another Prize") but soon had to withdraw from the competition because of the distraction all the fuss around them was causing. Sawley arranged one or two other public appearances for her.

The first was at an un-named Dirt Track, what we would now call a motorcycle speedway. The sport had arrived just a few years before and was something of a craze. The Albion track in Salford for example attracted 10,000 spectators on a good day to watch Sid Newiss and A J Ward, battle with "Broadside" Burton, "Buster" Breaks, "Skid" Skinner, "Riskit" Riley and the Langton brothers. So, wherever the Dirt Track was, quite a lot of people may have seen Win present the Silver Gauntlet to a grimy winner, decline a congratulatory kiss but then sit on the back of the machine and do a circuit with her skirt in the air.

The next was at the Albion Dog Track, as a favour to one of Sawley's pals: the Chairman of the Track. Greyhound racing was another very new sport, introduced from America in 1926 at the purpose-built Belle Vue Stadium in Manchester, and in Salford was run on the same track as the speedway. Its arrival was the subject of vigorous opposition; "greyhound racing, with its probable attendant evils, is not wanted in Salford" (Salford Sunday School Union). The main evil they had in mind was gambling, not maybe unreasonably since greyhound racing offered all the opportunities to lose money that horse racing did but in a convenient urban setting most days of the week. We can guess that this was right up Sawley's street: somewhere he and his girl-friend could hang out with racy friends while

Elsie stewed at home, not much more than a kilometre away. It may even have accounted in some degree for the financial decline he experienced. Win was welcomed to the Directors' Box with a floral aeroplane and after the big race, won by a dog called Constance, was invited to parade the animal around the track. This went well until the dog stopped and relieved itself, bringing laughter and cat-calls from the crowd.

There were plenty of other invitations. On 9 August she invested the Rose Queen at a small un-named Lancashire town and went on to be feted at the first crowning of the Silk Queen — a young lady called Lilian Jarvis[1] — at the Macclesfield Carnival. Macclesfield was at one time the largest producer of finished silk in the UK but the industry declined from the middle of the 19th century when the Chinese started to export the finished product themselves; in the 20th century artificial fibres effectively finished it off.. Some of the traditions survived and the coronation was one of them. Win was in the parade, led by the Town Band, after the Queens, Princesses, Heralds and Trainbearers, the Comical Characters, the Decorated Motorcycles, the Dogs and the Morris Dancers and many more in the three mile long procession. She travelled in the private car of Mr Walter Brown JP, shared with Mr John Remer, Conservative MP for Macclesfield, and Mr Walter Brown Jnr and was personally ser-enaded with a song celebrating her King's Cup win.

This was not Win's first visit to Macclesfield after the King's Cup success. The *Macclesfield Courier and Herald* for 2 August reports ("Air Queen Visits Silk Queen") that, on the previous Wednesday after-noon (30 July), 1000 people had paid threepence each (about 1p) to see Win land in a field for a visit to the town. Win flew in and did a few circuits of the field, a side slip and two loops before making a slow low-level pass and then heading back to Woodford. The on-lookers were assured that she would return by car but "The crowd did not receive this information too pleasantly and several caustic comments were made." Why she did not land was explained later: first there had not seemed enough room in the field and second a man had been seen standing in the field and waving a red flag as if to warn her off. The man had in fact been warning the crowd that she was about to land.

She and Ron toured a silk finishing factory and she picked out some Macclesfield ivory satin to have made into a dress, she met the Silk Queen and attended a reception at the Town Hall. Whether this mended the relationship with her fans in the field we are not told; whether the were refunded their threepences also remains a mystery.

There had been even more prestigious events to attend. Win had been invited to the House of Commons on 21 July as guest of honour, introduced to the Prime Minister, Ramsay MacDonald, and Stanley Baldwin and afterwards entertained in a private room by David Lloyd George. This, knowing the Welsh wizard's womanising skills, could have gone badly but happily the Speaker and Lloyd George's daughter were present. As it was Win said she lost her heart to him.

Win, if she did chat to Baldwin, would probably have learned that he had been at an aerial garden party at Hanworth arranged by his wife just two days before. Organised for one of her charities, the guests saw races, flying displays (including a slightly alarming one by an autogyro) and Baldwin may have been lucky enough to see the inevitable John Tranum step out of a plane to float down and, this time, land in a cabbage field.

Another event, which Win omits all mention of in her autobiography, is a talk she was asked to give on 8 July from Manchester on the BBC wireless. At 6:35 that evening she talked on the National programme for five minutes as the winner of the King's Cup. Sadly, no record of the talk seems to survive and we know of it only through its presence in the newspaper programme timetables.

Her fame spread to the letters page of the *Daily Express* in a letter printed under the title "A Joke from Hendon":

> In view of the achievements of women like Miss Marjorie Foster, Miss Winifred Brown and Miss Amy Johnson, why not appeal to the women of England to supply the bowler we need for the next Test match?

WINIFRED BROWN

B W Secretary
Sydney-grove, Hendon NW 4[2]

She took up an offer from the *Manchester Evening News* of £100 to do some simple aerobatics over some seaside piers as publicity for the newspaper. The trip to Rhyl in North Wales was made in low cloud and drizzle but the display went down well. On the next day (24 July) she went to Southport, the next to Morecambe (where she became involved in a drinking and poker session with two newspapermen and a barmaid, the barmaid cleaning up) and then on the Saturday (26 July) to Blackpool and Lytham St Anne's. She was lunched by local worthies, admired gardens, played push-ball and was taken for a spin in a small motorboat on the Morecambe boating lake by the mayor. At Rhyl she opened the new outdoor pool but declined a persistent invitation to swim a length. The little tour seems to have been a success; it boosted sales of the newspaper and her picture was on the front page of every one sold. She was always wearing, curiously, what looks just like a football scarf.

The oil company BP gave a dinner in her honour at the "Midland Hotel" in Manchester on the 1 August. The alcohol flowed and as she climbed out of the car on return to Lodore the box containing the King's Cup slipped and fell on her foot. By the morning this had swollen so much that the doctor told her to stay in bed — if she stood she might lose her leg. So she had to cancel her plan to fly down and attend the welcoming lunch to be given at the "Savoy" hotel by the *Daily Mail* for Amy Johnson on 6 August. According to *Under Six Planets* she sent a telegram saying she had dropped the Cup on her foot. The newspaper report of the grand luncheon puts her absence down to "illness" — and says that she had a special mention from Amy.

VARIETY

But the most remarkable development was her stage career. It started with a week appearing at the Blackpool Palace of Variety, an impressive theatre on the Promenade next to the famous Tower, starting on the 4 August. She flew there with her swollen foot; Ron carried her to the plane and even piloted the plane between take-off and landing. She topped the bill of *Twice Brightly* with George Formby, the Lancashire comic singer, Percy Honri "A concert-in-a-turn", Kharum "The Persian Pianist" and Ted Ray, later to be established as a major comedian, particularly on the wireless. Jennie Hartley shared the bill. An established revue actress and singer she was to become a friend. Jennie seems to have been made of similar stuff to Win. At the opening night of *Sinbad the Sailor* in Melbourne in 1920 she had paused in the middle of one of her songs to confide that "this is the worst song I've ever sung in my life." The audience, according to the *Melbourne Argus* of 20 December 1920, "did not contradict her."

Win was introduced to the audience by the Ringmaster of the Tower Circus and hobbled on, supported on two sticks, an instantly heroic figure in the attentive spotlights, dressed in her flying gear and to the tune "She's a Lassie from Lancashire". The details of the performance are not known but it may have started with a Pathé News film — certainly later ones did. We do know that Win "in her characteristic happy, laughing style"[3] chatted to the audience about flying and the Race. She then answered questions, sitting in the cockpit of VZ, which shared the stage. Before the week was out an offer of a tour came from Sir Oswald Stoll, the theatre owner, with dates at the Manchester and Bristol Hippodromes and the London Coliseum. The Manchester date was the following week and it meant that VZ had to be dismantled early on Sunday morning, taken to the local airfield, flown to Manchester, transported into the city centre and reassembled on the stage of the Hippodrome. This became a regular routine during the tour. It not only meant an early morning and a late night but the constant niggling worry, as they were flying, that some bit had been left out or damaged and that VZ might just crumple in mid-air.

At the Manchester Hippodrome Win found that one night Sawley had booked seats for his entire staff and, after the performance, she was presented with a giant bouquet from them. She was about to dismantle this and arrange the flowers in water when she was reminded that Hippodrome management's policy was that bouquets remained intact and were presented at every performance until they died. The Lancashire Aero Club turned out in force on the Friday evening, demonstrating her popularity at the club, even if she had theoretically won the Cup for Hanworth.

The London Coliseum appearance was not without its upsets. First when they ran her film at rehearsals it proved to be the wrong one. It featured archbishops and a baby show and they had to dash to the Pathé offices for the right one. Then there was confusion over the music. And then Ron made an unscheduled appearance in "Parisian Novelties", an item with scantily-clad ladies which had already drawn the attention of the local censor. He stumbled off the Coliseum's renowned revolving stage after pushing VZ into a corner and staggered into the middle of the dancers, who had started their act. His convalescence in Win's dressing room was interrupted by a screaming trumpet from just outside the door, where a rather scruffy musician had been sent to make distant trumpet calls for a war play going on on stage.

They had stayed at Hartley House in Gower Street, an establishment run by Jennie Hartley's sister. Good value and intended for theatre folk, it was just six and sixpence (32p) a night for bed and breakfast. Baths were extra and the maid told Win that the the price depended on how much water you had; the choice was between a penny (½p) one and a tuppenny (1p) one. The maid studied Win's ninety kilograms and said "Cor blimey, Miss! I don't think a penny 'un would cover you!"

The Coliseum week went well in an unexpected way. A handwritten letter arrived from Sir Sefton Brancker congratulating her on what she was doing on stage (there were some in the aeronautical press who thought it not quite right) and saying he would come and see her if he could.

She flew down to Whitchurch near Bristol on the Sunday to find that the lorry provided for the plane (suitably decorated with Win's name) was too small. The only solution was to tow VZ behind it, wings folded. The plane could only be got out of the aerodrome by digging up part of the railings at the gate and then the road was narrow and VZ caused a large traffic jam. It had to be dismantled outside the theatre with children poking the fabric and one swinging on the propeller and was finally reassembled on stage. At the end of the week at Bristol, where she shared the bill with Dave Willis, Mamie Soutter, Little Joey, 12 London Girls and others, Win ended her stage career. A proposed Scottish tour fell through perhaps because Amy Johnson was now the big attraction. Nonetheless these theatres at Blackpool, Manchester, London and Bristol were large 2000 plus seaters (Blackpool could hold 2800) and with a strong "supporting programme" (which had no doubt been booked to fill the seats before Win appeared on the scene) and the holiday period, they must have been well-filled. So "performer" must definitely be added to Win's skills.

Elsie's role in the events surrounding the Race had been strange. As the day approached she packed her bags and went to stay at a hotel in Germany. Quite why is a mystery. When the hotel proprietress told her that Win had won, she was dismissed as mistaken. The following morning when the lady tried to convince her with a photograph in a newspaper (a poor photo of Win with her blackened face) she was told that it was not Win — it was a Japanese woman.

It is just possible that Elsie had had enough of Sawley rather than of Win because it was around this time that Win met "Sweetie Pie", as the family called Sawley's girl-friend. Win went along with Sawley to a pub where he was President of the Bowling Club and a well-liked and generous patron, suggesting he had an active social life away from Elsie. Since Sweetie Pie is reputed to be have been a bar-maid, this may have been the pub she worked at. Anyway there was a rather raunchy game of musical chairs which involved the women sitting on the knees of the men; Sawley seemed to enjoy himself not least because he always seemed to be last man in — an arrangement Win thought. Win's later chance meeting with Sweetie Pie at a hotel ended badly with the lady throwing pieces of her turkey about and complaining that Win had been given a nice-looking piece of sole — too good for turkey! Sawley took Win home saying that Sweetie Pie was drunk. How much Elsie knew about the situation we cannot know but she was having Sawley followed on his night-time excursions at the time.

Sawley was tortured. One evening he asked Win if she would look after Elsie if he left. She thought immediately of what the newspapers would make of it ("Airwoman's father in divorce"), accused him of causing enough scandal already and stalked out of the room. She realised later, probably much later, that she had missed the opportunity to understand what he was going through and to help him. Anyway, the matter was never mentioned again.

PRESS CLUB

Win was invited to attend a dinner at the Press Club in London on 13 December 1930 in honour of famous sportswomen.[4]. She was a guest along with Marjorie Foster (who had just won the King's Prize for rifle shooting at Bisley, beating 1000 men); Diana Fishwick (the year's ladies open golf champion at just 19 years of age); Betty Nuthall, the US tennis champion; and Joyce Cooper, the swimmer who had won a silver and two bronzes at the 1928 Amsterdam Olympics. In *Under Six Planets* she says that Caroline Haslett, the leading electrical engineer, was being honoured too but this may have been another event or she may just have been there because she is not mentioned in press reports of the dinner. Whatever, Win and Ron arrived and downed half a dozen gins in the bar before they realised that Win was a guest of honour and the whole event was being delayed in the belief that she was late. In a short speech she made a joke in which a child thought the massive rolls of news-print that then arrived in Fleet Street on lorries were giant toilet rolls: *everything*, he thought, must be on an enormous scale in the newspaper industry. It went down well with the hacks.

Marjorie Foster and Caroline Haslett were two remarkable women of the time. Foster took up shooting at an early age and after her Bisley success frequently represented her country. With her partner, Miss Blanche Badcock, she kept a chicken farm in Mytchett, Surrey. On returning from Bisley she was driven in triumph on the Frimley Fire Brigade tender while a local band played "See the conquering hero comes". She was given a car bought with money raised by public subscription. Haslett started life as a secretary but, with the opportunity provided to women by World War One, became a respected electrical engineer and a pioneer for women in professional and engineering circles. She was convinced that electricity could take much of the drudgery out of women's lives. She was made a CBE in the 1931 New Year Honours and received many other honours.

OTHER LIVES

Win was Secretary of the North Manchester Hockey Club and a dictatorial and socially elitist Captain. To get into the first team it was reckoned by her enemies that you had to own a car and a fur coat, as well as being a county-standard player. She was the first-choice pick for Lancashire goalie until, in the winter of 1930, she was dropped. Perhaps she had been too honest about the prospects of not being able to play because of her expected theatrical work; maybe the time she spent talking to her young fans during the county trials had been taken as a sign of a casual attitude. Perhaps she seemed to be taking her place for granted.

She seemed ready to take this in her stride and play for the second eleven but Elsie was not. She was furious and persuaded Win to resign as Secretary and gave up her captaincy. She played for one season for Cheshire (someone realised that she had been born in Cheshire and thus was eligible) but failed to get into the North of England team. She continued playing club hockey but, at the end of the season, she decided that, at 31, her career at higher level in the sport was over. She played on Wednesdays and Saturdays in club games but the rest of the week was devoted to a new passion: golf.

GOLF

She joined the "Old Manchester" Club — the Manchester Golf Club — and took lessons from Bob Leather. She was soon winning prizes and led the Bronze Division (with her handicap of 25) at the annual open meeting for women at Stand in Yorkshire in June 1931[1]. Bob encouraged her to join a bigger club and this she did, choosing the North Manchester. She was soon playing for their team and, with near daily tuition, reduced her handicap to a very respectable 12. It was soon time to enter the Lancashire Ladies'

Championship at Formby and she got as far as the quarter finals. In this match she was well ahead of her opponent at the twelfth hole when her ball lodged half way up the face of a sand hill. She hacked away gamely at the ball, which was at shoulder height so she was swinging the club horizontally, but wasted (she says) twenty strokes trying to hit it. Naturally she lost the hole but she was now discouraged and the opponent (now encouraged no doubt in the mind game that is golf) went on to win the remaining holes and the match. Something came from the disaster because the fact that she had reached the quarter finals impressed the selectors and she was picked for the Lancashire second team — and occasionally played for the first.

She joined Blackpool Golf Club and again did well, winning the Gold medal and playing to a handicap of just four on the last occasion. Buoyed up by this success she decided to enter for the British Ladies Open in May 1934 at Royal Porthcawl Golf Club. She came to the last hole with 129 strokes on her card — perhaps 60 over par for the course — and in a quite hopeless position as far as qualifying for the tournament was concerned. She ignored her playing partner's suggestion that they give up and insisted in playing the last hole and completing the round. Her approach shot landed among the spectators sitting in deck chairs on a small hill short of the green. The prudent next shot was to putt the ball down the hill and onto the green but Win decided to finish with a flourish and chip the ball onto the green — giving it plenty of back-spin to stop it rolling past the hole. The conception was that of a master — the crowd could sense that. Winifred addressed the ball and struck it with her niblick. All eyes followed the trajectory as it pitched unerringly towards the hole. Unfortunately what they were all following was the divot Win had taken. She had missed the ball altogether and it still lay at her feet. She knew it was really bad when nobody laughed.

WINIFRED BROWN

ICE HOCKEY

As she retired from hockey and took up golf she also started playing ice hockey.

The Manchester Merlins was the first women's team in the country, playing at the Manchester Ice Palace to some initial opposition on the grounds the the sport was too physical for ladies. It was formed in the winter of 1929/30 and within a year there were three other teams to play against: Queens, Sussex (Brighton) and the Lambs. The Lambs was the female counterpart of the Lions and they played at Grosvenor House, Park Lane in London. Win's friend Connie Willan was a founder member of the Merlins and, their being short of a goalie, asked Win. Initially thinking that the inability to skate would disqualify her, she was soon convinced that she would spend more time on her knees than on skates. What would count was her sheer bulk filling the goal — and presumably her hockey experience.

Quite when Win first played is uncertain — it was a match against the Lambs — but by January 1931 she was Captain of the team sent to France and Switzerland to tour. When an England team was proposed, Win and Connie (and a Miss Eckersley) were selected after the trials at Grosvenor House (the selectors were all men as they were supposed to know more about the game). They played in the first ever international against France on 28 February 1931.

The Manchester Merlins were reckoned by many the best of the British teams. Their defence was solid but they struggled to score goals. So, many of their matches were goalless draws. They were undefeated in their southern tour in January 1932 but against foreign opposition they (and England) were generally found wanting.

The Manchester tour to France and Switzerland in 1931 was another example of trouble seeking out Win. She and Ron flew VZ to Le Bourget near Paris with a plan to complete the trip by train. This went well until they reached Le Bourget where they found it difficult to make themselves understood; presumably everyone spoke French. They were rescued by an Englishman called John who offered to get them to the city — and, at Win's prompting, to show them the night life. They visited a bar decorated as a miniature golf course; the fashionable but basic Jockey Bar in Montparnasse, decorated with paintings of American Indians (where she punched a customer on the nose); Fred Payne's bar in Pigalle which offered afternoon bridge and all-night cabaret, and finally a place where the dance floor was a mirror. She woke in John's flat with Ron on one side of her and John on the other. The other occupants were two love-birds in a cage and an Aberdeen terrier. Reflecting, no doubt, that this was an unconventional way to start a hockey tour (what would Miss Thompson have thought?) she realised that they had already nearly missed the train for Switzerland. However, after a frantic taxi ride around Paris to collect their stuff from their hotel, they just made the train, Win slumping into the corner of the compartment and, straight away, falling asleep. When they got to Chamonix they found that Connie, the team captain, had been left at an earlier stop when she went to a bookstall. Ron got the blame, having been appointed team travelling manager — which seemed to mean being in charge of the 49 suitcases the young ladies had filled. They left Connie's ticket at the station and went to their hotel.

The tour gave them experience but not success on the field. Win and Ron were struck by the number of injuries sustained in winter sports in Chamonix: broken legs and arms, people hobbling around on crutches. They thought curling looked safe until one of the sweepers fell over and was stretchered off with a cracked skull.

Win seems to have given up ice hockey in 1932 or 1933. By 1933 she disappears from accounts of games. The goalie at the 15 March 1933 game Manchester played with Paris (they lost again) was Miss N Scott and the captain was Connie Willan. Also in March 1933 the England goalie was Miss B Umney. Soon after that Connie Willan was playing for the London Lambs and the Merlins disappear from the press.

But Win was of course playing golf and still flying.

WINIFRED BROWN

FLYING ON

The faithful VZ faltered in late 1930. During a race from London to Blackpool Win detected something strange with her engine and pulled out. Ron could hear nothing wrong and mechanics at Blackpool gave the engine the all-clear. However when Win took the plane for a test run from Blackpool aerodrome the Cirrus engine failed catastrophically and Win was forced to make a crash landing, managing to avoid children playing in Stanley Park. The engine was replaced but, as Win says in *Under Six Planets*, the plane was never the same again.

Fortunately the new plane (a Sports Avian, a much faster all-metal racer) promised by Sir John Siddeley after the King's Cup race was not long in coming. Win asked Sir Sefton Brancker if he could arrange for her to keep the combination VZ for the new machine. He declared that he could not possibly influence the allocation of registration codes, she thought with a twinkle in his eye, but when it was issued it was G-ABED (Win says Elliott-Lynn's was G-ABUG[2]). Although Win was not specific about dates we can conclude it was in the autumn of 1930 because Brancker died in the R101 crash on 5 October 1930. G-ABED was named *Jerry* by the Avro staff; it seemed appropriate as jerries (a nickname for a chamberpot) went under beds.

In 1931 Win flew *Jerry* at numerous events: displays at Coventry and Skegness in May, a race from London to Newcastle in June for example. In July she and Ron took part in the King's Cup race. This was generally a disaster (only half the 40 starters finished because of the poor weather) and nearly for Win and Ron a fatal one. In poor visibility they ran into a hill at Hickleton in Yorkshire. They only damaged one wheel of *Jerry* and could probably have continued but Win had had enough and they spent the night with the locals and continued the following day.

Jerry's engine had a habit of occasionally cutting out without warning. It could be started again without any trouble but the fault was never pinned down. It seems (perhaps surprisingly) not to have caused a major problem until Win was giving a display in the Isle of Man in June 1932. The engine stopped and, in trying to get back to the aerodrome, Win landed on the boundary hedge . She was un-hurt but quickly realised that there was a woman lying on the ground, obviously hurt if not dead. To Win's relief the lady sat up and it was found that *Jerry*'s wing had broken her thigh bone. She was taken off by ambulance and it later emerged that things could have been much worse. The woman had thrown her son, whom she had been holding, to her husband just before the crash. The plane was repaired in time for the 1932 King's Cup[3] and Win came 21st out of 34 entrants.

In the autumn of 1932 Sawley complained that business was hard and wondered whether Win really needed a car, two aeroplanes and (surprisingly) a caravan. Clearly he was still funding a number of her activities. According to Win she sold VZ to John Tranum, the parachutist, to form part of a flying circus he was planning to set up. It certainly made an appearance at the Medway Towns Air Rally in mid-October flown by a Mr W M Wood.[4] It was written off in a crash a few years later.

UP THE AMAZON

The Booth Line ran a regular seven week cruise every two months advertised as "1,000 MILES UP THE AMAZON IN AN OCEAN LINER."[1] Various ships were used and there were sailings from London, Hull and Liverpool to Brazil via Portugal and Madeira. The cost was £75 to £100 including all the organised excursions. Elsie had decided that she needed another holiday, perhaps an accompanied tour of the Italian Lakes, but Win, seduced by the brochure for the Amazon with its yellow waters, luxuriant vegetation and exotic birds, decided that South America was just the place. She somehow had her way and they signed up for a cruise on the SS *Hilary* leaving Liverpool on 7 February 1933. Ron was to come too.

Quite how the Press became involved is not clear but Win later told the story that there was a farewell party at the Lancs Aero Club at which a member who was a newspaper reporter was present. He was not well liked because he always seemed to turn up first at any crashes and it was decided to play a trick on him. He was told that Win was in fact not just cruising to the Amazon but would be exploring it too, promising stories of head-hunters and giant snakes. The excited reporter dashed off and returned with a photographer and Win was kitted out in a cowboy hat, shirt and riding breeches to pose for him as the intrepid adventuress. This done the party continued into the early hours.

The next morning, hungover, she dragged herself from her bed to take a phone call from the editor of a newspaper. He had presumably heard from the reporter and wanted to buy the story of the adventure. When she heard they would pay, she quickly agreed to change her plans. This was 5 February, just two days before the ship sailed. She had no plans or equipment for an expedition but was sure something would turn up. She told Ron about the intrepid holiday extension and, the following day, drove over to the Booth steamship company in Liverpool and changed her ticket and Ron's; they would leave the *Hilary* at Manaus, 1600 kilometres up the Amazon, have their adventure and then catch another boat back home. Elsie, not being a canoe sort of woman and with little interest in head-hunters and large snakes, would stay on the ship and return alone. While at the Booth offices she met the British Consul from Iquitos, Peru, on leave in Britain, who persuaded her that she should visit his city and Peru. It was only another 3200 kilometres up the river. Before she left the offices she had made up her mind: Peru it was to be.

The next morning they caught the Liverpool train from Manchester, Win waved to an imaginary throng for the benefit of some pressmen who had come to photograph her farewell and the three of them settled back into their seats for the short journey to Liverpool and the *Hilary*. The loading was soon finished and the gangways up, the ship's whistle (more a blasting fog-horn really) sounded and the ship slipped away.[2]

PORTUGAL

The first stop was Leixoes in Portugal ("a depressing god-forsaken place") where they hired a car and drove the dozen kilometres to Oporto along the banks of the Douro, the locals waving to them and cheering them on their way. At Oporto the zoo made the greatest impact because the cages were populated mainly by dogs which were tormented by local boys throwing stones at them and poking them with sticks. Some of the animals prowled back and forth, snarling and some cowered in the corners. One large dog was just skin and bones with sores up his legs and blind in one eye; one of the passengers was so upset they tried to buy him. It turned Win against zoos and animal captivity.

The next stop was Lisbon and here they visited Sintra ("village of palaces" and a historic royal retreat), a few kilometres to the west of the city. In the Sintra Palace she was taken by the legend of the Sala de Pegas, the Magpie Room. Here the ceiling is decorated with 136 magpies with the words *Por Bem* (For the Best) issuing from their beaks. Win relates the tale that, in about 1400, one monarch, John I, was caught kissing a pretty peasant girl by the court ladies who ran off and told the queen. The ladies then persisted in prattling and even sniggering at the king and he became so annoyed that he had one magpie painted on the ceiling for each court lady with those inspiring words coming from its mouth. They may well have carried on sniggering, reflecting that if that was the best an absolute monarch could do, they had little to worry about. John I was remembered as a kind and benevolent monarch; his wife Philippa of Lancaster, daughter of John of Gaunt, wielded considerable power in the court and seems to have been a figure of influence on the international stage. Their marriage was the culmination of the process that made Portugal Britain's "oldest ally".

Perhaps uplifted by a story that had a Lancashire lass (at least in name) playing a major role, Win returned to the *Hilary* and they left for Madeira, a two-day passage. The quote below, and most others in this chapter, comes from Win's unpublished *Yellow Waters* manuscript:

> The sky is so blue and the rock so white, the palms so refreshing, the mule tracks so dusty, the markets and cafés so full of "picturesque" dirt! And the flowers and lizards and children, so gay. I liked to watch the native boys dive stark naked into the harbour for silver pieces thrown by the passengers. Their bodies flash so greedily, like long brown fishes streaking into the water, and they never miss their prey, even if the tiny coins are embedded in the sand at the bottom.[3]

In their brief stop on the island they visited the wine factory, where Win was impressed by the modern method of making wine which eschewed tramping feet and instead relied on "charcoal, milk, glass and ice". They then took the funicular up a mountain and tobogganed back down a cobbled track being showered with petals and blossoms by locals. She was bitten by someone's pet monkey and it "affected my vaccination" so she had to spend a few days resting with her arm in a sling as the *Hilary* struck out across the Atlantic on the 2600 mile crossing to South America that would take eight or nine days.

THE CROSSING

As they crossed she helped produce the ship's newspaper using the daily bulletin's radioed from Rugby in Morse code. Atmospherics produced some inaccuracies (the radio operator told her that on another ship the newspaper had announced the death of the actress Clara Butt, leaving passengers surprised when she actually boarded the vessel at the next stop) the most serious being mixing up the football scores and undermining the football pool run on the ship. She spent some time on the bridge and learned some navigation and followed a medical emergency on another vessel through the radio signals sent back and forth between it and *Hilary's* doctor.

> And so the voyage went on — until one morning a Lancashire voice called excitedly into my cabin, "Miss Brown, come quickly! The seas's gone like the Manchester Ship Canal". I followed him up on deck , and sure enough, although we were still 120 miles from the mouth of the river, the blue sea had changed to a yellow mud colour, the sky was heavy and sullen, and the air hot and sultry. The Amazon had come out to meet us.[4]

PARA

They picked up a pilot a few miles off the coast at Salinas 50 miles east of the mouth of the Para River during the night and then in the morning steamed up the river, thick with yellow mud, to Belem (which Win, in common with many English at the time, called Para). She was disturbed by the beggars but liked the Grand Hotel, enjoyed the cinema, was puzzled by the apparent popularity of golf given the prevalence of unpleasant skin-burrowing insects in the rough and alarmed and exhausted by the carnival in progress when they visited. As usual she persuaded strange men to take her to raucous and unseemly night-clubs.

Strangely, writers and explorers were, according to Win, unpopular in Brazil. For explorers this seems to have been because they turned up claiming to be searching for Colonel Fawcett. Percival Harrison Fawcett, a Lieutenant Colonel in the artillery and later member of the British secret service, undertook a number of expeditions to South America and came to believe that there was a lost city he called "Z". He disappeared on an expedition to find this in 1925.

There were many subsequent expeditions to determine his fate and that of his small party. Even as late as the end of the twentieth century there were disputes about whether he had died at the hands of natives, from natural causes or whether he had survived to found a religious community. Some thought he had become a great chief among the locals. At the time Win visited, just a few years after the event, sensible people seem to have thought that further searches were pointless but still expeditions, seeking publicity or money or both, turned up with little intention of actually doing any looking.

Fawcett lives on as the inspiration for Professor Challenger in Arthur Conan Doyle's fantasy *The Lost World* and may just have been the basis for Indiana Jones too. They left Belem on 27 February 1933.

TO MANAUS

From Belem the *Hilary* went up the Para River and, after about 60 miles, through the Passo de de Goiabel to the west. Then they headed for Os Estreitos, the maze of narrow channels that leads to the Amazon. *Hilary* probably took the channel that leads past Breves and snakes along for over 100 miles, first north and then west, until it joins the Amazon at Ponta do Vieira. It is then around 300 miles to the city of Santarem.

The narrow parts of the river were by far the most interesting: the forest closed in on both sides and they could see monkeys swaying the branches of the trees, brightly-coloured birds criss-crossed the river, screeching, and butterflies and insects shimmered in clouds. Sometimes they passed a hut built on poles and people in "exceedingly scanty clothing" came out in boats, clapping and yelling as the wash of the ship threatened to capsize them. And the ship bore on up the river, ever turning and sounding her whistle as she came to particularly sharp bends.

There was a storm every afternoon. Once, sick of her daily bath in yellow muddy water, she put on her swimming costume and stood on the top deck, letting the rain beat down on her until she was so chilled that she had to be revived with a hot whisky. The climate began to take its toll: passengers developed rasping coughs and their energy began to seep away as "Amazonitis" gripped them. There were tales of men so overcome by lassitude that they had to be stretchered to the sea to recover.

After two days of this, they came to the Amazon and the river opened out and it all became rather less interesting. The muddy river stretched far away on either side and then the distant forests were uninterrupted, seeming to infinity.

On 1 March they passed Santarem where the River Tapojoz joins the Amazon, its blue-black waters unwilling to mix with the copper-coloured (Win of course says yellow) ones of the main stream, the two staying startlingly separate well downstream from the meeting, swirling around but hardly mixing.

There was something about 80 miles up the Tapojoz that rather intrigued Win enough for her to plan an Appendix on it for the book she was thinking about. She called it the Ford Concession, Boa Vista; later it was known as Fordlandia.

Henry Ford had been granted a concession of 1 million hectares (10,000 square kilometres) of forest by the Brazilian government to grow rubber plants on the west side of the Tapojoz. He thought he could grow enough rubber for tyres for two million cars each year and it would relieve his dependence on the far east and predominantly British suppliers. Since the rubber business had started in South America and thrived there until some seeds were smuggled out and planted on the other side of the world, it seemed plausible and potentially good business, breaking the dominance of the British colonies. The workers started clearing the forests in 1929 for the 300,000 saplings Ford intended to plant and the company invested heavily in improving health and providing accommodation for them. There were, however, soon problems. Heavy rains washed the nutrients away from the roots of the plants, there were droughts and insect and fungal attacks on the trees. There were labour troubles too. The managers were all drawn from the Ford factories and had no experience of agriculture. The company provided free food, but based it on that supplied to factory workers back in Michigan. They organised square dancing too.

The 1930 riots started when the company tried to introduce self-service in its cafeteria, which until then had used waitresses. The cafeteria was destroyed by the affronted employees. There was more trouble when Ford brought in Barbadian workers.

Nineteen thirty three happened to be a turning point. It was then the company acknowledged that there was much wrong and swapped part of the Concession for a site closer to Santarem and started again with new stock. Fordlandia was abandoned completely in the 1940s and the new site, Belterra, staggered on, never reaching anything like its expected potential. In 1933 the future still looked bright:

> The finest rubber plants have been selected, and set on wide terraces, and in a few years Mr. Ford hopes to produce all the rubber necessary in the manufacture of his cars.[5]

On the night of 2 March they passed the mouth of the Amazon's largest tributary, the Madeira River. In *Yellow Waters* Win refers to the railway, finished in 1912, that was supposed to circumvent the rapids on the Madeira river and allow rubber to be transported from Bolivia down the Amazon to the outside world. Somewhere between six and ten thousand workers lost their lives in its construction and its completion came too late; by then the more efficient Asian plantations dominated the rubber market.

After this they entered the black waters of the River Negro and continued up to Manaus (Manaos as it was generally called at the time).

MANAUS

There is something sad about Manaos. At first sight it appears prosperous, and it comes as a surprise after a thousand miles of rank green forest, so far from civilisation. Close investigation however, reveals the tragedy of a lost city, lost again to the ever encroaching power of the jungle. The Opera House, where once such world famous singers as Caruso sang, is now deserted and crumbling to ruin. Many of the roads, built at the cost of thousands of pounds, are overgrown. The eternal jungle is claiming its own.

Early in the nineteenth century, when Brazil exported over 30,000 tons of rubber, and controlling the entire market, Manaos was one of the richest cities in the world, and boasts that its residents once lit their cigars with bank notes, and that — a thousand miles up the Amazon — it had an electric tram service before Liverpool. But in those days the rubber fetched over fourteen shillings a pound — today it is less than fourpence! So has Manaos fallen.[6]

The British colony numbered thirty men and four women and they entertained Win and Ron (and maybe Elsie) at their homes and at the town and country Club. It was at the Club that they (they probably meaning Win and Ron) killed their first snake. They were relaxing on the verandah with a coffee after a morning horse ride when wild screaming came from the direction of the chicken coop. They rushed to investigate and found a green and yellow snake, over a metre long, which had already killed one chicken and was clearly considering the possibility of despatching a second from the panicking flock. But, with her riding crop, Win struck it across the back of its head, killing it instantly. It turned out to be a particularly poisonous specimen and Win had it bottled in rum to take back to Manchester. She called it "Rastus".

She did learn why writers were so badly thought of. It seems that they turned up in significant numbers — and quite famous ones at that — and accepted all the generous hospitality on offer before returning to Britain and writing untrue and exaggerated accounts of the colony's private lives. It seems that Win suffered from an additional burden: a photograph of her dressed as a cowboy (presumably the joke one taken in Manchester) seems to have appeared in a local newspaper and it probably mentioned that she was to write an account of her trip.

Troubling too was the possibility that they might not get a visa to go further up the river and into Peru. This was still a risk when they waved off the *Hilary* with Elsie on board on 9 May, a rather depressing experience not least because Win had had an ulcer cut out from under her vaccination that very morning by the ship's doctor and felt "desperately ill". Luckily, later that day the visas for Peru were issued[7], though at a cost of five pounds (nearly two hundred pounds in today's money). So they bought a ticket for a passage to Iquitos for the following evening, 10 March, and booked into a hotel for the night; the bed was so uninviting that Win slept fully-clothed in the hammock they had bought earlier in the day.

THE BELEM

They were booked on the *Belem* for the journey of 1300 miles and seventeen days to Iquitos. It proved to be built in the style of American river boats with open decks and two tall funnels side by side. Its speed of seven knots or so meant that it ploughed up the river against the stream at little more than two knots, towing a small barge filled with coal. Win and Ron shared it with around 180 soldiers and sailors off to war, a dozen other men (who included two clerics and a bearded German) and two Brazilian women. The top deck was occupied by the Captain and the Navy, the second by the Army and the smarter passengers (including Win and Ron), with small four-berth cabins, and the bottom deck by the Third class passengers and the crew. The bottom deck also had stacks of wood as fuel for the voyage and the provisions. These comprised pigs, cows, hens and turtles to be slaughtered as required; a butchered cow was hanging from the roof by the following morning, clothed in flies.

After seeing this, lunch was unsatisfactory. Win skipped what she described as an "oily mess" and could eat only a little rice and some beans cooked in gravy. They stopped to collect grass for the animals — extraordinarily, the men who cut it were wearing Everton football kit — and then wood for the boiler.

Once they got going again a young Brazilian spoke to her and from somewhere conjured gin and vermouth mixed with ice and lemon which they drank as the sun set. After this they had dinner and Win ate everything put before her. Later, the boat drew up to the bank and the young man slipped mysteriously away into the dark forest with a gigantic umbrella and an oil lamp, not to return.

She also met the ship's doctor.

> I was surprised to discover that one of the Brazilian women was the ship's doctor. In a country of much venereal disease it seems incredible that a woman should he chosen in this capacity, especially where she will rarely have a patient of her own sex. On the whole, Brazilian women are quiet and retiring, and not very ambitious, but this doctor seemed to be an exception. Flying into terrible rages she made the men — even our captain — afraid of her, and she practically ruled the ship. All the same, I had cause to be deeply grateful to this woman, for she cured my arm. Seeing me dressing it one day, she promptly entered my cabin, and although unable to read a word of English, clearly had no use for our antiseptics which were thrown about in an alarming fashion. Finally with a cry of triumph she seized the Keatings [an insecticide], and it was only with the utmost difficulty I prevented her from sprinkling the insect killer upon my wound. In a rage, she then dragged me to the ship's hospital, and

producing what appeared to be a jar of mud, flung some on my arm and threw me out.

Later that day the second woman [the other woman travelling on the boat] collapsed unconscious on the deck. Soldiers carried her to her cabin, and to my horror the doctor sent for me to assist. For almost an hour we worked on the poor woman, and I felt certain she would either die or I should have to assist a young Brazilian into the world, which latter prospect did not particularly appeal to me. The doctor was clearly worried.

Finally our efforts were rewarded by a faint spark of life, and the doctor, after administering an injection, dragged me from the cabin. I presume the woman was cured, but I never saw her again![8]

Win was tortured by insect bites and found sleeping difficult. She was astounded that each little village they stopped at was lit at night by electricity. She was, on the other hand, dismayed by toilet arrangements that saw the used paper thrown out of windows or onto the floor so as not to block up the primitive sewerage systems. On the other hand she disregarded warnings about drinking the water, using crockery in restaurants, swimming in rivers, putting bare feet on the ground and sleeping in beds. Although she did observe that "With beds one must use discretion as in any other country."[9]

She even began to enjoy the food which was mainly thick chicken soup, salt fish, liver and tongue always with beans and rice. There were cheese and bananas or cheese and *goibade*, a kind of fruit jelly. She admired the way the Brazilians could eat an orange with a knife and fork, spearing the fruit with the fork and then peeling it perfectly with the knife before carving the juicy flesh into nice chunks. Her own attempts at this ended in a mess she had to eat with a spoon.

They did make friends with some of their fellow passengers (the Italian monk, the French priest, the German and a Brazilian soldier) even though they had little language in common. The main joint pastime was leafing through old magazines, pointing at the pictures and saying a relevant word in his or her own language. So a water scene brought aqua, eau, wasser and agua. When this paled as a distraction they wandered around the ship for a while then came back and started again.

On 15 March they stopped at a mission outside Teffe (now more usually called Tefé) to leave medical supplies for a hospital. And it was here she saw the tugboat *Delio* built by Isaac Pimblott and Sons of Northwich in Cheshire in 1906 just forty kilometres from Win's home. But time began to hang heavy and the flies and mosquitoes came in increasing numbers and the mosquitoes seemed to be getting bigger. There were still twelve days to go to Iquitos.

They disembarked some of the soldiers and some cattle at Tonantins on the 19 March and then chugged on through two days of torrential rain; the chill damp bringing mould to grow on their shoes and suitcases and even their spare clothes. There was some excitement when they found a steamer stranded on a mid-stream mud-bank, pathetically sounding its siren in the dark. How long it had been there they never found out but they learned that food was low and handed over flour, rice and beans to the starved and dejected occupants. Win gave the captain some cigarettes and they left them — a tow was out of the question — and steamed on for Esperanza, the civil frontier between Brazil and Peru. They arrived at the settlement of a church and a few huts on 22 March.

> As we approached the lights of a Brazilian warship, the *Floriano* could be seen, and she obligingly flashed her searchlight to lead us in. Here we were to unload both our coal and the members of the Navy, so there was the usual excitement, clamour, and embracings, and as usual all the ragged inhabitants of Esperanza, crowded aboard the *Belem*, trying to sell dirty looking sweets and cakes. During the night we set off up the Yavary river to deliver supplies, but when I woke next morning, we were back in Esperanza again, and spent two days moored alongside the *Floriano*, disposing of the coal, which was shovelled into small baskets, and passed

along a human chain into the bunkers of the war-ship. It was a filthy job,and very soon we, and everything on board the *Belem*, became covered in a thick layer of coal dust.

We made several trips ashore, for we had now learnt to somewhat thwart *mocuens*[10] by covering our bodies with carbolic soap; but there was little to see, and we merely returned covered from head to foot in mud and slime. One afternoon, to break the monotony, the warship sent shells screaming through the air, while the crew applauded noisily, and the inhabitants gathered in awe and wonder. Several of the sailors were doubtless descended from the African negroes, originally brought to S. America as slaves, chained to the ships, and at night one heard the rhythmic beating of tom-toms, mingled with another sailor's efforts to play "Goodnight sweetheart" on an ancient cornet, and the officers' wireless blaring out the American stock prices!

Next day we said "Adeus" to the remainder of our troops at Tabatinga, the military frontier, and — now a small company of five — we entered the territory of Peru.[11]

THE WAR

Win and Ron were stepping into a war zone centred on the town of Leticia. A grumbling dispute had been going on for decades: the locals felt they were Peruvians but Leticia was a key access point to the Amazon for Colombia. A 1922 agreement between the governments had handed over the Leticia region (a few hundred square kilometres between the Amazon and the Putumayo rivers) to Colombia in exchange for Peruvian rights elsewhere but the problem flared up in September 1932 when some 400 Peruvian civilians occupied Leticia. Peru then sent a small army into the region to support them. Popular outrage led to a fleet of the Colombian navy sailing (some of it over 5000 miles via the Panama Canal) up the Amazon. There were various skirmishes on the way (including an attempt to bomb the fleet by the Peruvian air force and similar attacks by the Colombians) until the Colombians attacked and occupied the town of Tarapaca on the Putumayo River about 100 miles north of Leticia in mid-February.

By the time Win and Ron arrived in the region the League of Nations had become involved and there would be a ceasefire in May 1933 and then permanent resolution of the problem by restoring the territory to Colombia. The war cost several hundred lives, most of them probably from disease. Brazil was not involved but sent troops, warships and planes to the area as an interested neutral.

PERU

Once they passed into Peru the north bank of the river was, for nearly 200 kilometres, the disputed territory so it was hardly surprising that Win attracted attention when she got out her camera and took photographs. Secret policemen watched her but she did manage some pictures, even of Leticia itself, through the porthole in the ladies' toilet. The excitement of being seen as a potential spy at least made up for the growing tedium of the journey; the green forest slipping by unchanging with now just a few passengers as distraction.

They had haircuts from one of the stewards; Win's left the back of her head effectively bald; Ron's extended to having his nose and ear hair trimmed at the barber's insistence. They were disturbed by the games the Amazonian children played: frog stoning and burning of live rats soaked in petrol.

When the *Belem* stopped at Chimbote on 26 March for wood, she and Ron wandered off.

> Two days before we reached Iquito, the *Belem* stopped at a small clearing named Chimbote, for wood, and on learning we should be there most of the day, Adams and I decided to go ashore and explore and were fortunate in finding a thin rough trail, winding precariously through the jungle. Marking the trees so that we should not lose our way on returning, we must have covered two or three miles, when I sud-

denly had the uncomfortable feeling that I was being watched. We paused and looked round. Platform after platform of thick green foliage, blotted out the sun and sky above our heads, and we stood listening in the weird half-light among the giant silver grey boles and trailing creepers, but could hear nothing but the strange sounds made by birds and insects.

It was a horrible feeling, and I could not shake it off, even a rustling in the undergrowth made me turn suddenly, my heart in my mouth, to find it was only a lizard. I breathed again, and reassured myself that it was only nerves, but even then I could not stifle the feeling that many eyes were peering at us. At the best of times it is not pleasant to feel you have unseen watchers, but in this jungle with the queer light and odour of musty dampness, there was an uncanny atmosphere that began steadily to get the better of me, and I cursed myself for ever leaving the boat. I asked Adams for a cigarette to steady my nerves, but the moment his hand felt in his pocket, the undergrowth parted and suddenly became alive. Evil faces smeared with orange and red paint peered at us from everywhere. We were in the centre of a ring of savages.

I don't think I have ever felt so frightened as at the sight of these grinning painted devils, more beast than human, and imagined something infinitely worse than death at their hands. They were dressed in tan-coloured fibre which hung from their waists, neck, arms and legs, their bodies being dyed a hideous yellow brown. My horrified glance fell upon a piece of raw flesh hung round the neck of the Chief, and similar decorations on the shoulders of his followers. These proved to be the wings of birds, freshly torn off and various portions of internal anatomy, probably obtained from animals. We stood still and stared at one another, and years seemed to pass. Then Adams had an idea. He presented the Chief with his tobacco pouch , a yellow oil-skin affair with a

zip fastener. The Indians could see the golden brown tobacco inside, but could not make out how it got there,and
passed it on to each other in amazement. Adams signalled
for them to return it, and with the mysterious movement of
a conjurer he demonstrated the zip!

That settled it, any danger we might have been in vanished. To the superstitious minds of the savages we were
clearly some kind of gods. Over and over again Adams had
to perform his miracle, and fortunately the zip not being
particularly good, required a certain amount of knack to
make it work, or otherwise they might have realised the sim-
plicity of the trick. as it was they were delighted and could
not do enough for us. We discovered later, they were
Yaguas — Indians who inhabited the high ground several
miles inland. Curiosity rather than bad intention must have
prompted them to follow us through the forest, for the
Yaguas are at peace with the white man, although they still
indulge in frequent wars with neighbouring tribes. The Indians we met were actually en route for the *Belem*, where they
hoped to obtain a little food in return for their services of
loading wood. We certainly felt rather foolish as we watched
our "war-like" savages at work, and although our scare had
been real enough at the time, we were forced to laugh afterwards at this unromantic conclusion![12]

The Yaguas, Win tells us, are like most tribes living along the rivers,
harmless; civilised by missionaries. But there are still the Jivaros.

In Northern Peru, towards Equador, in the jungles of the
Maranon and Pastaza rivers, lie the Jivaros, or headhunters,
most primitive of Indians. The chief hobby of this tribe is to
remove the heads of visitors or past friends, shrinking them
to about one fourth their original size by pouring hot sand
into the skull. These grim trophies, about the size of an orange, are hung from poles as souvenirs to decorate their

huts, and young Indian boys are brought up in the belief that ill luck will follow their tribe until the heads of all their enemies are thus arrayed. These children accompany their elders to war at seven years of age, and on returning are smeared with chicken blood as a token of honour, for witnessing their first battle.

Later, on winning their first head, they are rewarded by a drug that is supposed to give them communication with the spirits of wild beasts. The wars are generally tribal or family feuds, in which everybody is killed by the victors except marriageable women, who are taken to weep over the heads of their relations, in the ceremonial dance that follows the battle. So strong is this feeling, regarding the head trophies, that the women of the losing side are said to decapitate their own relations rather than allow the heads to be taken by the victors. A successful warrior returning with a head is supposed to diet for six months, eating neither fish nor game meat.

Unfortunately, some traders discovered a market for these grim trophies, and the sale of heads began. Naturally the Jivaros were loath to part with their treasured possessions, and white men who entered the jungles of the Maranon to obtain heads, often had their own added to stock. Some tried to make the Indians drunk and then steal the trophies, others attempted to trade, and occasionally the promise of an old rifle would seal a bargain. The heads brought as much as £40 in England and America, and one man I met told me how he had taken two home as a present to his wife, thinking they would look well on the mantelpiece. Needless to say he was ordered out of the house until he had disposed of the grisly ornaments! Finally the authorities were compelled to step in and stop this horrible trading, and to-day it is practically impossible to obtain a shrivelled head![13]

Win showed considerable sympathy for the plight of the Indians although observed that the Chunchos threw their sick or aged parents into the river and killed or banished the children of any widow who decided to remarry. Several man-eating tribes were noted, the Cashibos singled out for their relish of the flesh of the white man. They believed that they would "absorb the cleverness and good qualities of our race." The Incas were "a fine race" but, exploited and persecuted by the white man, they "could not easily understand civilised religion, especially when it was accompanied by massacre." Small wonder she thought "if they bear animosity to the white race that has murdered and spoilt their people, and stolen their land."

IQUITOS

The *Belem* reached Iquitos on the night of 28 March and they were met by a Scotsman called MacRae, who was the acting British Consul and the representative for Booth & Co (London). He took the pair to his house, "Chalet Booth", which proved to be a civilised oasis with a billiard table, piano, ice box and even a swimming pool. They slept in comfortable beds between clean white sheets.

The next day they were introduced to the rest of the British Colony: an Englishman and "a Jew from Manchester" who had been sharing a house for 20 years. There were also two American lumbermen living in this quaint little town, aloof in the jungle with its one paved street and narrow tracks that crossed open sewers where it was wise to carry a stick in case of snakes. The entertainments were few. A walk along the promenade crumbling into the Amazon or a ride in a rented car around the square with bats whirling in the evening sky was all the entertainment available most days. But on Thursday nights and Sundays there was a special treat. Then, a steam engine was brought out with two open trucks and for a small sum people could ride this all evening, chuffing along at an alarmingly high speed (it seemed to have only STOP and GO settings), back and forth through the town. Win learned it was the only means of access to the cemetery and many of the revellers could expect to make their last journeys on it.

There were two cinemas that showed exclusively melodramas featuring men with black moustaches — the larger and blacker the moustache, the more evil the character — and women with long skirts and bustles (which may well have carried some moral coding too). The films were well-worn in every sense of the word and Iquitos seems to have been their last showing before they were taken away and burnt. In fact things were even worse than that cinematographically; the war had severely reduced the supply of films so the cinemas had resorted to showing the same film over and over again, each week changing the title to something more lurid.

The war was all around. Men were rounded up and sent off to the front with ancient guns. There were rumours of spies and that a suspect (who had travelled with them on the *Belem*) had been shot. Planes loaded with bombs flew over the Chalet; martial law was declared. When the *Belem* left on the 4 April, not to return for a month, they felt isolated. Perhaps more so when they heard of the emergency evacuation plan for the foreign contingent: if things got too bad they would all take to a raft built by the Americans and drift down the river — through the heart of the conflict.

They had originally hoped to take an Air Force flight to the Andes but this now seemed unlikely given the existence of a state of war so they decided to take a canoe trip and explore the smaller rivers and the jungle. First they obtained permission from the authorities and then MacRae found them a canoe, four Indian paddlers and an interpreter, Vasquez. After a farewell dinner at the house of the two Englishmen, they set off the following morning, the revolvers they had acquired (but which did not work) hidden, on their new adventure.

BY CANOE

Win was wearing riding breeches, a thick woollen shirt she had been given by MacRae and field boots. Her luggage was: pyjamas, a change of underclothes, a clean shirt, woollen blanket, "Flit" insecticide spray, a small medicine chest and a swimsuit. They were equipped with machetes, the revolvers (hidden), cameras (hidden), tent, camping equipment and some provisions. Win had a St Christopher charm strapped to her belt. They left behind other charms and mascots and two parrots they had acquired.

They stopped for lunch with the American lumbermen at the Nanay sawmills at the mouth of the Nanay River and after that paddled up the black Nanay (and then probably up its tributary the Manon) for several hours until Vasquez decided it was time to camp for the night. In spite of the apprehension that went before, the night was uneventful and they awoke shivering with cold, everything damp from the mist that hung over the river and the sodden ground around. Win put on her swimsuit and (after the Indians had been sent in for a swim to check for alligators, piranhas and other potential nasties) she dived in for a bath. This did not last long: something cold and slimy rubbed against her and she was back on dry land in an instant. Then, after a breakfast of oranges and eggs washed down with whisky, they set off again.

They paddled up the river until it turned sharply to the right and the Indians decided that there was shortcut through the swamp. It had them struggling to force the canoe through the trees with macaws squawking around them and black ants invading the boat, dodging wasp nests that dangled from the trees and disturbing alligators. They struck on a dark lake, plunged back into the jungle and then an hour later found themselves back in the lake again. Eventually after thrashing around in the flooded forest they did manage to get back into the main river (where Win took a swim) and they began to look for somewhere to camp for the night. Just as it looked hopeless and the light began to fail they came upon a small Indian village and pulled into the bank. Whatever, it would be better than sleeping in the canoe.

Win insisted that she and Ron would sleep in the tent in spite of an invitation to share one of the huts and, with suitable application of the Flit, they had a good night's sleep. The following morning, after Win's cleansing dip in the river, they set off again. They bought fresh pineapples at lunchtime and in the afternoon the Indians tried to shoot some game with their ancient guns without success. But that night they were given some fruit and eggs by an Indian and they gave her biscuits and paraffin in exchange.

And so they progressed. One day they hit upon an isolated village where they found a woman using a Singer sewing machine with Coates' thread. Her son was responsible for keeping a calendar, something learnt from missionaries who had set up shop in a nearby village for a while before disappearing in, Win presumed, mysterious circumstance. Another day they found a young mother suffering badly from malaria, her baby "like a shrivelled frog" and Win, under pressure from Vasquez to do something, administered quinine. She left a supply with instructions. One day an English voice called to them from the swamp but when they tried to speak to its owner he melted into the forest, presumably regretting his cry.

The sun shone, exotic birds flew around the forest canopy and swooped across the river and the butterflies became larger, more iridescent if that was possible. Win regretted not bringing her butterfly net and killing jar. One of the birds sang snatches of the tune "Sonny Boy"; the phrase "there may be grey skies" floated through the forest often enough to be irritating. Win reckoned they might nearly be in Ecuador.

There were storms and, after one particularly violent one, they woke to find it as bright as day at 2 am, the birds singing and their companions awake and puzzled. After a while night fell again — and then dawn broke again around 5 am. They put it down to the storm. It was Good Friday, the 14 April.[14]

On the seventh day in the canoe they left the main river and headed for the Napo River to the east. They saw sloths, heard howler monkeys and saw *Make-Sapa* (long-armed intelligent monkeys). She recorded with amazement the praying mantises and snakes, although it is not clear that she actually saw the boas and anacondas she described.

As night fell they left the canoe in a small creek and set off inland for an Indian village. It was to be a fascinating and disturbing experience.

YELLOW FANG

First they met the chief, a gigantic evil-looking man reputed to be 100 years old, who spoke no languages the interpreter knew and looked extremely displeased with these visitors: Win thought he had eaten white people in the past and remembered the indigestion that had resulted. His second-in-command they named "Yellow Fang" from the teeth that stuck from his deformed jaw. He took an instant liking to Win and was able to talk to Vasquez so they were invited to stay for the night. Win opted for the tent (in spite of a particularly violent storm that whipped the jungle into a frenzy and sent lightning crackling across the sky) and then decided to make a getaway from the threatening and rather creepy bunch. Her mind was changed when Vasquez said they could join the poison fishing the following day: she, for some reason, had always wanted to see that.

The poison fishing had been arranged by Yellow Fang, perhaps even to please his toothsome visitor — maybe he had been tipped off by Vasquez about her desire to see it. What it did not do was please the Chief who was firmly opposed to indiscriminate angling. It seemed to convince him that Win had brought the storm and now he found her responsible — acting through Yellow Fang — for the fishing. He apparently called her a messenger of the devil.

The fishing did take place. Some roots were crushed and pounded and the liquid that resulted was tipped into a section of a river that had been cut off with barriers of sticks. The fish were either killed outright or rendered unconscious or disorientated and could easily be speared from boats and from the banks by excited villagers. They seem to have collected a good bag and presumably feasted for a while. The downside was that the method was hardly selective: it killed fish (and perhaps more besides) young and old and left the river barren for several months. So the Indians ate what the could and smoked the rest.

After this they saw the tracks of tapirs and, after a "hurried lunch", six of them set off to find the animals. It was now about 15 April.

WINIFRED BROWN

LOST TEXT

Here the typescript that has been the main basis for the account of the Amazon adventure stops, after eleven chapters and twenty thousand words. Its proposed title was *Yellow Waters* and, while un-dated, it was probably written after *Under Six Planets* was completed in 1955. A pencilled note on the front says there were 15 packets of black and white illustrations — but these have been lost. She wrote an account for the newspapers but it was probably for a northern edition of one of the *Express* newspapers and has disappeared, so far, without trace. There were a few newspaper articles over the fol-lowing decades that briefly describe the Amazon adventure but they mention nothing that is not in the typescript. There are two pub-lished photographs from the period: one of a plane in *Flight* and an-other in a newspaper, very blurred in reproduction, of her looking at some war graves. Ron's daughter Hilary has a number and some of them are reproduced here.

THE RETURN

Whether they found tapirs or not is something we may never know. But it is possible to piece together the elements of the return.

They looked for the tapirs but then, rather quickly, they must have started back for Iquitos, going roughly the way they had come.

But the farther they got into the interior, the more hostile the In-dians became, and it is perhaps fortunate that the expedition ran short of food and had to turn back, otherwise Winifred's own head (shrivelled to the size of an orange) might have become a museum piece.[15]

We know they checked on the woman who had been treated for malaria and found she had made a remarkable recovery. Somewhere Win bought a *Make-Sapa*, one of the intelligent monkeys they had seen, to take home.

The only guides to their movements are the rather blurred stamps in Ron's passport. These include a visa from the Brazilian Consulate in Iquitos for travel to Manaus, in transit for Liverpool, dated 18 April 1933 which means that they were back in Iquitos by then, just four days after the Good Friday storm. The canoe trip must have lasted about ten days. It seems likely that they then caught the *Belem* at the end of the month on its regular run to Manaus because there are stamps for Chimbote on 30 March and Tabatinga (Leticia) on 1 May. They carried with them the monkey and presumably the two parrots but somewhere along the way Win realised that the monkey was distressed and left it. The fate of the parrots is unrecorded.

The final stamp from South America in Ron's passport is indistinct but suggests they set off (from somewhere) for home on 22 May.

Photographs show them travelling home on the Booth liner SS *Alban*, probably from Manaus because the *Alban* arrived in Para about the 15 May and had enough time in her schedule to go that far up the Amazon. They called into Le Havre and Dieppe on 19 June and landed in London the following day.

LEARNING THE ROPES

She continued to give flying displays after she got back from the Amazon; on 23 July 1933 she gave one at her old haunt, the Norbreck Hydro (she was billed as "of King's Cup and Amazon fame"). But her interest seems to have declined and there is no mention of her in *Flight* magazine after 1932 except as the woman who won the 1930 King's Cup. In 1936 she sold *Jerry* and gave up flying. It had been a miraculous nine years since she had learned to fly but something made her give it up. Did she feel she had done all she wanted to do? Was she increasingly aware of the dangers? Certainly, in a talk she gave, summarised in *Under Six Planets*, she rather dwells on just how many of her contemporaries had died in aviation accidents or been seriously injured. By then she seems to have stopped playing ice hockey and competitive golf but she already had a new interest: sailing. And she had a boat, *Perula,* which she had bought "more by accident than design" in the autumn of 1935.

Of course Sawley had been sailing in the Irish Sea for years and Win had made at least one trip across with him, so she must have had some idea of what she was taking on. Plus Sawley, as Commodore of the Manchester Cruising Association, a gentlemen's sailing club who met most weeks to discuss nautical matters and made the odd foray to sea, arranged for Win to become its first lady member. She gave a talk on flying and navigation and told the story of her Amazon adventure. So she had herself stepped into the yacht cruising scene. And of course there was all that sea and the Amazon she had seen. It must have all contributed to her choice of a new medium for challenge — and success.

PERULA

Perula was built in 1932 by A M Dickie & Sons at Bangor north Wales as a fishing vessel. Powered by a 36 HP Russell Newbery (RN) diesel engine she also had a bermudian rig for sailing. The main sail was loose-footed — it did not have a boom — and there was one head-sail. Built of pitch pine on grown oak frames, she was 15 metres overall and 12 metres on the waterline. Her beam was four metres and draught just over 1.5 metres. Her name initially was *Alec Randalls*.

She seems to have been a handy vessel and made several fishing trips but she suffered from the disadvantage that her fish-holds were too small so she was uneconomic. She was sold in 1935 to a house-builder friend of Win's who had her converted into a yacht and renamed her *Monavic*. She was changed to a yawl by adding a second mast towards the stern and a glass structure (which Win calls the "Tomato House") was added between the masts. The two sails were probably given booms at this stage. When Win saw her in the summer of 1935 she was in Jubilee Dock, Fleetwood; she bought her to help her friend who was in financial difficulty. She seems to have paid £300 so, in spite of her protestations, may have thought she had a bargain. She may have had one but there were expenses before *Monavic* was sea-worthy. It cost her £585 to remove the tomato house and have a teak wheelhouse built in its place and do other work; a third of it went on repairing the engine, which had seized. Even the toilet was a problem but that was resolved when a lampshade was found lodged in the system. They named her *Perula*, after an Amazonian goddess believed to "aid the sick, guard the sleeping and cheer the disconsolate." Win liked to pronounce it "pe-RULA".

She sold *Jerry* to pay for putting the boat into sea-worthy condition. She had to do that not least because she had announced to the Press that she would be sailing around the world in her. The work was done by Dickies at Bangor on the eastern end of the Menai Straits and when it was finished *Perula* was launched (on 10 June 1936) and taken to a mooring at Glyn Garth on the other side of the Menai Straits where Win and Ron were left to their own devices. The initial impulse, as they were drinking the launch champagne, to go for a sail was resisted; Ron pointed out that he worked for the company that was insuring *Perula* and he thought they should wreck her so soon. They tried the Primus stove but set fire to the paint and burnt the steak they were trying to cook. Eventually they decided to go ashore but even that was problematical — Win could not row. They seemed to master the activity between them but one day it seemed particularly hard work. It was only after twenty strenuous minutes that Ron realised that they were towing a bucket on a length of rope, dredging the Straits.

RMYC

By now Win had become a member of the Royal Mersey Yacht Club. Elected on 7 May 1936, she was sponsored by her father and seconded by E J Bowerbank. The following month, when *Perula* was launched, she was granted a Warrant to fly the club's defaced blue ensign. Ron had to wait until 20 March 1941 before he was let in — proposed by Dunstan Walker, a Menai man. Although based on the Mersey at Birkenhead, the club had a strong presence on the Menai Straits and a small clubhouse there. Win was to fly their burgee at her masthead throughout her adventures.

FIRST SAILS

Win was always one to get on with adventures so they had several sails over the next few days with local skippers but on 18 June they set off for Puffin Island, off the eastern extremity of Anglesey, on their own. They did not put up the sails but the 10 nautical mile round trip down the channel was anyway challenge enough for two novices in a heavy 15 metre boat in tricky and rather busy waters. They even managed, at the third try, to get back on their moorings afterwards. It was quite an achievement but they (and "they" means "Win" in this context no doubt) were soon ready to venture farther afield and they decided on a voyage to Douglas on the Isle of Man, about 50 miles away. They would go with Alfred Barker, an ex-Navy friend.

On the appointed day they set out by car for Menai from their homes in Manchester but stopped several times at pubs on the way and finally arrived not much before three o'clock. It would mean that they would arrive at Douglas well after darkness had fallen, not, Alfred pointed out, ideal for a first visit. However Win argued that they had never been in daylight and did not know what it looked like so they might as well go in the dark. So they started the engine and left, rounding Puffin Island in a dead calm.

They first saw the Isle of Man ahead at 20:45 and arrived off the harbour entrance just before midnight and then hung around outside in fear of meeting the midnight steamer right in the entrance. They finally went in at twenty past midnight with Win at the wheel, narrowly missing several boats as they leapt out of the night. They anchored but the anchor dragged so they found themselves right in the middle of the harbour, were yelled at, got the anchor up and then managed to drop it and a second one for luck in a quieter corner. They turned off the engine at 1 o'clock in the morning and went to bed.

Win was woken early the next morning by a loud crash and, assuming that the anchor had dragged and they had hit something, bounded from her cabin in the darkness and tripped over Ron and Alfred who were lying on the floor. The crash had been nothing more than Alfred falling out of his bunk. It had made Ron leap out of his and fall over him and brought Win tumbling in the scrum that followed. So disturbed were they that they decided to stay awake so had breakfast and spent the morning riding on a horse tram "to mend our shattered nerves."

We know from the logbook that they left at 9:30 in the morning but which morning is not recorded (for some reason the dates of the trip are not given) but they must have spent another night there at least. The return trip must have been slightly less comfortable than going out; they headed south into a brisk south-westerly wind which kicked up a choppy sea. They motored all the way back to

Glyn Garth arriving at 11 o'clock at night. It was their first proper voyage and it gave them confidence for more efforts on their own. However, they must by now have realised that *Perula* had at least one shortcoming: her sailing qualities were very poor. In subsequent voyages they would rely almost entirely on the engine, which could push them along at a respectable 5 knots. The sails could help them along when there was a good strong breeze behind but if the wind came from ahead they were there just to steady her motion through the waves.

The next adventure is not recorded in *Duffers on the Deep* but is in *Perula*'s logbook. On 16 August they left their moorings at 8:55 in the evening and spent the night at Caernarfon. This means that they would have passed through the Menai Straits and the notorious Swellies, where the tide rushes furiously through the narrow rock-strewn chasm of the Straits, in the dark, a challenging undertaking even for an experienced yachtsman. According to the brief notes in the log, the strong south-south-west winds made the dangerous Caernarfon bar impossible to cross the following morning so they abandoned their plans — which seem to have been to go on to Abersoch — and returned to Glyn Garth. The timings are right for a passage through the Swellies to pass through at slack water but it was a foolhardy passage for beginners in the dark. Perhaps they did have someone to pilot them; perhaps there is a mix-up in the log (which is very sketchy) and they did it in the morning.

A few days later, on the 20th, they did sail solo to Holyhead, the ferry port on the north-west corner of Anglesey. The tides on the north coast can run at 3 knots or more at spring tides (and it was just after spring tides when they went) so it is important to catch them as they sweep west and south-west for a reasonable passage time. It means the difference between a real speed (over the ground) of say 7 or 8 knots and one of 2 or 3 knots. They left their moorings at 12:47, just the right time, headed past Puffin Island and then began to work their way west round the north of the island, leaving the rocky Skerries well to the south and being swept on by the favourable tidal stream. There was a kind northerly breeze and the sea was calm as they motored on, leaving the sails for another time. Less than six hours later they were anchored in Holyhead harbour.

The return the following day was almost as satisfactory. Again they caught the favourable tide by leaving at just after 9 o'clock and arrived back at Glyn Garth just over six hours later. They had put up the sails after they left and, Ron understanding that a ship under sail would look after herself, they had gone below for lunch. After an enjoyable meal they returned to the wheelhouse to find that *Perula* had quietly turned herself around and they were nearly back at Holyhead.

HEYSHAM

For some reason they had wanted to sail to Heysham, the ferry port in Morecambe Bay, but found it difficult to get anyone to go with them on account of the Bay's reputation. Its extensive sand banks and tides that swept across them faster than a horse can gallop seemed to put people off. Until they asked Dickie Hughes that is. "Nothing to it," he said and even generously offered to bring the necessary chart. However, when he did turn up for the trip he was chartless. We do not know the date of the voyage (somewhere between 21 August and 16 September) but we do know that it started in reasonable weather and they left at 06:30, putting up the mainsail fairly promptly. However visibility soon deteriorated and by the time they approached Morecambe Bay entrance at 16:30 they switched off the engine to listen for fog signals and picked up the siren of the Morecambe Bay lightship.

The bay is full of sandbanks that dry out at low tide and at other times have little water over them. They extend like spread fingers south west out of the bay. Between the fingers are channels of rather deeper water but most of them are still shallow and anyway peter out as you head up them. There are two that are marked and safe: the one to Barrow-in-Furness at the north of the bay and the Lune Deep at the south that leads to the fishing port of Fleetwood and to Heysham. Most yachtsmen would not set off for this area without a chart and, of the few that would, all the sensible ones would turn back if there was a threat of poor visibility. But they followed other boats that seemed to be heading in their direction until these turned off for Fleetwood. Then our adventurers simply made a sketch chart from the pilot book they had with them and, followed the buoys (which were flashing in the fog) towards Heysham, ticking them off as they went. This was a dangerous strategy, because if they missed just one they could be completely lost, but at 18:45 they found themselves outside the harbour.

They seemed not to be welcome in this commercial harbour with its large railway ferries plying the route to Ireland but were finally moored up to some kind of raft at the lower end of the harbour. Here trippers were rowed out to see the lady (was this real fame again or were yachts so foreign in Heysham?) and her yacht for a few pence. The stay was fairly eventful. When they went ashore in their dinghy they left it tied up to the harbour wall only to return and find it had disappeared, sunk by discharge into it from a waste pipe. Dickie retrieved it, falling down the slimy harbour steps in the process.

They left early the following morning, cleared the harbour just before 8 o'clock in a gentle south-westerly breeze and motored home, rounding Puffin Island at 18:25 and picking up their moorings at 19:25.

When she did see a chart of the Bay, Win thought that the goddess Perula really had looked after her.

TO FALMOUTH AND BACK

Their next adventure was bolder still — but they did have charts. With Alfred Barker they decided to head for the South Coast and, on the evening of 16 September, they set off in a stiff breeze and had rounded the Skerries before the first sign of conflict appeared. It seemed that Win and Alfred both regarded themselves as Navigator and had not agreed a route between them. Alfred had decided that the first port of call should be Dublin while Win had something more directly south in mind. So, as soon as Win's watch came round, she altered course accordingly. As they sailed on through the night some kind of resolution was agreed (or imposed): Win and Alfred would never be awake together. Ron would mediate. So they sailed on during the night, Alfred aiming for Milford Haven but on the afternoon of the 17th Ron found himself in Fishguard, Win's preference. On the 18th they set off brightly at 07:25 with Alf having St Ives in mind. Sometime in the middle of the afternoon Win decided that Falmouth was more suitable so, in falling rain and poor visibility, they headed to round Land's End. Passing the Longships on the inside the following morning, further dissension became apparent: Alfred was planning on stopping at Penzance while Win was heading for Falmouth. Inevitably they arrived at Falmouth, tying up next to HMS *Dart*. Here Alfred did strike back.

As the Navy observed the colours ceremony, the raising and lowering of the ensign at sunrise and sunset, so Alfred insisted it should be observed on *Perula*. So he made Win and Ron line up to raise or lower *Perula*'s ensign whether it meant dragging them out of a cosy bunk or hauling them out of the pub.

During the day they were in Falmouth they also filled up with diesel. They ordered 300 litres (no doubt the engine had been run all the way from Menai) which arrived by train, a small engine pulling a tank along the quayside. A large pipe was thrown down to them covering them in fuel and then pumping began. They managed to find a funnel so got most of it into the tanks and, as Win put it, *Perula* and the harbour were both refuelled.

On the 21st they started the return voyage and set off for St Ives with a calm sea and mist. For the trip home no conflict is recorded between the Navigators but Ron must have been unsettled from the trip down. After they anchored at St Ives he rowed across to buy some fish from a boat nearby and came back, fish-less and rather perturbed, to report that the fishermen did not speak English. Had the navigation feud continued and they had ended up in France perhaps? Not so it was pointed out. It was a French boat at St Ives for the pilchard fishing.

The following day they left at 11:33 and after another misty passage anchored at Newquay for the night. Then early the next day they set out north, sighting Lundy Island mid-afternoon but decided that with the wind freshening from the south-east the anchorage there was not safe for the night. So, they sailed on in a south-easterly force 3 (so it did not freshen much) and, under overcast skies, at just before 6 o'clock on the afternoon of 24 September they sighted Holyhead Hill. By 20:10 they were anchored in the harbour. The next day, a misty and rainy one, they returned to their Glyn Garth moorings. They had finished their first substantial cruise without any real sailing incidents. They had now experience of poor visibility but not yet of strong winds. These were to come before they ended their first season.

ROCK FERRY GALE

Win seems to have fancied a real test of *Perula* — she had never seen rough weather in their hands — and decided on a late October cruise to Scotland and Ireland. They engaged an experienced skipper , H Griffiths (the best on the Straits she said), at a rate of 15 shillings a day and were ready to set off north on 23 October. The wind was a south-westerly force 6 and Griffiths may have realised that there was worse to come because the weather charts show a depression over Iceland and a high over France squeezing the isobars between them, suggesting even stronger winds on the way. Whatever, he refused to go to the Isle of Man, the first planned port of call north and after some argument they agreed on Liverpool. So they set off, planning to enter the Mersey through the Rock Channel, a shallow entrance through the sandbanks off the coast of the Wirral. Of course it was not completely without incident. Win did not have a chart and Griffiths did not know the Rock Channel. However, they arrived at the Channel mid-afternoon around high water when it was at its deepest and widest and with the help of the Admiralty Sailing Directions, the book that lists navigational information, passed through into the Mersey with darkness falling. They went up the east side of the river and anchored off Rock Ferry where there would have been shelter from the wind and waves.

The following morning they left and sailed north up the main shipping channel in the fresh south-westerly wind that was still blowing. Griffiths had agreed on Fleetwood as a destination. With the wind on the beam *Perula* must have been a fine sight on the first leg down the Crosby Channel, sails full and spray flying. After a few miles of this they had to turn west to go down the Queen's Channel. It meant turning into the wind. *Perula* would have heeled over even more and would now have been sailing much more directly into the waves, with the full mainsail still up she might well have felt rather out of control. It was now that Griffiths chose to point out that the seal for the propeller shaft was leaking and suggested that they might return to Liverpool to have it fixed, perhaps a diplomatic way to say this was madness (even for 15 shillings a day). Win would have none of it. If they were going anywhere to have repairs done it was going to be Menai and at 11:00 she turned to the south-west, directly into the wind and sea. Griffiths disappeared below to lie down.

The wind strengthened and the seas grew bigger as the day wore on. It was too rough to take the mainsail down and reefing was "quite beyond us." The lacing that attached the sail to the boom came away and they managed to repair it; then the radio aerial was blown down. Their logbook records winds as building from force 7 to force 10 at 23:00 and, while this latter figure was probably an overestimate, it was strong enough to break the lacing again and rip out some of the sail battens. They used the engine and tacked as best they could, the heavy boom crashing wildly from side to side as they did. Off Great Orme Head around midnight Win lost control, the wheel wrenched from her hands, and *Perula* turned broadside onto the seas, a very dangerous situation with waves breaking across the deck and the boat lying nearly on her side. The boat did recover herself though and, as they approached the Straits, Griffiths was summoned to pilot them back to Glyn Garth in the dark. By now the seas would have moderated as they were in the shelter of land and they were back on their moorings at 03:00 in the morning. The whole passage from the Mersey had taken over 17 hours; they had spent 15 of them battling across the bay making an average speed towards their destination of around 2 knots. They had eaten only biscuits since leaving Rock Ferry but had drunk quite a lot of rum.

Afterwards Win was elated; they and *Perula* had coped with terrible weather on their own. Griffiths presumably had his own thoughts which may have included a reflection that there were easier ways of earning thirty bob than sailing around in a gale with a head-strong, mad woman.

SMALL LESSONS

As well as the actual sailing there had been some peripheral lessons. First that tides are a force of nature and need to be watched. While at Glyn Garth they had to use the dinghy to get ashore and seemed always to find a problem with tying it up and leaving it. One evening in mid-July they were roistering in "The Gazelle", the waterside pub at Glyn Garth between Menai Bridge and Beaumaris, with some rather snooty American guests, sampling fine wines and local ales until 3 am. They emerged to find that the tide had come in and the dinghy was floating some hundred metres out. Without much hesitation Win stripped to her pink underwear and plunged into the Straits, swimming out to the dinghy and then diving to release it. Darkness, drink and five knot tides were no deterrent for her.

They also learned that outboard motors, if not actually a force of nature, have minds of their own. Sawley had given them a French outboard motor for the dinghy. Naturally the instructions were in French. They managed to fit it to the dinghy and start it but stopping it was beyond them and they careered around the moorings, Win trying to read and translate the stopping instructions in the lurching dinghy. It stopped only when it cared to, maybe after running out of petrol.

It also, like most of its kind, had an ambition to plunge into the sea. One day as they were lifting it into the dinghy Ron stumbled as the wake of a passing steamer hit them and it saw its chance. It was only Ron's instinctive leap that kept it on board but the leap took

Ron into the Straits in its place. Fully dressed with oilskins he was lucky not to be swept away by the tide.

They also learned that dinghies have their thoughts too, waiting for the sailor's slightest forgetfulness to cause trouble. One day (it was the one after the incident with the outboard) as they reversed off the moorings Win forgot the dinghy tied to the stern. Quickly, seizing its chance, the dinghy's painter — the rope attaching it to the boat — wrapped itself around *Perula*'s propeller and the dinghy was wound in towards the boat. Win was mesmerised but Ron leapt into the dinghy and cut the rope, just saving the dinghy from being dragged below *Perula*'s stern. They managed to get back to the moorings and then Win once more stripped off and plunged in with a knife and, clinging to the rudder, sawed away at the rope. With a little further work from Ron they removed six or seven metres of it.

LAYING UP

The trip to the Mersey was the last one of the season and it was soon time for laying up, the process of preparing the boat to stand idle ashore for the winter. This kept it safe from winter storms and would allow essential work to be done but it meant that it had to be emptied of all its contents and the mast and rigging had to be re-moved. The contents would be stored away from the ever present risk of dampness and mildew. The masts were removed to lessen the danger of the boat, standing ashore, being blown over. Sails and rigging needed careful checking anyway in the age before synthetic materials. The engine would have to be prepared for the winter. It and the water system would be drained to avoid the dangers of freezing.

Win motored *Perula* across to Dickie's yard: "...everything I touched was covered with Vaseline and we had but one plate to eat off, and we only had that because it had been left out by accident." The masts were lifted out and then "dozens of men in large boots leaped aboard" and she was manoeuvred onto a large wooden cradle. Then "most of the men swung down the trestle into a waiting boat, and the big winch was started and slowly pulled us onto dry land."[1]

They spent the rest of the day and much of the night climbing up and down a ladder humping coils of rope and packages across to the stores, picking their way between the parked boats. Darkness fell and everyone went home and still they were ferrying things down from the deck across the now desolate yard and into the stores. Finally *Perula* was empty and they propped open lockers and cupboards against the damp. They stood back and wondered, as sailors have always done, how on earth so much stuff fitted onto and into such a small vessel. Then, in the early hours, they climbed into the car and drove home, their first season over.

TO NORWAY

Over the winter they decided that in 1937 they would go to Norway, chosen apparently as somewhere they had not previously visited. No matter that it meant sailing much further than they had ever sailed alone before (to Holyhead) and that it involved a very long sea crossing of the North Sea. Sawley suggested something slightly less ambitious like a circumnavigation of Britain but Norway and back it was to be.

In preparation Win spent £50 on new steering to replace the system that had proved such hard work in the Liverpool Bay gale and had two new fuel tanks fitted that could carry enough to give *Perula* a range of 3000 miles (she did rather more than a mile to the litre). During the winter she brushed up on the navigation she had learned for flying at Captain Dobson's Nautical Academy, concentrating this time on how it might be used at sea, and Ron studied seamanship and diesel engines to complement her knowledge. Then, winter over, on 22 April 1937 they set off back to Bangor. The car broke down and they were forced to send telegrams to Dickies saying they would be late, imploring them to load the boat with all the gear they had taken off. This the understanding Dickies did and when they finally arrived they found *Perula* not only loaded but afloat.

VISITORS

Then came a hitch. Ron's father had to undergo serious surgery and so he had to return to Manchester to look after things, leaving Win to finish the fitting out and bring the boat back to a sea-going state. Win lived alone on the boat on her mooring, an axe at hand to repel boarders. While she was waiting for Ron to return she had visitors.

Her old friend Margery Walsh, now Margery Pearce and married to a wholesale baker, brought bread to feed the seagulls when Win had invested in deadly armament just to keep them at bay. Margery developed an attachment to one particularly large specimen she called "Bold Willie" and was saying a fond farewell to him at the end of the visit when he did what seagulls perhaps do best, all over her new jumper.

Don and Len were friends from flying days and they came to spend the week of the Coronation of George VI with her and on Coronation Day, 12 May, they tried to dress the ship. This involves stringing the signal flags together in a prescribed sequence (to look their prettiest) and hauling them up the masts, the ends attached to the bow and stern. This started well but seems to have defeated them when they tried to haul the chain of flags up the masts. The string kept breaking and, even after several hours of trying, *Perula* remained un-dressed. They left for the pub.

Here they joined in the celebrations which included crowning a fisherman. Back on *Perula* they were drinking and playing cards when Win sensed there was something wrong. Disorientated for a start, she soon realised they were being swept backwards down the Straits. She started the engine, managed to miss the Menai Bridge pier and got the boat back under control just in time to avoid being swept into the Swellies. They tied up at Bangor pier after hitting it head-on, throwing Don over the bow and onto the pontoon. It seemed that the mooring had somehow failed.

The next visitors were Captain "Dash" and his wife. The Captain held an Extra Master's Ticket and had spent 20 years at sea. He and Win seemed to disagree over most things nautical and she had little aptitude for those prized activities of splicing ropes and painting. He, on the other hand, was used to blind obedience and not used to being so close to the water, happier high on the bridge of a steamer. He also hated being rowed by a woman. The situation was saved when he was called back to his ship.

In preparation for the voyage they adjusted the compass them-selves. This was a troubled process much removed from the adjust-ment that took place for aeroplanes but they did finally manage to get a good enough result to get them to Norway. Then there were the charts. Win knew which ones they needed for British waters but was quite mystified by what she should have for Norway. The names of the places being in Norwegian did not help, nor did the fact that she was not quite sure where she was going. It was difficult to pick the right ones from the catalogue. Finally she resorted to a feminine wile by writing to the chart agents J D Potter, explaining who she was and where she wanted to go and asking they sent the charts she needed.

Within two days she had a bundle of charts. Whether they were the right charts she could not determine so she took the ones for England and Scotland and put the rest away for later. As she said, "Never trouble trouble until trouble troubles you."

WEATHER

By early July Ron's father was on the road to recovery and Win's attention turned to the weather. She listened to the daily weather forecasts for farmers and shipping broadcast at the remarkably civilised hours of 10:30 and 21:00 by the BBC and the "Weather London" ones directly from the Air Ministry. They did not paint an encouraging picture. A series of depressions was sweeping across the Atlantic and passing across Scotland, bringing with them fronts, strong winds and rain. There was poor British summer weather. The maximum temperatures in the resorts of North Wales and Northern England were seldom more than 20 °C; it was cloudy with long periods of rain and drizzle. In the Irish Sea the winds were from the west and generally moderate or fresh and the sea was moderate to rather rough. To put this in some perspective the term "moderate" means "moderate for large ships"; for small boats like *Perula* moderate seas (with average wave heights of between 1.25 and 2.5 metres) are quite enough.

TO IRELAND

Win followed the forecast with some dismay. But, when Ron arrived on Saturday 10 July, he was told that they were leaving for Norway in half an hour — explaining why people in the Gazelle were buying him farewell drinks. The wind was blowing a force 5, with no immediate prospect of improvement, and it was coming from the north-west — more or less the direction they intended to set off in. They walked down the jetty in the ever-darkening gloom of overcast skies and dusk. Win ignored suggestions from locals that they wait until the morning and soon they were on *Perula*, casting off. They motored away from Glyn Garth and soon Puffin Island was abeam and they turned onto a course that would take them towards the Isle of Man. The wind strengthened to force 6 as they were passing Lynas Point, on the north-east corner of Anglesey. As they passed through the stream of shipping headed for Liverpool, Win (who was on watch on her own at the time), confused momentarily about the rules of the road, had a close encounter with a steamer. The sea was now rough and white crests of large waves appeared out of the blackness; spray beat against the wheelhouse and slashed across the windows. The crash of crockery came from below and her legs ached from bracing herself against the constant and violent lurching. Her eyes ached too from staring into the blackness, watching for lights that meant danger. She thought for a while of turning back.

Ron appeared and took over the helm as the sky began to lighten. He had a large lump on the side of his head from being thrown out of his bunk during the night. Win went below, wedged herself in and slept for four hours, waking to find leaden skies but wind and a sea that had both moderated a little. They now had the Isle of Man in sight.

After some debate (which may have involved Ron) it was decided to head for the Irish coast and calmer seas so they changed course, passing to the west of Chicken Rock on the south of the island at midday. The target was Strangford Lough, the 150 square kilometre inland sea just south of Belfast connected to the Irish Sea by a narrow eight kilometre long channel. By 15:00 they could see the Irish coast ahead and the seas were quietening down as they moved into the lee of the land. When they arrived off the Lough entrance at 18:00 the wind had dropped and it was calm. Sanctuary and a peaceful supper seemed just a short motor away but Win had made a mistake.

The waters of the Lough rush in and out through the channel twice a day and they had arrived at the middle of the period when they rush out. For several hours entry by a boat with a top speed of just a few knots is practically impossible; at spring tides (which these pretty well were) the rates of ebb tides can hit 7 knots for a while. Enough, as Win records, to drive *Perula* backwards. It was either wait for the tide to turn or go somewhere else and Win choose to go on to Belfast. Perhaps she had little information about Strangford tides or perhaps she knew that a night entry would be easier into a large port like Belfast. So they motored on, covering the 40 miles in another 9 hours. They eventually anchored in Whitehouse Roads at 03:00 the following morning.

Their first major solo voyage had lasted 30 hours and they had covered around 120 miles. Much of it had been in rough conditions driving into large seas and strong winds. Setting out when they did had probably been a bad idea, it was a definite mistake arriving at Strangford when they could not get in and they had nearly been run down by a steamer. Also, they might have had a more comfortable passage if they had put up the sails to steady *Perula* as she ploughed through the waves — something that occurred to them only afterwards. However, as they may have reflected, they had done it and they were learning fast.

SCOTLAND

After a rest, they left that evening. The weather had quietened down and the sea was calm but it was now very misty as they cleared the Irish coast and headed north. In the night Win caused an alarm by mistaking the reflection of the red glow of her cigarette in the wheelhouse window for distress signals. For a while they charged full-speed towards the distressed vessel. Ron was woken up to prepare to receive shipwrecked mariners with tea and what blankets he could get together.

They were abeam of Kintyre just after dawn and heading north up into the Sound of Jura. For some reason at 10:15 they went into Lowlandman's Bay on the east coast of Jura and then "left immediately". They missed the notorious hazard of the whirlpool of Corryvrecken and negotiated the difficulties of Fladda and the Sound of Luing as they were carried by the tide towards Oban.

Win was writing a letter while helming when she missed the Sound of Kerrera so they passed to the west of the island and approached Oban from the north. Here they picked up a mooring in Ardantrive Bay, opposite Oban. It turned out to be a sea-plane mooring but they seem to have stayed the night anyway. The following day they went on to Fort William where they enjoyed two nights before setting off for the entrance to the Caledonian Canal at Corpach.

This 60 mile long canal joins the west coast of Scotland with the North Sea through the Great Glen, a valley caused by an ancient geological fault in the earth's surface. Some 40 miles of it are through three natural lochs: Lochy, Oich and Ness. The man-made parts that link them and the seas together were constructed in the early 1800s as part of a programme of public works to bring employment to Scots displaced by the Highland Clearances. From Fort William in the west to Inverness in the east, it was built with 29 locks, generally in staircases of several together to reduce costs. Designed for sea-going vessels, it allowed sailing ships up to 46 metres long and with beams of up to 10 metres to avoid the difficult and sometimes stormy north coast and the Pentland Firth. With the threat of Napoleon, it offered safe and reliable passage for warships too. Started in 1804, by the time it was completed in 1822 ships had grown in size and were often steam powered so it was never fully used. Napoleon had left the scene for good the year before.

It was not something Win had been looking forward to; negotiating *Perula* in its narrow confines would be something quite new. It started badly.

The lock-keeper of the first lock told her to keep plenty of speed on as she entered the lock from the river to avoid being swept sideways by the tide. She did this on the approach towards the half-open entry gates (the locks were more than 10 metres wide and the gates were seldom fully opened) but then suddenly saw the closed exit gates of the lock. Although the lock was nearly 60 metres long she panicked, thinking she might not be able to stop before the second gates, and throttled back. This allowed the boat to be swept by the tide and, when she once more opened the throttle, *Perula* hit the first gate with a heavy thud.

The narrow ribbon of water with green fields on either side seemed an unnatural place for a boat like *Perula* to be. Win found it difficult to concentrate on keeping in the middle (remember she had gone the wrong side of an island a day or two before because she was writing a letter while steering) and ran into the bank several times. Locks and lifting bridges were a particular nightmare because they often meant trying to keep *Perula* stationary while a lock filled or emptied. Like many boats of her type she was really not good at reversing; going astern meant going somewhere in the general direction of backwards with very little control. The so-called paddle wheel effect on such boats quite often kicks them sideways with the real possibility, especially with a little help from the wind, of making a complete pirouette. Win did in fact manage to get *Perula* broadside-on across the canal while stopping for the railway swing bridge at Banavie not long after they entered the canal.

Apart from some nasty moments when *Perula* was nearly drawn into Inverness Weir, they reached the town without real incident, stocked up with food and visited the Customs House to clear customs. This could have been a nominal procedure but Win made something of a fuss because she wanted some papers to display for foreign officials. So she invited the full rigour of the revenue men and was required to complete No 7 (Sale) Declaration and No 35 (Sale) Victualling Bill. These produced wrangles over who was who on the boat and how to declare the coffee and the paint they carried. There was also the question of rebate on oil. And then they were visited by a Customs Officer to check everything and sign that all had been done correctly.

Since they were setting out on a 300 mile-long sea crossing Win decided to get a forecast from Weather London so she sent them a telegram with a prepaid reply "Desire to cross North Sea small yacht kindly wire forecast when weather favourable." This was part of the Weather London service (which provided forecasts for a variety of purposes including hill-walking) and a reply was quickly received "Southerly wind moderate sea." It seemed a little curt to Win; the amount she had prepaid would have covered a more fulsome response. But, brief as it was, it sounded all right so they "made a large stew and prepared to sail at dawn."

FIRST TIME CROSSING TO NORWAY

They locked out of the canal at 9 o'clock on 17 July 1937 in bright sunshine and took the North Channel out into the Moray Firth. Avoiding the notorious banks and shoals was not a problem at high water. By 11:30 the were passing the entrance to the Cromarty Firth and could feel that the passage had begun and with the usual mixture of trepidation (which was fading as they had things to do) and excitement (which only grew), they tossed the log (the device that would tell them how far they had travelled) over the stern and lashed everything down. Just after 17:00 they put up some sail and headed for the island of Utsira, rather less than 300 miles away. In fact, with the wind from a south easterly direction, they could only manage a course around ten degrees north of what they wanted. It meant that they were beating into the wind and, with the moderate sea, it was uncomfortable. As the afternoon turned into evening the strength of the wind grew. At 21:00 the engine was turned off and soon the wind veered slightly and reached force 7. It meant they could now sail directly for their destination and their speed was a respectable 5 knots.

In the early hours of the 18th they turned on the engine for some extra speed and left it on for the rest of the day and by noon they reckoned they were almost half-way across. It seemed to be getting rougher and Win's attempt at a sight with her sextant, to find their position, was spoiled by a large wave which made the boat lurch and threw her over. She cut her ankle on the wheelhouse door. *Per-ula* throbbed and ploughed on, a cloud of spray and a small boat on a rough and desolate sea. The seas, sweeping across the deck from time to time, sent trickles and drips of water into the saloon. Everything was quickly damp.

That night on watch alone around midnight (she usually took the stretch from 22:00 to 02:00) Win stretched out on the wheelhouse settee to ease her painful ankle and watched the stars to check that *Perula* was keeping her course. While she was lying there the news came over the radio that the search for Amelia Earhart, missing for days in the Pacific, had been abandoned. She looked out at the empty sea and wondered if Amelia, on the other side of the world, might still be alive and doing the same, desperate for rescue.

The next morning the wind seemed to be easing a little and the sea was not quite as rough and, at 09:00 they sighted the Norwegian coast. Two hours later they identified the island of Utsira just two miles away. They were almost exactly where they wanted to be after 300 miles sailing on the course set soon after leaving Scotland. This was remarkably accurate navigation although Win had to admit (at the time only to herself) that she had forgotten to allow for the time they had headed a little north and had not accounted for the change in magnetic variation there was between Scotland and Norway. Still they were there and, from the J D Potter collection, she dug out the chart that would lead them to Haugesund. It was something of a shock.

The entry did not look at all straightforward. There was a good sprinkling of islands between them and their destination and the passage was through narrow and winding channels that were marked on the Norwegian system, something they had obviously not encountered before. Win in fact soon worked out what it all meant but, in this first meeting, red marks with blunt tops, black ones with pointed tops and others striped in black, white and red danced before her eyes. Somehow she managed to find the main harbour in the Smedsund and, after excitement with spectators, helpers and customs at the busy commercial quay, they moved to a quieter mooring buoy on the other side of the Smedsund, away from the town. After treatment of her swollen ankle they went ashore and took a nauseating walk (their bodies thought they were still at sea) to send a telegram to Elsie. They returned, went below to rest and listened to the scampering feet of inquisitive local children on *Perula*'s deck. Sometimes men came too, climbed aboard and wandered around the deck for a while until they had seen enough. That night Win slept in comfort on her sprung mattress for twelve hours without stirring — but only after opening the curtains and reassuring herself that they really were in Norway.

HAUGESUND

They stayed in the quiet and liquor-free town (they tried to buy cocktails) of Haugesund for three days. They might have moved on if the harbour master had not warned them each day of an impending gale. When they did leave on the 23rd it was to weave through the Indreled, the sheltered passage between the mainland and the offshore islands that runs up much of the coast, to Hardangerfjord.

> For a few miles, whilst traversing Sletta, we were exposed to the open sea, but the weather was good and we turned into Bommelfjord, the entrance to Hardangerfjord, without experiencing any difficulties. This was our first real glimpse of Norway. A sky, blue beyond description, white fleecy clouds mingling with snow-capped mountains, a sun so hot that it was almost painful to walk the deck in bare feet. I lay aft on a cushion, my feet up against the mizzen mast, and marvelled at the beauty of the Norwegian scenery, as *Perula* threaded her way between grey rocky islands, patched with the dull green of pine trees. [1]

They passed through Storsund, where sculpted rock walls plunged vertically down into the water and, further off, waterfalls sometimes thundered and sometimes floated down the mountains. A beautiful sunset entranced them. So magical was it that Win was almost pushed to poetry but the spell was broken by alarming noises from the engine so they struggled nervously on until they found some-where shallow enough to anchor at Rosendal. Here meadows sloped gently down to the water.

They arrived just after 19:00 and promptly started to dismantle the engine and when time had passed and there were a sufficient number of pieces on the saloon floor, not having found the source of the problem, they put it back together again and started it. While it did work there were now dense clouds of smoke as well as the alarming noises. Win quickly identified it as a fuel problem and in searching around they did find that fuel was leaking from a broken pipe, not the source of the problem they were working on but non-etheless an important discovery.

It was midnight when Ron started, to Win's disapproval, to dis-mantle the fuel pump but he was forced to stop when a spring leapt out of it and landed in the wheelhouse. So they gave up and, after Win had listened to some music on the radio, went to bed.

Next morning Ron was convinced they had not put the engine back together correctly so took it apart again. It was true that they had installed the inlet valve cages upside down but he found also that one of the push-rods was bent. This was the source of the noises and smoke. With no spare readily available, it needed to be straightened. (Although they did not realise it at the time, the wrong lubricating oil had been used in the engine and this had turned into a sticky substance that had gummed up a valve, causing the rod to jump out of position and get bent.)

Wandering rather forlornly around Rosendal with the broken fuel pipe and the bent push-rod they eventually found a blacksmith who could straighten the rod. This required a game of charades that had Ron first imitating the sound of a diesel engine, then crouching to create "bent" and finally standing to attention and articulating "straighten". These final actions seemed to convey perfectly what was wanted and the blacksmith plucked the rod from his hand and threw it into the glowing coals. Soon it was as good as new. The blacksmith showed himself to also be a master of charades when he indicated that the broken fuel pipe would have to be sent to Bergen by steamer for repair. It would take a few days. They spent them enjoying Rosendal, then as now a pretty and popular tourist resort.

The parts came back from Bergen and, since the blacksmith refused payment, they entertained him and two of his mates on *Perula*. The whisky flowed that evening and the Norwegians zigzagged back to shore in their rowing boat.

The following morning, the 28 July at just after 9 o'clock, they upped anchor and left for Sundal. The party may have had after-effects because while Win had the departure time right, the logbook says they reached Sundal just after midnight. For a 15 mile passage this seems a long time — and Win corrected it in *Duffers*.

They anchored at Sundal after some trouble. A Norwegian motor boat owner told them what to do. They dropped their anchor 30 metres from the shore and then took a line from their stern to a mooring post ashore. *Perula* was then pulled in to make sure the anchor gripped and ended up, quite safely, just a metre or two from the shore. They entertained the helper with alcohol but, stocks depleted, Win had to produce a cocktail of various wines, apricot juice and added Eno's, a foaming indigestion and flatulence remedy, to give it some bite. It seemed to go down well and they were invited to the Norwegian boat to enjoy sun-dried lamb, boiled salmon and sweet liqueurs. It may, of course, have been intended as some kind of revenge for the Eno's but Win and Ron enjoyed the mix and were well enough afterwards to walk the four kilometres up to see the Bondhusbreen glacier, a spectacular cascade of blue ice reflected in a limpid lake.

BERGEN

By the following evening they were in Bergen. They had come via Lokksund, where wooded mountain slopes swept down to a channel that narrowed to just 100 metres, and then across Bjornafjord and up the island-strewn channel that leads to Bergen. They put on their city clothes, shopped and went to the Post Office to pick up four spare push-rods Through sheer and, to the staff no doubt incomprehensible, resolution Win got them for free, refusing to pay the £2 cash-on-delivery charge. There was a trip on the funicular railway up the side of Mount Fløyen. Here, 300 metres up, they could look out across the fjords, mountains and islands and, as yachtsmen always do, pick out their boat moored in the Puddefjord. They left this smart and cosmopolitan city, that washed like the water up the valleys between the mountains, on 1 August for Ålesund 170 miles away.

The land was much lower here so sailing should have been possible but the wind was strong and dead ahead so they motored into quite rough seas and spray flew once more over *Perula*. After ten hours they had covered little more than 40 miles so they anchored for the night in the mouth of Napsvåg, a small creek off Undelandsund.

The next day they travelled much further (75 miles) and by 21:00 they were anchored on the north side of the island of Skavøy. The passage through Krakhelle had been interrupted by a loud crack from the engine (predictably thought Win, given the name) so it had to be partly dismantled again — but otherwise it had been straightforward. The following day they set off for Ålesund. Before they had really got going, a bank of fog swept over them.

While fog is unnerving enough in open water it is a nightmare in confined channels like the ones they were facing. The trickiest spot was soon after they entered Ulvesund where the channel narrowed to just 100 metres with rocks not far off on either side. Luckily Win had prepared carefully the night before and had worked out her compass courses and this bottleneck and the rest of the sound were negotiated nervously but safely. When they left Ulvesund it was to round the Stadlandet headland and this brought them into the open sea. It is an area notorious for rough seas if the conditions are wrong but it seems to have been reasonable as they passed the headland — although rocks and white water kept appearing out of the lingering fog. Win had planned to duck quickly back into the sheltered Indreled after this but instead, with the poor visibility, elected to stay at sea until they were off Ålesund. Of course, soon after this the fog cleared and they arrived at Ålesund at 18:20 after an 11 hour passage and tied up to a large buoy north of the rocks in the middle of the Aspevågen, the natural harbour to the south of the town. They did try the harbour to the north but found it dirty and full of small fishing boats chugging about and throwing out clouds of black smoke from tall exhaust pipes. The large buoy was quieter until the early hours when more noisy fishing boats arrived and tied up to it.

ÅLESUND, MOLDE AND THE TROLLSTIGEN ROAD

They spent a day in Ålesund (Win records in the logbook that there were good shops) and then, just after midday on 5 August, left for Molde. "A pleasant little town" in the logbook, Molde had been a resort smart enough to attract the Prince of Wales with spectacular mountain views, colourful wooden houses, lush gardens and luxury hotels but much of it had been destroyed by fire in 1916. By 1937 it had recovered and maybe deserved its nickname as the "Town of Roses" but just three years later it was virtually wiped out by the fires following German bombing raids in 1940. The raids were pre-cipitated by the stay of King Håkon, his family and his government who stopped there for a week as they fled north before being evac-uated to exile in Britain. It is now known as the "City of Jazz and Roses" in recognition of its famous annual jazz festival. The "City" title is slightly misleading: it has around 25,000 inhabitants so is still rather a pleasant little town. It was also their furthest north on this voyage.

However, the attractions did not detain them long; they left the following afternoon for Åndalsnes at the head of Romsdalsfjord, a 25 mile trip south-east. The next day, the 7th, they took a bus up the Trollstigen road. Opened just a year before by the King, the Troll-stigen (Troll's Ladder) climbed the side of the the 1800 metre Bis-pen (Bishop) mountain in a series of eleven hairpin bends. Towards the top of the climb, where the road levelled out, they got off and decided to climb the Kongen (King) a mere 1600 metres high. Al-most as unprepared as it was possible to be without being arrested for indecency, they set off up the bare rock-face. In their deck shoes they managed to climb some way, the wind getting stronger all the time and the face getting steeper, until Win looked down at the road far, far below. She lost her nerve, grabbed hold of a fern and would not let go.

Ron reasoned with her over a cigarette but she clung on, even as it started to rain. It was only the sight of a huge blanket of cloud rolling towards them and the thought that they might never get back to *Perula* at all if it enveloped them that got her moving. The only way she could travel was on her bottom and it was thus that she slowly edged down the mountainside and, sometimes sliding on ice, reached the road. After a walk they managed to find a tourist hut where they had coffee while they waited for a bus. It took them through a thick fog down the unseen but still vertiginous road and thus they regained *Perula* where they wrote in the logbook "Take bus to Trollstig — worth seeing."

The following morning they returned to Ålesund for two nights and then sailed for Stordal. The 27 mile trip took them through Borgenfjord, Humlesund and the very narrow but well-marked Vegesund (not much more than 50 metres wide in places), weaving between the small islands out into Storfjord. Stordal was then 20 miles up the fjord. They spent the night anchored there and then at 08:10 next morning set off for Geiranger fjord.

GEIRANGER FJORD

By 13:00 they were photographing the Seven Sisters waterfall half way up to Geiranger fjord. The log records them as spending two hours doing this and *Duffers* gives some indication of what they were up to.

It was decided to lower the dinghy and for this they had a specially designed derrick installed by Dickies. It functioned beautifully but, as Win was leaning over to release the dinghy, Ron arranged for its boom to strike her on the head, rendering her insensible (in her version). When revived she took charge of *Perula* while Ron clambered into the dinghy with the camera; he would take photographs of *Perula* and Win actually beneath the falls. This was not a simple as it sounded. The dinghy was nearly turned over by a steamer's wash and it proved very difficult to line up for the required shot. *Perula* nearly collided with the bank several times as Win manoeuvred and she decided that the falls were not that impressive anyway, picked up Ron and motored off up the fjord. However, when she looked back she thought the view magnificent and went back to try again. This time things worked and the result can be seen in *Duffers*. So, after a finally-fruitful two hours, they did motor on to Maråk at the top of the fjord and dropped the anchor, staying for two nights.

The logbook records[2] that on the following morning, the 12th, they sailed back down the Geiranger fjord and Sunnylvsfjord and turned into the dead end of Norddalsfjord and Tafjord. The peaceful waters and soaring mountains of Tafjord had been, just three years before they visited, the site of one of Norway's greatest natural disaster.

In the early hours of 7 April 1934 an existing fissure 700 metres up the face of Langhamaren mountain suddenly opened and between 2 and 3 million cubic metres of rock slid into the fjord. It sent three enormous waves, 62 metres high near the landslide itself, sweeping up and down the fjord destroying villages, indeed everything, in their paths and killing 47 people, mainly in the villages of Tafjord and Fjora. The scar was visible to Win — and is still visible. Such slides, mercifully much smaller, are a recognised hazard in sailing some of the fjords and Win's Sailing Directions advised keeping in the middle as much as possible.

It was in Tafjord that Percy joined them. Percy was a whistler and an invisible one at that. He whistled just as Win and Ron did to call one another and he whistled several times that day. Several times one or other of them dashed up from the cabin to see what the other wanted in the wheelhouse. Each time it was nothing other than Percy, the ghostly visitor. Percy kept them busy until they anchored in Honningdalvåg, a small bay on the north shore of Storfjord at 19:27. A trip ashore to Honningdal left Win unimpressed and she recorded "one shop — of sorts!" in the log but the shop did provide her with "Teddy" cigarettes[3]. "You ought to try them some time" she suggests in *Duffers*. Perhaps they brought back memories of the Swearers' and Smokers' Club. Perhaps she recalled Sawley's herbal cigarettes that she so enjoyed.

The next day was a longer one. They left early and went down Storfjord and then Rovdefjord. They then picked their way through Åramsund and Storsund and headed out to the open sea to round the Stadlandet peninsula. They retraced their route through Ulvesund and headed east up Nordfjord. They anchored in the small bay of Davika on the southern shore of Davikfjord. In just under 15 hours they had covered 86 miles. Percy was still with them, whistling away. Once more the nearest village failed the test: "another cock-eyed place" wrote Win.

Not a place to linger apparently because they set off the following day up the fjord to the head of Innvikefjord and anchored off Loen (Win called it Leon). The first attempt at this was thwarted by the whirlpools created by the river that flowed into the fjord there and they spent a miserable time in the rain, which had been falling all day, waltzing around and going aground. Eventually they found a better spot. It was not much better but it served.

Next day they went to Eid in Eidsfjord, where they filled up with water by hand from the village pump, and then the following day, 16 August, they set out for Florø on the north side of the island of Brandsøy. They had thought of passing through Rugsund but "one look was enough" and they went the slightly longer route west around Rugsundøy. After that they probably headed down Frøyjoen, but we cannot be sure. Whatever, they arrived at Florø after a 7½ hour passage and, according to the log, anchored (in *Duffers* Win says they tied up to a buoy).

FLORØ AND KINN

They liked Florø. At first sight it looked rather dilapidated but they were won over by the surroundings and the people. They stayed the following day and entertained the Lloyds' agent and the harbour master, passing on in *Duffers* the tip that Norwegians like plenty of water with their whisky; they dilute a single one with a whole tumbler full of water. At midday on the 18th they left and sailed the 15 miles south to Kinn. Here they dropped the anchor in Kinnesund on the east shore of the island.

They had two visitors there. First they looked up from the galley and saw momentarily "a most odd-looking child" with lips trembling and eyes full of tears framed in the wheelhouse door. He vanished to be replaced by a man with a large knife who was wearing only swimming trunks. Whatever the first figure was (there is no explanation) the second one was real. He was a student from Oslo University who went to Kinn each summer for a few weeks of solitude to climb, swim and build his small house and grow potatoes. He stayed for coffee.

They walked up to the 12th century stone church on the island. It looked out over the sea and the strange mountain, the Kinnaklova, that had a great notch in it. Once the most important church around, until a new one was built in Florø in the late 1800s, it had served the needs of the pilgrim traffic up and down the coast and been sustained in its richness by the tithes on the herring caught nearby. In the 19th century 15,000 fisher folk lived on the island but when Win visited there were very few and by the end of the 20th century there were barely a dozen.

As they approached the church they heard a mournful wail and saw that it came from a scruffy old man wearing a red cap who was wandering among the few untended graves around it. The student explained that the man was calling to his dead wife, an explanation that rather shook Win, perhaps understandably given her experience with Percy (who was still with them) and the fleeting, odd-looking child. When the old man started grubbing around in the soil she must have been even more rattled (Could she have thought he might drag out the wife to welcome them?) but it soon became apparent he was digging up a large key to the church. Once they got into the church it seems to have been the triptych that caught Win's imagination. Although, it had been made in the Netherlands in the early 16th century and the three figures were supposed to be saints, it had somehow been adopted as a representation of a local legend.

This was of an Irish princess, Sunniva, who had fled the country with two of her servants to escape an arranged marriage. Each had vowed to build a church wherever they landed. They travelled in three ships and the princess landed at Selje, a little north of Kinn, and began her work. The project was not going well until a troll, putting aside the usual lustful and malevolent impulses of his kind when he saw how beautiful she was, helped her finish it. The story could have ended well but, alas, Vikings were in the offing and, knowing their legendary evil intents were only increased by the good looks of their intended victim, she prayed to be spared. She was hiding in a cave at the time and the wish was granted when the rocks above her crashed down and killed her. She may have been hoping for a better outcome but they were, after all, different times.

They left Kinn just after 16:30 and by 21:30 they were anchored in Skivenesvåg, a long narrow east-west inlet, for the night. They entered in the dark and it seemed snug enough but, come the morning, they were horrified to see rocks all around. So nasty was it that they had to reverse out. As they set off they had engine trouble and they had to throttle back and then Percy started and was with them as they motored south and then east up Sognefjord the 58 miles to Balholmen where they anchored in Esefjord. Unspoiled and magnificent, Sognefjord seemed to sum up the best of the region. It was, Win thought, the place to go if you only had a week or two to spend in the Norway.

That night Ron dismantled the engine yet again, presumably to sort out the problem they had had all day, and in doing so he simultaneously eliminated the whistling Percy — with a drop of oil. The following day they dined at a hotel as guests of a Lancashire yachtsman they met on the quay and Win took full advantage of the buffet and then danced the night away. The following morning she was sick over the side and they set off for Fjaerland, somewhere that turned out to be their favourite place of all.

WINIFRED BROWN

FJAERLAND

They anchored off the Mundal Hotel, hired a car and drove off to see some ice, the Fjaerland region being famous for its glaciers. The ice was the Suphellerbreen glacier, two masses of ice split by thundering waterfalls. Win strode off, drawn to the ice cave beneath a veil of water, to stand in its translucent blue depths. Ron had different ideas and grabbed her, dragging her back, indignant. When she learned later that another Englishwoman had died the year before, acting on a similar impulse, she saw it differently.

They went to the Mundal hotel in the evening. Built out of wood at the end of the previous century, the walls were lined with tapestries and a log fire sparkled and crackled. They joined in the dancing led by a man wearing a large top-hat and followed by girls in national costume, all embroidered bodices and fancy aprons. They whirled in circles, careered around the hotel in something like a conga, went through a complicated routine of passing beneath arches made by other dancers' arms and finally made uni-sex circles. The singing had started slow, become frenetic during the conga section but was now mournful and slow. Another dancer explained that they were currently looking into the grave and it seems then to have dawned on Win that they were at a funeral which was also, as she put it, "a real good 'do'".

The next day being a Sunday, locals came from miles around to the church in the village with its stumpy square tower, the dark red painted wood and crisp white window frames looking at their best after a recent refurbishment. Old women came in shawls, children in national costume; they came by cart and boat and on foot. Perhaps they came from the cows and goats and cheese-making; perhaps they came from the silver-fox farms established in the area for three decades using Canadian animals. From wherever they came it was probably the highlight of their week; Fjaerland was then completely cut off from the outside world except by boat.

On the Monday Win and Ron held a farewell party on *Perula* for fifteen locals, reflecting no doubt on just how convivial the Norwegian funeral had been, and left mid-afternoon to go back to Balholmen for the night. On the Tuesday they sailed to Gudvangen on Naerofjord, perhaps the most awesome and gloomy of them all. Here they were amused by the preparations for the arrival of a cruise ship:

Ashore next morning we found the village a mass of "stolkjerrer," small traps pulled by the cream coloured ponies. There were hundreds of them, awaiting the arrival of a German cruise ship.

> It used to amuse me intensely to watch some tiny village preparing for the arrival of a big ship. First, boatloads of cars would arrive from the neighbouring fjords on what we called "Adams's ice breaker", for at the first sight of this car transport, which was blunt at both ends, Adams had spent a considerable time getting agitated about the "proximity of ice." All available means of transport having been unearthed and dusted, stuffed polar bears, reindeers and such like, were carefully placed outside the shops, and the more picturesque inhabitants dressed up for the occasion. The ship would then arrive and the peaceful village became an uproar. The roads were impossible; if you were not run over, you were blinded with dust. Motor horns shrieked out and the pony traps swept by with the tinkle of bells. Everybody was arguing, bargaining and taking each others' photographs. As soon as the big ship left everything was whisked away to the next village. Orange peel and chocolate paper still floated about the fjord, but otherwise all was peace again.[4]

TO SCOTLAND 1937

By now it was the 24 August and it was time to think about going home so on the following day they left. After one night in Balholmen they headed for Bergen with an overnight stop at Sildevåg, on the east coast of the island of Fedje, on the way. The weather news in Bergen was not good with a series of deep depressions sweeping across northern Britain bringing gales and so they sat for a day, despondent. But then on the morning of the 28th they were told there was a small window for the crossing when winds might not exceed force 6 or 7 and should be northerly rather than dead ahead.. This was not ideal but good enough in the circumstances so within half an hour, at 1255, they were off, down the fjord to pass north of Marstein Island, their kicking-off point for the 240 mile crossing. It nearly went terribly wrong soon after: Ron spotted breaking waves ahead and they quickly realised that they were heading straight for Marsteinboen. This isolated rock, three-quarters of a mile west of the island, lurks just below the surface, ready to rip the bottom out of a boat, and Win had missed it completely when planning her course. After this, a night spent picking their way through a fishing fleet apart, the crossing was without incident. After 44 hours, just before midday on the 30th, they sighted Kinnaird Head on the south of the Moray Firth. They changed course for Banff on its southern shore and then not liking it went to Portknockie, 10 miles further west, where they tied up.

The winds on the crossing had never been more than force 5 and they had been from the north or north west most of the time giving them a quick crossing. The forecast stronger winds did not turn up and for the last day there was not much wind at all and they motored into the Moray Firth. Port Knockie was small but welcoming and the charges were very reasonable at 6d (2½ pence) per ton according to the logbook but there is a note saying it cost considerably more if you include the cost of entertaining the harbour master.

The following day they left and by the evening they were back at Muirtown on the Caledonian Canal. After a day there dealing with the formalities they pressed on through a wild and rough Loch Ness to tie up at Fort Augustus. It was here they met the man from Bilbao.

Ron had met him; he knew a lot about boats. So they went to dinner with him and then invited him back for a drink. He gave them a photograph of the main road in Bilbao with a cross marking the spot where "the first bomb fell."[5] in the Spanish Civil War. He sat and talked and drank into the early hours and beyond: Win found he was still there when she woke up at 0900.

He was there again the following evening and even invited some people who had arrived on a steam yacht aboard *Perula* for a drink resulting in another session lasting until well past midnight. They eventually threw him out, turned out the lights and locked the doors. The man from Bilbao was not one to take a hint and there was thumping and banging as he stormed around *Perula*'s deck, crying out that he had been locked out of his hotel. Suddenly there was a loud splash and then silence. Win was desperately worried that he was drowning but Ron forbade her going outside to look. So she didn't and carried on worrying all night.

The following morning as they were motoring off they saw him blowing the horn of his car on the bank, trying to attract their attention. They ignored him and that night, after leaving the canal, they anchored behind an island opposite Fort William, hiding.

The following day they sailed to Oban where they were stuck for five days waiting for the weather to moderate until, on the morning of 10 September at 06:40, they left. By the following afternoon they were back on their mooring at Glyn Garth, swept down the Irish Sea by a brisk northerly wind that kicked up large and frightening following seas. It did moderate after the Isle of Man and as they arrived at the Straits a couple of sirens were sounded and the Beaumaris ferry dipped its ensign to them in salute. At 15:15 they picked up their buoy, having easily shooed someone off it, and the adventure was over.

The total distance was 2500 miles and they had run the engine for 450 hours — meaning that they had it running most of the time. They had spent 1 shilling (5p) on harbour dues and just £8 on fuel and oil. It had been "a good and cheap holiday".

Perula was taken out of the water for the winter on 6 October and they must have learnt from the previous experience because the process is dismissed in just a few words. There was some work to be done and before they left Dickies they asked for the ballast to be refastened, the topsides to be painted and a chair to sit in at the wheel rather than a stool. This done, they left for Manchester and their families.

TO SPITSBERGEN

No doubt they had discussed what they might do the following year but it was on Christmas Day that it was decided. Ron had forsaken his own family for Christmas lunch with Win, Elsie and just possibly Sawley. Win was poking around in the fire for a chestnut when, perhaps influenced by the snowy scenes on the mantelpiece Christmas cards, she announced that they should sail to Spitsbergen. Ron, perhaps just drifting off into a warm and enveloping well-fed haze, uttered a startled "What!". Elsie looked up from her book and told her not to be a fool.

Spitsbergen is the largest island of the Svalbard archipelago, a frozen wilderness just 600 miles from the North Pole, surrounded for much of the year by ice. To the north east of it is Nordaustlandet and below this are the islands of Barentøya and Edgeøya. Storfjorden lies between Spitsbergen and these two islands. There are a number of other, smaller, islands in the group. Win fetched an atlas, checked the distances and decided it would be "a cinch". Bear Island (Bjørnøya) was a convenient stop, just 220 miles north of the Norwegian mainland, and Spitsbergen a mere 122 miles further. It must have been decided then. Ron perhaps settled back for a doze, knowing that there was little he could do to change things anyway; Elsie probably returned to her book, resigned to more worry about her daughter. Win, for her part, started planning.

First, improbably, she wrote at length to the Norwegian State Railways offices, then as now, in Cockspur Street, London. She gave her life story, making sure no doubt that they knew they were not dealing with a nobody, and asked a string of questions about the weather, what clothes she should wear and, generally, whether the planned cruise she outlined was practicable. The scheme worked.

The letter could not be ignored, coming from a well-known figure and no-one in the office felt able to reply. So it was forwarded to the National Travel Association of Norway in Oslo who, equally intimidated or flummoxed, sent it to someone in the Norwegian weather service. It was thus that a report came from Hr Winther-Hansen in Tromsø, their expert on weather in northern Norway. It was sobering reading.

First there was the ice on the west coast of Spitsbergen. While the region to the north of Isfjord, about half way up was, because of the warming Gulf Stream, normally free of ice in summer, the coastline to the south might not be. This happened because ice released from Storfjorden on the east coast was sometimes swept round the south of the island by north-easterly winds and then drifted north up the coast. Sometimes it even reached Isfjord and blocked it. This was bad news since Win's plan was to sail up the west coast to Isfjord and then up the fjord to Longyearbyen, the capital. There may have been some comfort from the fact that Hr Winther-Hansen said that this had happened in 1915 (was there no more recent example?) but it was unnerving that his remarks were based on ships designed for ice, something *Perula* was not.

The ice news for Bear Island was slightly better. The island was normally free of ice after the end of May — but there were times when there was ice until July.

Overall the Norwegian expert recommended sailing in July or August to have the best chance of avoiding ice. However these were the worst months for fog; it was around Bear Island for one day out of two. But, he suggested, it was the lesser evil. And winds? Well, gales of force 9 or more were infrequent in the favoured months — but should not be ruled out.

Hr Winther-Hansen's notes[1] extended to five typewritten pages (and cost her £1) and those pages must have been pored over in those winter evenings in Lodore. Was the plan challenging, foolhardy or just plain madness?

Other sources of information were not encouraging. She read the *Arctic Pilot*. Its advice on sailing among ice floes suggested striking them head-on if you had to strike them, anchoring to one if you became trapped and clearing out if the ice began to crush you. This hinted at the bleak reality if things went wrong. Professor Rudmose-Brown of Sheffield University, who had served as surveyor to the Scottish Arctic Expeditions to Spitsbergen in 1909, 1914 and 1919 and was now a respected polar expert, was helpful but advised against the enterprise. He doubted that the Norwegians would allow it anyway. Major Smales, who had cruised the north Norway coast around the North Cape, advised against it too.

A modern pilot describes the summer of 1994, the worst for 32 years and so an example of how it just might be, with "an intrusion of heavy pack ice off the south-west coast in mid-July, day after day of thick fog, substantial blizzard snow-storms and more than a few days of sustained winds to force 8–9 with topographically caused sustained gusting to force 12."[2]

It must have been February or March when Win and Ron had a "committee meeting" to discuss whether to go. It would be a grand adventure said Win. Ron agreed that it would, provided Win had the sense to turn back in time if necessary. So they decided to go "towards" Spitsbergen and not necessarily "to" it. Unleashed, Win went straight to the press and sold the story. She was guaranteed at least £70 for it.

She ordered the charts for the voyage from Jacob Dybwad, the publisher and bookseller in Oslo, choosing this time the Norwegian ones rather than those produced by the Admiralty. She needed 80 altogether and when they arrived she spent weeks studying them, planning the passages as far as she could using the Sailing Directions. She hoped that this would save time on the actual voyage; during the previous voyage she had been passage planning into the early hours so that they could press on day after day.

Ron had also been busy travelling back and forth to *Perula*, fetching and carrying all the bits and pieces that needed cleaning, painting and repairing. He even brought the sails home and sent the mainsail to the laundry where it was spread out and scrubbed with fresh water. He did the mizzen and the staysails himself. He did them twice because the clothes-line broke under the weight the first time and they ended up in the mud.

On 11 April they both went to the boat for a week and spent three days painting the inside. This proved difficult; it needed the skill, Win said, of an ARA (an Associate of the Royal Academy of Arts) but whether even a determined one of those could perform lying on his back with the constant risk of being stuck to a bit he had just painted may never be tested. They used their own concoction of enamel and house paint to save time and the results were disappointing if not distressing. They decided that they would know better next time and hoped it would look acceptable once the hull was filled with the usual gear — and their paintwork had been covered up.

Perula was launched on the 27 April and on the 10 May, with it seems no sea trials, they started the engine and, just before 11 o'clock left. In the logbook, after the firm line she had drawn under the last entry for the previous year, Win started a new page and then wrote "SPITSBERGEN" after the word "towards". Then she wrote the first entry for 1938: "Engine started, cast off, circled jetty." On the jetty stood a farewell party of pressmen and the waiters and maids from the Gazelle. They waved to them, nearly rammed a ferry and set a course to take them up the Irish Sea.

ELECTRICITY AND GOLF

Over the winter she had still functioned as a public figure. On 28 January she had given a talk at the eleventh annual conference of the Manchester and Salford Branch of the Electrical Association for Women at the Town Hall. The Association was set up in 1924 to educate women about the potential of electricity, particularly in the home, and to put the woman's point of view to suppliers and government. Dame Caroline Haslett (who Win may well have met at the Press Club dinner in 1930) was a founder and there were branches in many towns and cities and, as well as pamphlets and talks, they had other means of disseminating information: for example, *"Watts" In A Home (A Play in Four Acts)* was published in

1929. The organisation brought women together in an exciting modern cause and created, at its height, an almost religious zeal for a future without manual drudgery that released women for more serious endeavours. Manchester City Council was caught up in the national fervour and Alderman R W Shepherd announced to the conference that in four month's time the "finest electricity show-room in the United Kingdom" would be opened in the Town Hall extension. They had perhaps been encouraged by the "All-Electric House" built and furnished by the EAW in Bristol in 1935.

Win, the chief speaker at the conference, talked of how lost pilots could be directed by wireless and how electricity made weather forecasts available to sailors, giving her own return from Norway in the predicted finer-weather window as an example. There were problems of course. On a flight back from Belfast she had had a mysterious electrical problem that could have been fatal had she not been on the shortest route and nearly four kilometres high at the time. Electricity lines strung across the country were a hazard to aviators — and she had had a narrow escape herself. But there were pluses: an atmospheric electrical disturbance akin to the Northern Lights had made hostile Indians flee instead of attacking on the Amazon adventure.[3]

She must have seemed an exotic creature in this rather earnest world of labour-saving household appliances and may well have been seen as an example of what women could do when released from domestic toil. The fact that Win had never, like most women driving the EAW at the time, had to actually do much around the house was not too relevant. Indeed some have argued that an important benefit of electrification was that it made it easier to retain servants because the appliances made their lives a bit more tolerable.

She also played golf until just before they sailed off. She reached the last eight of the *Bystander* Ladies' Northern Foursomes Tournament at Sand Moor, Leeds with her partner Mrs Brooks. They were beaten on 7 April three and two by Mrs H Somerville and Miss D

Green — who had the advantage of being members of the home club.[4]

TO SCOTLAND

Those things must have already seemed an age away as Puffin Island slipped by, *Perula* rumbling along across calm water heading out of the Straits and turning north, the Welsh mountains dissolving into a haze. Summer clouds patched a blue sky and, as they went on, *Perula* swayed a little more and they knew they were once more at sea. It was so calm that they had lunch at the saloon table, leaving the boat to look after herself, and when Win returned to the wheelhouse she could already see the Isle of Man 40 miles ahead. Of course the idyll had to end. It had been dented by a forecast of freshening winds and they turned off the engine to listen carefully to the afternoon one. It predicted the stronger south-easterly winds that were to build up after dark and last through the night.

They had put up the sails in the afternoon and, in the middle of the night with Win on watch alone, the boat gybed, the heavy boom swinging dangerously across as the wind caught the sail from behind. The seas had now increased to moderate and, breaking their rule about working on deck alone, she went up to adjust the sheets without rousing Ron and very nearly fell in. Saved by her lifeline, she struggled back to the wheelhouse, much shaken.

The wind came and went, it rained and the visibility was very poor at times but by just before midday they passed the Mull of Kintyre and at 18:30 they anchored in Crinan harbour, more of a rocky inlet than a harbour.

Leaving the following morning, they passed through Dorus Mor (narrowly avoiding being swept westward through the Gulf of Corryvrecken) and up the Firth of Lorn. To this point it was much as the previous year but now they passed Oban and turned northwest up the Sound of Mull and at 16:45 anchored off Tobermory on the Isle of Mull.

The Gulf of Corryvrecken is between the islands of Jura and Scarba to the north-west of Crinan. The tides can run as fast as 10 knots over the uneven bottom of the narrow strait which is in one place over 200 metres deep while on the north side an underwater pinnacle of rock rises to within 30 metres of the surface. As a result there can be standing waves up to 10 metres high under the right conditions and water swirling around the pinnacle gives rise to a world-class whirlpool. The roaring waters can sometimes be heard 20 kilometres away. The writer George Orwell and members of his family nearly came to grief in 1947 when the small boat they were travelling in capsized and they had to be rescued by fishermen. On the other hand his one-legged brother-in-law Bill Dunn did manage to swim across the gulf. Orwell was living on Jura writing his novel *1984* and, in one version, Dunn swam across in the year 1984 to celebrate this.

They left Tobermory for Portree at 09:15 the following morning heading west out of the Sound of Mull. They rounded Ardnamurchan point and headed north-north-west. Win estimated that the wind was a south-westerly force 6 when they set out and, before they had been sailing long, there was a warning of a southerly gale. It started rather badly. For the first ten miles or so there was little protection from the open Atlantic so Win was keen to get that behind them. Unfortunately she had made some kind of error with the tidal calculations so it took a long time to get round Ardnamurchan Point with *Perula* seeming stationary at times, rolling wildly around in the lumpy seas. After this, with the strong south westerly winds behind them, they left the islands of Muck, Eigg and Rhum to port (Win had a rum at this point) and headed into the Sound of Sleat which separates the Isle of Skye from the mainland. By now the wind had risen to force 7. They were struck by violent squalls which swept down from the mountains, whipping up the sea into a local frenzy, knocking *Perula* onto her side and bringing rain so heavy that the land on either side disappeared. Even in the half-mile wide narrows of Kyle Rhea they could see only water all around, below and above.

At the head of the sound they turned west down Loch Alsh (narrowly missing a ferry) and swept the last 20 miles up the west coast of the Isle of Skye in sheltered waters, the strong winds and squalls now blowing them along. They anchored at Portree at 20:40 having covered the 71 miles in 11½ hours and were very pleased with themselves that they had beaten the promised gale and would be safe and even snug as it blew through. It was almost a disappointment when the wireless told them that it had arrived a little early and they had just sailed through it.

The following morning was spent trying to buy fresh vegetables in Portree only to learn that it was too early in the year that far north. So Win spent some time dividing up the tinned ones they already had to make sure they did not eat them all at once. At just before midday (there was no point leaving much earlier because they would meet foul tides north of Skye if they did), with no wind, they started the engine and motored off towards Stornoway. There was no wind for the whole nine hour passage and the passage was quite uneventful until 18:00 when, off the coast of Lewis, they encountered some basking sharks. Primed with stories of them sinking small boats, they were alarmed when one swam straight at *Perula*, its wavering shadow passing right under the keel. But soon enough they were chasing them for photographs, even though the apprehension never quite left them. At Stornoway they had some trouble with their anchor and Ron had to carve a wooden pin to replace the metal one that had fallen out. With all the messing about and the attention it was attracting from the locals Win decided to anchor well away from the town. They did go ashore in the evening to discover that they were the first yacht of the season; like the cuckoo thought Win, a herald of spring.

The next day, again in a calm and after the early morning fog had cleared, at just before 11:00 they left to round Cape Wrath, planning to arrive off the headland when the tide was slack and so the seas would be slighter. Unfortunately, as Win might have put it, the fog didn't know it was morning fog and returned. So they were just half an hour into the trip when they could see nothing of the land that lay close by on the port side. They narrowly missed Holm Point but it meant that Win could work out a course to leave the Hen and

Chicken Rocks, just three miles away, safely to port. Feeling their way through the fog, eyes straining, fog-horn blasting and circled by sharks, the rocks put in an unexpected appearance on the starboard bow prompting a quick change of course. It was a relief when the fog cleared about midday but hardly had it done so when the light northerly wind began to increase in strength. By 16:45 it was about force 4 with an uncomfortable swell and it was hard work maintaining a course that would take them safely round Cape Wrath. It looked as if the weather was going to get worse so they turned east and headed for Loch Inchard about 10 miles south of the Cape. As they did so the wind steadily increased and the sea started to kick up. By 18:30 the wind had reached force 6 and the sea was rough when they saw the coast, about half a mile ahead. Win soon identified the entrance to Loch Inchard. The wind reached force 7 and the rain began to lash down, as they struggled towards it, the boat lurching about in the heavy seas. It was not long before she realised there was something wrong: all around them were rocks and breaking water. For a moment she was frozen in horror, not knowing what to do. It was Ron's shout that made her steer for clear water. When they reached it they took the mainsail down, working on deck in the bitter cold stinging rain, and took stock of where they were.

For a while all Win could conclude, even with the help of the chart, was that they were lost. Then she slowly realised that they were around two miles south of Loch Inchard, somewhere south of Handa Island around the rock-strewn mouth of Loch A'Chairn Bhain. So now they turned *Perula* north and made for Loch Laxford, directly into the wind and seas. At full throttle *Perula* seemed hardly to move and the seas were leaping green over the bow. It took an hour to cover the two miles into Loch Laxford, just south of Inchard, where they anchored in Fanagmore Bay tucked away behind a headland and sheltered by islands. In the logbook Win wrote "Found! Anchored L Laxford and very glad to be."

Exhausted as they must have been, Ron decided that he would develop the photographs he had taken of the sharks. This of course involved chemicals and a developing tank system that should have

155

allowed him to do it in the light but something went wrong and they had to sit in the dark, counting off the seconds (all 1320 of them) for the chemicals to do their work. When it was finished they found the photographs were a dismal failure. All round it had not been a great day.

NORTHERN ISLES

The following day they set off just before 14:00. The wind had dropped but there was still a heavy swell to lift *Perula's* bow as they set off to round Cape Wrath. They passed the little group of islands and the rock called Whale Back and Win looked back to Laxford and, as she often did, made some notes that might help her find it another time. They passed Bulgie Island (Am Balg) and by 18:00 they were off Cape Wrath. After studiously avoiding Stag Rock (Duslic Rock), a mile to the north-east of the Cape, they made their way 15 miles to Loch Eriboll. They anchored in the wide bay of Camas an Duin, five miles up the loch on the eastern side. They thought it a desolate spot (they christened it "Loch 'Orrible") and were excited when they saw a car go by on the road that crept around the loch.

The next morning they upped anchor and set off for Stromness, fifty-three miles away in the Orkney Islands. The part of the voyage that bothered Win most was Hoy Sound on the west of the islands. They had to pass through this gap between the islands with the tide with them. That meant arriving after 20:00; before that, it being spring tides, the tide could be running against them at more than seven knots making progress impossible. In the wrong conditions such strong tides could lead to very nasty seas, even if the timing was right.

As it was, the voyage was without incident and they passed through Hoy Sound just after 20:00 at more or less the optimum time and anchored well up Stromness harbour just off the North Pier. They stayed for three nights and then on the 20th left for Lerwick in the Shetlands, 120 miles away. The Orkneys surround an extraordinary natural basin, Scapa Flow. Some seven miles in diameter with depths greater than 30 metres it is accessible by just a few quite narrow channels between the islands. So it is a natural harbour, well protected from the elements and from intruders and was the base from which Britain ruled the northern seas. Littered with the remains of some of the 74 ships of the German High Seas fleet, scuttled there on 21 June 1919, (a few of which appear like dotted ghosts on modern charts), its entrances were protected by block-ships and anti-submarine nets.

Win had chosen to go directly east across Scapa to pass out through Holm Sound, not a recommended route because of the block-ships strung across the approach at Kirk Sound.[5] With the current bubbling along at eight knots, they were swept through, Win following the rather sketchy directions she had managed to get from the locals. It was easier than they expected; in fact, disappointingly so.

They turned to the north in the rather gentle breeze and by 21:00 they saw Fair Isle, and passed it in the early hours. At dawn they were abeam of Sumburgh Head at the south end of the main island of Shetland and a few hours later they anchored in Lerwick harbour just off Victoria pier. The long voyage had been accomplished without any real incident.

TO NORWAY AGAIN

They did not linger in Lerwick too long. In the afternoon they cleared customs and a little later the telegram arrived from Weather London in response to the one Win had sent that morning. It warned that winds locally would be quite strong but that elsewhere it would be fairly quiet. By the time they received it the winds were already strong, howling in the rigging. Anyway, the telegram advised waiting until dawn to set out and this they did. So early on 22 May they motored out of the harbour. Win had originally intended to head to the Arctic Circle directly, well up the Norwegian coast but, instead they went east towards the entrance to Sognefjord.

The winds were light with heavy rain for a start but by the afternoon dropped away to virtually nothing, bringing fog. They crept forward until the fog cleared at teatime. By 22:30 it was back and, with the arrival of darkness, they could not see a thing. They struggled on with one of them sitting in the bow, bitterly cold and peering into the fog and periodically sounding the bell with a hammer. Vast ships of the imagination charged towards them in the foggy night and they swerved many times to avoid them but they heard no fog horns and slowly relaxed enough for Win to fall asleep on a sail in the wheelhouse, much to Ron's disgust when he returned from lookout. Daylight brought rain and improved visibility and they saw the Norwegian coast at 09:45. Quite where they were was not clear and it took several hours of motoring up and down before they identified the Hellisøy beacon at the south end of the island of Fedje. Then they entered the Indreled and went north about 20 miles, anchoring at Nåra on the north of the entrance to Sognefjord where there was a telegraph station marked on the chart. Sending the telegram to Elsie was surprisingly difficult because the operator, who did not speak English, insisted on understanding what he was sending. Most words were eventually resolved with the help of a dictionary but "Salford" was a sticking point for a while.

After they had returned to *Perula* the telegraph operator, who was the shopkeeper too, turned up in a grey cloth cap as the Customs Officer. He seems to have been deeply suspicious of this couple who had arrived at this tiny place from the Shetlands and rushed straight away to send a telegram containing the word "Salford". First he spent a long time inspecting the ship's papers without seeming to understand a page of them and then he nearly fainted when he saw the scale of the bonded stores they had. He decided to search the boat and did this until everyone became fed up and they filled out the various forms required, almost at random, until he seemed to lose heart and left. Win was convinced, on reflection, that she had declared a ton of pickles.

He came back the next morning to complete the work on the bonded stores and it was 14:00 before they left for Florø.

They seem to have been welcomed back at Florø, remembered from the previous year. The news of their appearance as smugglers from the Shetlands had gone before them. So there was a warm welcome — but nothing to what they received at Ålesund when they went on there the following day. They arrived on the 26 May and were there until 1 June. Invitations to breakfast were followed by more to lunch and then more again to dinner.

One evening they were entertained at a "Sailing Hut" set on the top of a hill on a small island a few minutes away by ferry. With a backdrop of snow-capped mountains mirrored in silent fjords, the party-goers threw pine logs on an open fire as the sky dimmed around midnight. They seem to have eaten and drunk their fill again.

At the weekend they inducted the harbour master Capt Christiansen and his wife as crew and set off on a trip up the fjords. The fjords were firmly touched by spring, lined with blossom and flowers. Higher up was still white, gripped by the last of winter. They arrived at places that had never seen an English yacht before and were yet again lavished with hospitality and with cream and cheese and home-brewed beer. The villagers came aboard *Perula*, the men in a group and then the women, to stand and look at the English pair while the Captain explained and translated.

> In return we were invited to their homes, spotless little wooden farms and houses. Many had picturesque grass-covered roofs, with buttercups and meadowsweet growing round the chimney stack. Often the bed was in the parlour, with beautifully embroidered quilt and cushions. Old-fashioned lace mats draped the furniture, but the floor was usually bare. The women were served with coffee and home baked biscuits; the men with more home-brewed beer, accompanied by the usual "skåls" and "takks."[6]

When they returned to Ålesund a circus arrived on a schooner, the animals walking off and the tent set up on the quayside. They were taken one night and Win saw an act she had seen in Morecambe.

On the night of 31 May Win wrote her notes for *Duffers* and then they decided to have a fire and had the stove going nicely with some locally-purchased "smokeless" fuel when it started to emit acrid fumes. Moments later the bulkhead burst into flames. Ignoring the fire extinguishers, they put it out with a kettle of water and a soda syphon (the latter a nice touch on a boat). No serious damage was done but Ron had to excise a section of the bulkhead leaving a hole that Win thought she might conceal with an aspidistra, another nice touch.

Early the following morning, after a week in what they reckoned to be the best spot in Norway, they slipped away, seemingly telling no-one.

The next leg took them to Kristiansund through a section that was supposed to be one of the most difficult parts of the Norwegian coast, rock-strewn and open to the North Sea. One of the more disconcerting experiences in sailing is when you expect to find a buoy you have based your navigation on and it is not there. It can put the whole business of where you are and where you are going in question. Only the supremely confident or the foolhardy can shrug this off even these days with satellite navigation. On a rocky, foreign shore it is the stuff of nightmares. This time the dismay did not last long; Ron remembered seeing a notice before they left Ålesund that it had disappeared and, just to confirm, the buoy, called "Kolbeins-flu", put in a surprise appearance shortly afterwards. All they had to endure now was five hours of being thrown around in seas that swept over the deck. After that the wind dropped but soon, at around 20:00, a thick mist descended, making the last hour a nervous affair motoring down a narrow channel with rocks threatening on both sides.

They arrived at Kristiansund after what Win called a "disgusting passage" of 14 hours.

The sail to South Leksen the following day was exciting: a clear and open passage with no worries from rocks and even a race with a Norwegian fishing boat. After a night at anchor they set off for Namsos the following day in a fairly uneventful 100 mile passage. It was not without incident though because, as they passed the island of Valsøy, Win handed over to Ron without giving him a full briefing on where they were. She went below to take a bath and was in the middle of this when Ron cried out that there was a rock that was not on the charts. Win's response was rather casual, telling him to mark it on the chart for future reference. But moments later she saw through the porthole two large rocks pass close by. Wrapping herself in a small hand towel she leapt onto deck to find they were surrounded by rocks. Rushing around with a hand-bearing compass in an attempt to find where she was, she saw a Norwegian fishing boat nearby. "Follow that boat" she cried to Ron in desperation. But the fisherman stopped his engine and called his crew together to watch the near-naked Englishwoman cavorting in the bitter north-easterly Arctic wind.

They arrived at Namsos in the early hours of the following morning and slept for a few hours but it was raining and the town, a timber port, was not too attractive so, in spite of a low barometer promising strong winds, in the afternoon they pressed on north. The wind was not far behind them and soon the sea was churning and they were being swept north at 10 knots. It was a dangerous coast with no place of refuge, everywhere surrounded by rocks. Eventually they did find a small creek, Edshaug, that seemed to offer shelter and they made their way into it and, after several exhausting attempts to anchor and tie up to tree trunks, they came alongside a rough timber jetty and sat for a while eating cakes and drinking hot whisky. It was now 04:30.

After they had had a rest, some Norwegians helped them move *Perula* to a better berth and then they were invited to a fishing picnic. With the aid of a bamboo pole and several worms Win caught seven fish, the largest a two kilogram salmon trout. They ate *eggedosis*, a dish of eggs (using several yolks per egg white) whisked with sugar and rum, round a fire while local girls sang sad folk songs as the sun sank to kiss the horizon.

From here they went uneventfully (except for a near-miss with a seaplane) to Brønnøysund[7] and then to Sorvik, to see a famous group of mountains (the Seven Sisters), where they were nearly

161

crushed by a mail steamer. It was now one month since leaving
Menai and they had covered 1400 miles.

On the following day, 8 June, at 16:46 they crossed the Arctic
Circle in bright sunshine from a clear blue sky. The vast Svartisen
ice field was to starboard and ahead they could see the red rocks of
the island of Rødøy, called the Red Lion because it looks strikingly
like a lion crouching. That night they anchored at the foot of the
Svartisen glacier.

> *Svartisen. Midnight:* We are anchored in the most beautiful
> place I have ever seen, almost at the foot of a gigantic glaci-
> er. *Perula* rides alone in milky blue-green water, and all
> around us tower rugged mountains. The glacier lies just
> ahead; at the top I can see the snow on the ice-fields, pink in
> the setting sun. From it sweeps down the blue ice, like an
> immense river of breaking foam, casting a reflection on the
> water that reaches right up to us. As I write, the sun, instead
> of sinking, changes its mind, to rise again; the glacier is
> turned to gold.
>
> We are both badly in need of sleep, yet we are sitting in
> the wheelhouse, fascinated. It is made all the more beautiful
> by the absence of civilisation; no hotels or shops, hardly a
> cottage. [8]

Later they climbed onto the glacier and took photographs (which
they successfully developed) and then they set off for Bodø.

They spent three days in Bodø where they were entertained by
the harbour master, an old sea captain who grew trees for a hobby
and spoke some Welsh as a result of being shipwrecked on the
north Wales coast. He had the mail for them with no doubt some
version of the instructions sent to most harbour masters by Elsie
telling them to pass on the money and warm clothing enclosed.
They were also taken out by Hr Sannes, a man who knew the legendary ice pilot Captain Schjelderup of Tromsø and gave them a
letter of introduction to him. Schjelderup knew Svalbard well and
could be useful to them.

TROMSØ

They set off north again on the 12 June and arrived at Tromsø on the 14th without too much trouble although the whirlpools in the narrow Rystraum kept sweeping them into the path of a mail-steamer that tried to pass them. Win had not only misjudged the tides but had missed the passage in the Sailing Directions that read "Sailing vessels should always have a boat ready for towing them out of the whirlpools."

Tromsø marked an important psychological milestone for them because it was from here that it was planned to set off for Spitsbergen. Win hoped to talk to Hr Hansen, the meteorologist, and Captain Schjelderup, the ice pilot, before making a final decision about going on. It weighed on her mind:

> As usual, it looks as though I am going to put everybody to a great deal of trouble on my behalf but I feel it is too great a decision to make unaided. I am quite entitled to set off and drown myself if I want to, but I have Adams to think of and am beginning to feel keenly the responsibility of being "Captain" of even a baby ship.
>
> I think this attitude is perhaps typical of a woman. I have found it in aviation as well. Most of us can key ourselves up to do something spectacular, but when it comes to the steady job of piloting an air liner or commanding a ship, day after day, through all kinds of weather with the lives of passengers at stake; then I think very definitely it is a man's job. I know personally I live on nervous energy, going blindly on without stopping to think until I reach the goal I have set myself. By that time I have probably smoked a few thousand cigarettes, drunk a case of rum and need a rest cure. Of course, I am fortunate in having Adams, for while most of the hairbrained schemes are mine, he, poor man, gets dragged along and provides the necessary stable influence; although, as usually happens in life, I get most of the credit.[9]

When they arrived at Tromsø they managed to find Schjelderup who was only too willing to help them. First he went to see the master of a coal steamer, which had recently returned from Spitsbergen, to establish the state of the ice. This was, by his standards, good in that it extended only 25 miles west of the south of the island. His instructions to the couple were to sail to within a few miles of the west of Bear Island and then to head directly north until they saw evidence of ice ahead. This evidence would be "ice blink", a lightening of the clouds that occurs from light reflected up from the ice below. When they saw this they should head west until the blink disappeared and then it would be safe to turn north towards Prince Charles Foreland. This would lead them to the entrance to Isfjord and they should sail up this to Longyearbyen. Of course, ice is not entirely predictable, so it might be necessary to sail more than 25 miles to the west to avoid the ice that sweeps round the bottom of the island but, if they kept going they would find safe passage, the Gulf Stream would see to that. And then there was the possibility that Isfjord would be solid with ice. Not to worry; they should just hang about off the entrance for a few days until it cleared.

This last part of the advice worried Win most. She had come to accept that there would be no stay-over at Bear Island to break the voyage. The deviation to the west to avoid ice would not be too long. But the prospect of several days hanging around waiting for the ice to clear out of Isfjord was unwelcome; the conditions could be very bad and there would be no accessible haven, or even shelter, for hundreds of miles.

Of course there was also the prospect of fog but this Schjelderup explained was nothing to worry about. All you had to do was turn off you engine and listen. Ice can usually be heard.

It had been the plan to see Hansen, the weather expert, but Schjelderup seemed to steer them away from this and relayed the forecasts to them himself. But he approved of *Perula* and his cool and quiet manner (and possibly his "tanned face and blue eyes that twinkled with laughter") led Win to think she would go to the

North Pole if he said it was safe. So they enjoyed Tromsø. Known as the "Paris of the North" for its cosmopolitan quality, it sounds more like a frontier town with the sealers as the wild cowboys. They wandered around marvelling at the constant comings and goings of boats in the perpetual light, patted polar bears in wooden cages lashed to the deck of a ship, saw Lapps in rather ragged costumes and the sealers drinking away their earnings before setting off to club more of the creatures and skin them on the ice for their bloody pelts.

And then on the 16th Schjelderup came and told them that the forecast was good for at least a few days with winds of no more than force 2 or 3. He was rather vague about what would happen after that but said that storms did not happen in summer (and any- way they had a sound boat) and promised them that they would be safely in Spitsbergen in a week's time. So that evening they left.

THE CROSSING

By the early hours of 17 June they were in the open sea and were shortly discovering some navigation problems. First Win found that the tables she needed to correct her compass did not extend this far north. Then the deck watch for timing her sextant readings was not working, then they could not pick up the radio time signals they needed and finally the sextant itself was scratched and cracked. Somehow she overcame these seemingly insurmountable problems and recorded some positions during the passage.

In light winds they made good progress north and by the even- ing of the 18th [10] they were looking anxiously for Bear Island., the log showing that they had run the expected distance of 250 miles. Win decided that it would help navigation to take a sounding (be- cause within about 20 miles of the island the seabed rises so depths are 100 metres or less) and had got Ron to hunt out enough rope to make up the 100 metre line required. While he was trying to sort out the tangle that inevitably resulted, Win saw a streak on the horizon that might be land and they motored towards it and found that it was indeed the island. They considered anchoring but, judging nowhere to be suited to the circumstances, they decided to press on to Spitsbergen. It was now 00:45 on the 19th and Win set a course to take them 30 miles west of the southern tip of the island (Sørkapp), to avoid the ice they had heard about from Schjelderup.

In the evening the wind picked up from the north and they just managed to avoid a large log hidden by the waves, one metre diameter and several metres long. These logs remain today one of the recognised hazards of the passage: colliding with one could do serious damage and even sink a small boat. But the log was soon forgotten as towards midnight the wind reached near-gale force 7 from the north and the sea became rough and confused. All through the following day the wind screamed and the boat lurched along; in fact on the morning of the 20th Win records in her logbook that it reached force 9. They were cheered up a little when a coal steamer passed them going north in the early afternoon but alarmed that seas sweeping onto their deck nearly carried away the meat safe (which contained six lamb chops and some butter) and the dinghy. They were saved only by Ron's frantic efforts wearing his pyjamas, roused from his attempts at rest. Motoring with only a scrap of sail up they covered just nine miles in nine hours that morning.

The wind stayed at force 7 for the rest of the day and did not begin to drop until late on the morning of the 21st; the sea stayed rough and they made slow progress. Then, at 10:00, the sky cleared and they saw Spitsbergen, ethereal white mountain-tops rising out of the haze to starboard. Win changed course towards them but after just a few hours they met drifting ice and had to turn away again, following a coal steamer that had come out of the ice. But at midnight they were back close to the coast.

They thought for a while they were close to Isfjord and headed into the entrance only to find a wall of rocks ahead, they tried again later and found they were trying to sail not into a fjord but between two mountains. At one point they thought they had found Bellsund, the inlet 25 miles south of Isfjord, and headed north up the coast, unable to make out convincing landmarks in the mist and mirages. They saw nothing but endless white mountains stretching away to the north with no sign of a fjord. The 21st changed to the 22nd and the only thing they were certain of was that they were lost. They were dismayed too because the wind picked up again and now they could see the waves crashing against the barren, wild and icy shore with no sign of an end to it all. At 09:00 Win wrote in the log: "Thoroughly lost — can't distinguish any thing." Ron even suggested giving up and going back to Norway.

But then, just before midday, their luck changed. They saw a beacon on the shore and guessed that it was Fuglehuk, there being very few to chose from on that coast. This was both good and bad news. The good was that they knew exactly where they were. The bad was that they had missed the entrance to Isfjord and were now about 50 miles north of it.

Soon after this they met a Norwegian fishing boat and tried to check their position. This Win did in Norwegian, addressing the entire crew of the boat who had assembled to see this woman rolling about on a small and strange boat so far from anywhere. There were 10 minutes of farce as Win shouted, clinging to the rigging, and the men looked dumbstruck and took her photograph. They offered no response until Win cried out in desperation "I want Isfjord". Then the Captain replied, in perfect English, "Isfjord Madam? I will direct you there with pleasure." Win's attempts at Norwegian had been mistaken for Chinese or Russian.

They made their way back south through the Forlandsund, the stretch of water between the island of Prince Charles Foreland and the main island, which was sheltered from the growing wind. It was not completely straightforward because just under halfway down it narrows and becomes very shallow except for one slim channel. They anchored in Adventfjord off Longyearbyen at 06:45 on the 23 June after sailing nearly 2500 miles from Wales and Win wrote in the log "What a hell of a place!" It was to be. In a way she could not possibly have imagined.

WINIFRED BROWN

LONGYEARBYEN

Win put on new trousers, a white cover on her yachting cap and white suede shoes and they rowed ashore. Clambering through the rubbish and slimy mud rather spoiled the new shoes but they headed for the town:

> Going up the hill was easier said than done, and before long we were breathless and filthy. There was coal everywhere, on the ground and in the air, as it swung down from the mines on the overhead cables. In one place the buckets crossed the "road", and a notice of warning requested you to "se op." I dodged beneath, feeling sure a load of coal would descend on my head. The "town" in view, I nearly had a fit. It was situated on a slope, and lining the two "streets" were rows of wooden buildings, mostly painted with oil and resembling old army huts. Outside them hung dead birds, odd blankets, clothing and muddy boots. One hut I noticed bore a painted cross, and was apparently the hospital. Near it were two or three glass frames in which a few lettuces, etc., were carefully tended, reserved, I suppose, for the sick. A building rather resembling a bicycle shed proved to be the fire station and, on the right, in the shadow of a mountain, was a small wooden church, painted white. The mountain was a reddish colour and along its side was a mine structure and the usual steel pylons. We found later that this mine, closed down after a disaster some years previously, was still on fire—hence, I suppose, the reddish colour.[11]

They trudged through the muddy town and found an immense heap of empty tin cans and more buckets of coal swinging across a valley from a distant coal mine. The dismal scene was minimally relieved by reindeer grazing far-off on patches of moss but they found that the post office and shop were both closed. The wireless station was open though and they sent Elsie a telegram saying they had arrived safely. Then they went back to *Perula* where Win expressed the view that Longyearbyen was "awful, awful beyond description" and no reward for a long and exhausting voyage. But everything changed the following day.

For a start there was hot sun so they could cast off their overcoats and walk around the town and then they met a man who described himself as the "Sysselmann" and said that he would like to visit the boat. Win, recognising a man of distinction, rather impulsively invited him not just to visit but to stay to supper. She later discovered that she had invited the Governor of Svalbard to share their limited supply of canned bully beef.

As they returned to the boat they were approached by a man wearing an old jacket and trousers with knee-high muddy boots and several days of stubble on his chin looking as if he had just come up from the coal mine. He asked them, in a tone of some authority, if they had all they needed and if he could be of assistance. They said they had and the man left them and they rowed back to *Perula*. A brief and rather awkward encounter — but Win noticed that he had nice blue eyes.

The meal with the Sysselmann, Wolmer Marlow, seemed to go well. He spoke excellent English and they discussed boats (he was having one built for his official duties), the history of Svalbard, the animals (many already protected by hunting restrictions) and life generally on Spitsbergen. He explained that most of the 600 men living in Longyearbyen worked for the Store Norske Spitsbergen Kulcompani (SNSK), the company which owned the coal mine. Longyearbyen, he might have said, was a company town. He did say that food, which he must have gathered they needed, was all supplied and rationed by SNSK but that he would take them to see the Food Controller the following day. He seems to have enjoyed himself and wrote on the last page of the log a comment in Norwegian which translates as:

> I have been aboard *Perula*, where I had a splendid supper. I
> have the greatest admiration for what *Perula* has achieved,

navigating from England over to Norway and on to Spitsbergen. 24/6-38.[12]

He might have seen the "What a hell of a place!" note on the facing
page but said nothing. His comment rounded off the logbook
rather well because it was now full so the following day they took it
to the post office and had it stamped. The neat circular stamp says
"Longyearbyen Svalbard 15°35'00"E 78°13'04"N."

The following morning they visited the Sysselmann at Government House, a small wooden bungalow overlooking the town
where they had cakes and tea served with fresh milk by a maid. His
wife, who was English, was holidaying in London after a long, bleak
and isolated winter on the island. Win felt "very proud that one of
my countrywomen has the courage to live away out here." They
were taken to the SNSK food offices and promised a parcel and
then to the company bakery where they were given large bags of
cakes and bread.

Then in the afternoon they started the engine and motored
across Isfjord, dodging the small icebergs and admiring the pristine
snow-topped Borebukta glaciers of the north shore. Ron got out
the dinghy and took some photographs. When they got back Win
wrote below the Sysselmann's note and the stamp "Cruising in
Spitsbergen To Borebukta Glaciers 40 miles(return) 25th June Total
Mileage 2502". They now definitely needed a new logbook.

The next day, a Sunday, finding there was no detailed weather
forecast available on the island, Win sent a telegram to Schjelderup
asking him to reply when the weather was suitable for the crossing
back. She delayed sending it until late in the day so that there would
be no reply to disturb their evening; they had been invited to dinner
with the Sysselmann.

There were two other guests, Hr Ross (an engineer) and the
Managing Director of the mine, Einar Sverdrup. Win had heard of
Sverdrup in Tromsø and was looking forward to meeting him.
When he arrived she did not recognise him until she saw those blue
eyes again. He was the scruffy man they had met on the quayside,

now clean-shaven, smart in a lounge suit and good-looking. They spent an evening eating, drinking whisky, talking and playing bridge. It was all so civilised; Einar and Ron even argued about the Irish question. It was in some way, in the little England created by the Sysselmann's wife, a bit like home. She fell asleep over bridge and at 11:00 the following morning found herself fully-clothed in one of the bungalow's bedrooms being brought tea by the maid.

They met Ross later in the day and learnt more about living on the island and the problems that arose. Some of Sverdrup's reputation was explained by the way he had handled a food strike.

> We did have food strikes. [Ross told them] The food is always good, but it is not easy to give great variety. As the men sat eating a few would start to stamp on the floor, in their heavy mine boots, until all joined in and the noise was terrible. The strike generally lasted for twenty-four hours; one shift off for every man, but Hr. Sverdrup, he is wonderful, he issued rubber boots, so now they cannot make the noise and all is well.
>
> Later I asked Sverdrup about it. "Yes," he said, "we did have food-strikes, but now all of us have more sense. You know, Win, and please understand it and do not blame the workers, for it is always easy to blame other people, but it is not always just; it was not in reality food-strikes. Of course, the food here can, as in other places, be more or less good; as a rule, everyone is satisfied. When we had these strikes it was other things at the bottom. In most cases the nerves were too hard pressed and something had to happen, that the whole bunch might get some fresh air, literally, or what you call it. Excuse me if I have expressed myself poorly—it is your impossible language and my impossible way of handling it."
>
> "But Einar," I said, "did you really stop the strikes by giving the men rubber boots?"

He smiled. "Well, have you seen a cat fail a mouse?" he said. "So it was." [13]

SVERDRUP

As Win may have learnt in these few days, Einar Sverdrup was rather well connected. His grandfather Harald Ulrik had been a Norwegian MP and Harald's brother had been Prime Minister of Norway for a time. His father Johan was a professor of theology and his uncle was an MP and Minister. Johan married Maria Vollan, daughter of Ole Vollan, a leading figure in the Moderate Liberal Party, in 1886 and then, two years after her death in 1891, he married her sister Agnes. Another Vollan sister married into the Grieg family and her son, Nordahl, was a celebrated and controversial playwright and poet who was a strong supporter of Stalinist communism and, during the war, a voice of the Norwegian resistance in exile in the UK.

Einar's siblings were not without distinction. His half-brother Harald Ulrik (1888–1957), born from the first marriage, was the head of scientific work for Roald Amundsen's *Maud* expedition between 1918 and 1925 and went on to a distinguished career as an oceanographer. From 1936 to 1948 he was Director of the prestigious Scripps Institute of Oceanography in California. He even has a unit used in oceanography named after him: the Sverdrup (Sv) is 1 million cubic metres of water flow per second. His sister Maria, as Mimi Sverdrup Lundun, became a well-known peace activist and campaigner for women's rights.

Finally his brother Leif Johan "Jack" (1898–1976) emigrated to the USA in 1914 and formed a civil engineering partnership that designed bridges. At the time of Win's visit the bridge designed by the partnership to cross the Mississippi at Atchison, Kansas, the birthplace of Amelia Earhart, was nearing completion. During the war he constructed airstrips in the Pacific and afterwards commanded an infantry division.

Einar had trained as a mining engineer in Norway and the USA. Win describes him as the mine manager but he was in fact a Director of SNSK, the company that owned and ran the mine and indeed Longyearbyen. As such he was the senior representative of the company on the island. This, combined with his impressive pedigree and solid political connections, must have made him a quite formidable and uniquely influential presence on the island.

Win chose a photograph of herself with Einar as the frontispiece for *Duffers on the Deep*. She is looking as girlish as she could in wellies, a firmly-placed yachting cap and bundled into a heavy overcoat. He commands the photograph, standing in its centre with a relaxed stance but a firm and even arrogant gaze into the lens, exuding breeding and self-assurance. So powerful a presence is he that it takes a while to realise that he seems to be wearing a cardigan that is a few sizes too small.

Ron is in the photograph too. To be precise, part of Ron is in it. His face makes it but nearly half his body has slipped out of frame — or been pushed out by Sverdrup's charisma.

FAREWELL SPITSBERGEN

On the 28th of June Sverdrup took them on a tour of the workers' quarters and showed them a road he was having built — the first on the island. When, afterwards they were sitting in the comfortable staff club, the telegram came from Schjelderup. It said that for the next five days there would be favourable weather.

Sverdrup insisted that they had lunch before they left and then took them for goodbyes to the Sysselmann who asked that they send a telegram when they arrived safely on the mainland. Sverdrup walked with them to their dinghy. He declined an invitation to a last drink on *Perula* and, after reminding her about the telegram, said a brief good-bye and left. These were sad moments. In the five days they had been on the island (it seemed much longer) they had made good friends and were unlikely to see any of them again. She would, in fact, see some of them but even she would not have known it or even hoped for it as, at 16:45, they upped anchor and set off for the south. Win made her first entry for the new logbook. She could not actually enter it *in* the logbook because they had yet to buy one. For the passage back to Norway she wrote notes on scraps of paper and cigarette packets.

By 22:00 they were at the mouth of Isfjord and could turn southwards on a course that she thought would clear the ice they expected off the west coast of the island. Within an hour or so they found themselves surrounded by it but by heading off to the south-west for an hour they found it thinned and they could make good progress. In the early hours of the 29th the wind started to freshen from the east and to make matters worse the ice returned in the afternoon and they had to slow down and pick their way through it in the now rough seas. In the evening the wind swung round to the north-east and increased further. Ron exhausted himself and scared Win taking down the mainsail.

It was now very rough with the wind building to a full gale. Waves sweeping towards their stern crashed on board and smashed against the wheelhouse. They were both frightened as they contemplated the possibility that a large wave would carry it away. If one did, they would sink quickly; both of them would certainly drown or die of exposure if that happened. They both sat and miserably contemplated death for a while as they lurched around. It was not helped when the engine faltered for a moment; losing it would mean that control was gone and they would swing round to take the waves sideways on, the most perilous situation of all in rough seas.

Then, at sometime around 05:00 on the morning of the 30th, they remembered the sea anchor. A sea anchor is something like an underwater parachute. Deployed, it fills with water the way a parachute does with air. If a boat is tied where the man normally hangs on the airborne version, the sea anchor slows its progress through the water and, if it is tied onto the bow, it brings the boat head-on into the wind and waves. It is a much safer situation than just drifting helplessly; the best way to take large waves is bow-first.

Having said it is like a parachute, it is made from thick canvas rather than featherweight material and attached not with fine lines but with heavy chain and thick ropes. Ron struggled to deploy it from the bitterly cold and swaying deck. But when he did, it transformed the situation and *Perula* rode the seas much more easily. So they turned off the engine and, exhausted, both fell asleep.. But not before Ron imparted some potentially very bad news. While on deck he had found part of the mainsheet — the rope controlling the boom — was missing and the chewed end of what was left sugges-ted it might be wrapped around the propeller. With breaks to check on things they slept until midday and then again that night, waking up for breakfast at 10:00 on 1 July. From time to time Win checked the barometer and the world outside but neither were encouraging; she drew the curtains and turned on the radio, filling the boat with hymns. The conditions had improved by now but, after breakfast, they found that the propeller was fouled with six metres of rope wrapped round it. In the afternoon they discovered that the sea an-chor had come adrift sometime during the gale and they had been floating free.

It was time to get under way again but it would not be wise to use the engine; it or the propeller or the shaft and seals might be damaged. So about 16:00 they hauled up the mainsail in the now light wind and turned towards Norway while Ron hung over the side and struggled to cut away the tangled rope with a knife tied to the boathook.

Win had been concerned about how much the gale had forced them off their course — particularly as the sea anchor had been lost at some unknown time. So she was pleased to get a sight of the sun just before 19:00. It suggested that they had been blown about 50 miles to the west-south-west

For the next ten hours Ron bent over the boat's side and fought to clear the propeller, breaking several knives in the process. The results were dishearteningly small fragments of rope but by 10:30 on the 2 July they decided that there was only about a metre still round the propeller and they would give the engine a try; Ron was too bruised and exhausted to carry on anyway. Their main concern was that the rope would somehow pull the propeller shaft out of the back of the boat (it happens) leaving a large hole for water to pour in. But, when they pressed the button and slowly edged the engine into gear, the propeller seemed to spin freely. So they motored off at half-speed heading for Bear Island about 80 miles away.

They were expecting to see Bear Island mid-morning the following day but when the time came there was no land in sight, just a few birds and fog patches, so they turned south and aimed for the Norwegian coast near Hammerfest, abandoning Bear Island. The night brought another gale, not quite as bad as the last one, and the day a vicious swell, squalls and poor visibility. Then, at just before midnight, Win saw a large mountain dead ahead. It was obviously the north coast of Norway but exactly where was a mystery.

A check against a coloured postcard they had brought along convinced Win that it was North Cape. This conviction did not last long; poring over charts she worried that they were too far east and had actually hit Russia rather than Norway. More study persuaded her that she was far west of North Cape at Nord Kvaløy and this, when they asked a fishing boat in the early hours of 5 July, turned out to be right.

They motored down the west of the island of Vannøy, and then probably turned south into Ullsfjord and then to Grøtsund and on to Tromsø where they tied up alongside a boat called *Zoe* at 12:40. They had travelled 600 miles by the log from Spitsbergen in a week. After a short walk ashore to send telegrams to Elsie and the friends on Spitsbergen, she bought some cream cakes. Then, so tired she was swaying as she walked, she made her way back to *Perula*, ate the cakes and fell asleep for 17 hours.

BACK IN NORWAY

They did not see Schjelderup, who had recently sailed for Spitsbergen, which was a disappointment. Win might have discussed with him his idea of reasonable weather for the passage.

Perula was in need of some care so they spent some time rubbing down and varnishing. The most urgent concern though was the propeller and its fittings still wrapped in rope. After debate it was decided to get a diver who turned up in a wretched affair of an old hull with a crude hut perched on the top. He sat in the hut while the dilapidated boat was towed by a rowing boat to lie alongside *Perula* and a heavy wooden ladder was then put down between the two boats.

The diver sat inside the hut in his diving suit looking quite dejec-ted as he was kitted out in his heavy boots, knife and gloves. Someone must have been turning the wheel of his air machine in the hut as his helmet with its tiny window was put on and he clumped towards the waiting ladder. The moment is caught in a photograph in Duffers. It is impossible to confirm the state of mind of the diver but everyone else seems to be enjoying themselves, smiling and laughing as he lumbers towards the ladder, climbs down it and flings himself into the cold water.

A long five minutes later he emerged and made the slow climb up the ladder. When his helmet was removed he was smiling: there was no problem. There had been only two turns of rope left after Ron's efforts and he had cut them off with his knife. There was no damage at all.

On 12 July they set off again but not to the south. A letter from Elsie had expressed some disappointment that they had missed Bear Island and the North Cape. Quite why she thought this is not clear. Maybe Bear Island sounded nice; Win had made something of her plan for a stop-over there. But whatever Elsie's reason, Win decided on a trip to the northern tip of mainland Norway.

Over the next few days they visited a Lapp settlement near Lyngseidet, Hammerfest ("dismal looking buildings formed the town") and reached the North Cape at midnight on the 15th, the sun shining low through thin cloud. They spent a few minutes looking at the desolate scene and then turned *Perula* to head back south, this time for home. After an overnight in Hammerfest they went on to Altafjord (or Altenfjord as it is usually known in Britain) and here they met a little bit of Britain earlier than they could ever have ex-pected. They tied up to a buoy off Alta close to an anchored long black ship with cream funnels flying the White Ensign. Ron thought she looked like a destroyer and they decided to salute her by dipping their own ensign[14]. The vessel responded likewise. A nice moment so far from home.

Later, while they were ashore, an Englishman came and introduced himself to them as "Westminster" and offered them any help he could give and invited them to visit him aboard. After he had gone Ron explained: it was the Duke of Westminster and the boat they had saluted was his luxury steam yacht the *Cutty Sark*.

The Captain of the *Cutty Sark*, Commander Mack, visited them later and offered them a bath. They accepted and stayed to supper. The next morning the *Cutty Sark*'s launch was again at *Perula* with an invitation to high tea with the Duke. After the meal they were taken by Mack to watch the Duke's party salmon fishing (it was presumably the reason *Cutty Sark* was there) and later the Duke sent them three fresh salmon and a parcel of provisions.

Over the next two days they made their way to Tromsø, troubled much of the time by fog. There they stocked up on supplies and, at last bought a new log book. The "Dagbook" was completely in Norwegian and they had some trouble figuring out exactly what all the column headings meant. Stopping no longer than they needed, they pushed on to Bodø reaching there on the 25th and staying for three days.

One day they visited the Saltstraum. This is where, a few miles to the south east of Bodø, a large fjord, Saltfjord, has just two narrow channels linking it to the sea. As the tide rises and falls the tidal rates can reach 16 knots (some think more) in one of these, the Saltstraum. The channel then turns into a turmoil of rough water and large whirlpools, swept along in the stream slurping in air and hoping for a boat or two. The noise it all made reminded Win of Niagara Falls; the spray generated a mist that hung over the scene. They watched the small fishing boats — the fishing was and is particularly good — dodging around but even they avoided the turmoil at its worst. Afterwards Win, showing her usual careless affection for animals, was nearly gored by a calf when it ran round and round her wrapping its tether round her ankles before setting about her with its non-existent horns. It was, she admitted, no bigger than a large dog.

On the 28th they set out again and decided to have a look at the Torghatten, the mountain with the hole they had not seen on the way down. After a long row and a stiff uphill walk (an injury from the calf encounter was turning septic and Ron had hurt his knee) they found themselves in this natural wonder, a 160 metre long tunnel narrowing to 35 metres wide and 20 metres high, piercing the heart of an isolated loaf-shaped mountain.

Over the next few days they worked their way down to Trondheim, hardly yet used to darkness after their time in the midnight sun, and impressed by the number of lighthouses that guided them down the Indreled. The weather was windy and progress was slow but on 3 August they reached Trondheim. Here they went to the railway station and bought a return ticket to Hell. Hell being a small village a few kilometres from the city.

They visited Trondheim Cathedral, the market and took a bus to see Lerfossen waterfall. They were taken out for a sail by the sailing club too.

On the 6th they left for Ålesund and arrived there on the 8th. They stayed for two weeks. The rigging was checked, the compass adjusted, a new sea anchor and lifebelt were made. They met Capt Christiansen once more and contacted Hr Pettersen for weather information. He agreed to send them a telegram the moment there was a good period of weather coming up.

The good weather was a while coming with fog and gales sweeping across the North Sea but they enjoyed themselves visiting the sights. On the 19th it was Ron's birthday and they celebrated with champagne, a dinner with the locals and a large cake, followed by dancing and drinking. They went to a film and, when they ran out of cash, they were lent some. Win visited an old sailors' home and enjoyed talking to the inmates.

On the morning of 22 August Ron looked unwell and Win suspected he was having a bout of malaria, something he picked up either on their trip to Australia or in the Amazon jungles in 1933. It was just then that the telegram arrived with its promise of a few days of good weather coming up. It was difficult to believe this as they prepared to leave, hauling the dinghy on board in driving rain. With Ron struggling physically and looking very poorly, they cast off at 15:30, hoping that the conditions would improve, as promised. The next stop should be the British Isles. They were going home.

THE VOYAGE HOME

They took the Indreled as far south as the Stadlandet peninsula and then set a course towards the Shetlands in a strong swell from the north and a moderate wind from the south-west. They motored through the night with just the mizzen sail but as the day progressed and the wind came round to the south they put up the jib and then the mainsail. Waves crashed onto *Perula* and the wheelhouse became wet — Win thought the deck planking had opened up a little as they moved south — but Ron seemed to be getting better; certainly the worst of the fever had gone. At one point he staggered below determined to check the engine but fell and sliced open one of his fingers on the spinning flywheel.

On the morning of the 24th the wind increased to a "litten kuling", a force 6, and, Ron being out of action for a while, Win motored slowly forward with just the mizzen and foresail. In the afternoon she hove to[15] with a little engine to prevent *Perula* turning broadside to the waves and stayed that way for the next 16 hours, drifting slowly to the west.

When the wind eased on the morning of the 25th they got under way again and, in spite of the fog patches that appeared about midday, they sighted the Shetlands soon after. They were slightly south of where they expected to be but it was a good result considering they had been hove to for so long. So they motored north up Bressay Sound and by 16:00 were anchored at Lerwick, 268 miles from Ålesund by the log.

They left Lerwick the following afternoon with a plan to pass north of the Orkneys but it was interrupted when they nearly hit

Fair Isle in the middle of the night. Win decided it was a slight mis-calculation of the tides and that now — it was raining and misty and the tide had turned — it would be better to retrace their steps on the outward journey and pass through Holm Sound and into Scapa Flow. Here they found that more block-ships were due to be sunk and that anti-submarine nets were being laid; the European situation had become more serious since they left.

They spent the night in Stromness and left early the next morning, rounded Cape Wrath about midday and by 19:20 they were anchored in Loch Laxford at Fanagmore Bay where they had stopped on the way out. An early start the following morning had them in Kyle Akin on the Isle of Skye for the next night and the next day they returned to Tobermory arriving in the dark.

There was no lingering now and they left Tobermory at 06:35, were abeam the Mull of Kintyre by 23:00 that night and by midday on the 2nd they were approaching the southern tip of the Isle of Man. Win decided to go through Calf Sound the narrow channel separating the Calf of Man, a small island, from the main island. The tide rushes through this narrow channel and Win wrote later that she had never been so scared; they seemed about to hit the rocks many time in the short passage. When she filled in the log-book she described it as "a foul place!" so they must have been pleased to reach Douglas at 15:40. It was not to be an extended rest.

Within a few hours they picked up a weather forecast suggesting that the weather would deteriorate with strong winds coming from the south. So, unrested but cheered to meet some of her fans on the quayside, they set off again at 20:45. By 07:45 the following morning, the 3 September, they were back at Glyn Garth. In total they had travelled 5192 miles since leaving 16 ½ weeks earlier.

The welcome home was quiet. A man appeared on a neighbouring boat, *Himeros*, and called out sleepily before disappearing again and there was a lonely figure pacing the jetty. This was a press cameraman who had been turned out of his bed in Manchester at 04:00 to drive down and record the reception for the lunchtime edition. He had taken some photographs of fishing boats as they arrived —

he had no idea what *Perula* looked like — and he now faced the need to create a Reception. This he did by stirring the Gazelle into life, the staff and owners making a show of being pleased to see them at this early hour. At last the photographer was grudgingly satisfied and he left for Manchester and his newspaper. A short report appeared in that day's *Manchester Evening Chronicle* but there was no account of the joyous homecoming and, sadly, no photograph.

Win and Ron rowed across to Dickies to see Bill Campbell in his office that smelled of oil stoves and drawing boards and later they saw Peter Dickie, to thank him. Win heard from a friend that the newspapers were prepared for the possibility that they would not return and he had seen an obituary, ready for the presses, for when the bad news came. Win thought it had been recycled rather neatly into the *Chronicle*'s "Britain's Adventure Girl, No. 1"[16] two days after their return.

They pottered around for a couple of weeks, living on the mooring but going nowhere, and then on 24 September, *Perula* was slid out of the water at Dickies and laid up for the winter.

SNOWDROP IN WINTER

Win returned to Lodore for the winter. She was offered a series of five articles in the weekly yachting publication *The Yachting World a*nd they appeared starting on 14 October. She had written about the voyage for the *Manchester Evening Chronicle* but these were much more for a yachting audience. Then something much more ambitious came along: a commission from Peter Davies Ltd to write a book about her voyages. She met Davies at the offices in Henrietta Street in London where, when she expressed doubts that her writing skills were up to it, he advised her to write the book as if she were writing a letter to a friend. She accepted the job (and the advice) and agreed to do it in just two months.

Peter Davies was one of the Llewellyn Davies children who inspired J M Barrie to write *Peter Pan*. His two elder brothers were befriended by Barrie during outings in Kensington Gardens when he conjured up the stories for them. Peter's name was taken for the title and he was known forever as the boy who was Peter Pan. The boys, there were five of them by then, were orphaned in 1910 after the deaths from cancer of their mother and father and Barrie took them under his wing. Peter went to Eton, was commissioned as a signals officer in World War One and won the Military Cross. In 1926 he founded Peter Davies Ltd and published Daphne du Maurier and many other authors, including the sailor Uffa Fox.

When Win got back to Manchester her first concern was to find a typist. She acquired Nellie, one of Sawley's regular customers at Cateaton Street, and then locked herself away in Lodore, venturing out only to deliver manuscripts to be typed.

She had written a thank-you letter to Sverdrup soon after getting back and mentioned the book. His reply was from Norway where he was spending the winter, presumably near Oslo with his wife and children. He offered to help with the book and Win took it up, asking all those questions about Spitsbergen, Norwegian names and the mines that had not been asked while she was there. She seemed to ask more personal ones too: of "your feelings, your hopes and disappointments." He replied answering her questions of fact. Her other questions, the more personal ones, drew from him over time, trapped as he was in some kind of Norwegian suburbia, his longing for the lonely and bleak island far to the north, the workers there and even the mines themselves. They were the letters of a homesick man — living with his family.

Win sent him chapters (presumably just the ones about Norway) as Nellie typed them for his correction and approval. Then, quite suddenly the days of frenzied writing, often all day in pyjamas, were over. The two-month confinement came to an end. No more Nellie and even no more Sverdrup: the excuse to write to him had vanished.

But the letters continued. Over the winter Win wrote long letters by the light of her bedroom lamp into the early hours, her face covered sometimes in face-cream, pouring her heart out to her Beloved, as he had become. The flirtation developed into discussions about commitment so it was a shock when the letters from Norway stopped. Win wrote three desperate letters, the third one blunt and maybe rude, before a reply came: Sverdrup had been very ill, close to death even. "As I lay there waiting for them to carry me off, I had to smile as I thought of their faces when they found your dear letters, for I have kept every one." Who "they" were is not explained; maybe they were his family.

Win sat and wrote back. The response stunned her: a telegram arrived saying that he was sailing for England and would meet her in Newcastle.

NEWCASTLE

Of course, she later wrote, she had no intention of going to Newcastle. It was never any more than a silly paper romance anyway; little more than a warm pen friendship. So she wrote several chilly, discouraging letters and telegrams for him to all the addresses she could think of, including the hotel where they were to meet. There could be no meeting.

It seemed to be settled when a letter from her lecture agent, Mr Tillimont Thompson, dropped through the door.

> Mr Tillimont Thompson had, in his youth, played Hamlet. A fine figure of a man although now slightly bent with years, he had a clear-cut profile, hooked nose and a high forehead from which swept a flowing mane of snow-white hair. When Tilly had had a few he would confide that the blood of seven nations ran in his veins and that every drop of blood was the bluest of blue. He certainly looked distinguished in his flowing cape (lined with silk), and he carried a long ebony walking-stick capped with silver. Tilly was my lecture agent; he was more, for it was he who had taught me elocution and first set my feet on the steps to the platform. The lessons had taken place in his parlour at Seaforth, aided by an ancient piano, a dusty poem that commenced "Hark to the Trump!" and a bottle of Green Goddess.
>
> Tilly's letter started as follows:
>
> 'Goddess! Nymph! Perfect! Divine,
>
> To what my love shall I compare thine eyne —
> sorry dear child — my Shakespeare you know! To
> be or not to be, that is the question———' [1]

He wanted to know if she could bring forward a talk she was giving in Aberdeen by a month and she agreed. Only later did she realise that the new date was the one on which Sverdrup's boat would be docking.

So now she had an excuse to meet Sverdrup. She could go to Newcastle on the way to Aberdeen . Her plans were to spend the night before the talk away anyway. She had Carlisle in mind but Newcastle would do nearly as well. Elsie would suspect nothing. The temptation tore at her until it dawned on her that Ron would be with her; he always drove her to lectures and looked after her slides. We will investigate the relationship between Win and Ron shortly but, whatever, Win thought it out of the question to involve him in this adventure. So, once more, Newcastle was out — even if she wanted to go.

This new equilibrium did not last long because Ron somehow managed to get a piece of coal (of all the possible minerals the most ironic in the circumstances) in his eye while poking the fire and announced he was unfit to travel. Win would have to go on her own. As she set off on the road to Preston and then Carlisle, on that clear March Sunday morning, somewhere not far north of Manchester, a firm invisible hand took the wheel and wrenched it round. She found that she was heading not north but east to Yorkshire and the road to Newcastle. Leeds came and went, Wetherby sailed past; then she was at Scotch Corner and then outside the appointed hotel. On each of the 200 or so kilometres she asked herself whether she was doing the right thing. She had constructed this man over the winter from pen and paper. Would the reality be unshaven and wearing an awful cap — a savage from the North Pole? Might he have fifty children? Would he, on a more practical level, know about contraception?[2]

In the hotel she booked a room and telegraphed, rather forlornly, Sverdrup on the ferry *Black Prince:* "Am at hotel alone. Any hope seeing you. Brown." She waited hours for a reply, reading distractedly in the ladies' writing room, until, as she gathered her books up to leave for bed, a small envelope was carried in on a silver tray. She opened it and on the slip of paper that fell out was the one word "Yes".

She met him on the *Black Prince* early the following morning. He walked past her at first. She thought he looked pale and rather ill but tall, distinguished and agreeably well-turned-out (no hat, shaven), a "highly polished specimen of manhood". The blue eyes were still there. Win's outfit had confused him for a moment. A squirrel coat, mauve dress and big black hat was very different from what she had worn on Spitsbergen.

In her account of what followed Win says she tried to escape — running to the car and trying to drive off without him. Somehow he was in the car beside her. At the hotel she bounded up to her room and slammed the door but the slick, highly-polished man had his foot in the way. They confronted each other, hunter and hunted, for a while and then he slid across the room, took her in his arms, tilted her head back and gave her a cigarette. Or rather a "cigarette", the code they had developed over the winter correspondence for a kiss.

There seems to have been time for little more than agreement that they would go to Aberdeen together and, skipping breakfast, they set off north. They stopped in Edinburgh for lunch at the "North British Hotel", the comfortable hotel built for the railway traveller beside Waverley Station in the city centre. They sat in the grill-room, drinking Gin and French cocktails and eating, whiling away the afternoon until Win suddenly realised that there was hardly enough time to get to Aberdeen, something over 300 kilometres away.

She drove manically, touching 110 km/h on occasions, taking one corner on two wheels but Sverdrup was calm throughout, even encouraging her to go faster. When they arrived in Aberdeen they checked into separate rooms but he sat with her as she changed into her evening dress, even zipping her in. They walked the short distance to the lecture hall arm-in-arm. After the talk, to the Young Men's Christian Association, they spent the night together.

SNOWDROP VISITS

The next morning they drove back to Edinburgh, had lunch at the railway hotel again, and then Sverdrup took the train to London. Win drove back to Manchester, depressed but confident in the knowledge that they would meet again soon, they had a plan for that. They had agreed that he would write to her rather formally saying that he was in England on business and wondered if they might meet. When he rang her later at home, he had already written and posted the letter.

When it arrived Win showed it to Elsie and explained that Sverdrup was the man who had helped them in Spitsbergen. Elsie immediately insisted that she wrote back to Mr Snowdrop, as she christened him, inviting the kindly man to stay. And not long after, that is just what he did.

In the entrance hall of Lodore Win shook his hand as if they had not met since Spitsbergen and Elsie asked her to take him to his room. Sverdrup was to have Win's room which for some reason had a second un-made bed in it. After an embrace or two she explained that it was her room and he asked which was her bed. Then he pulled back its green silk cover and kissed her pillow before they hurried back downstairs.

That night Win slept in the drawing room. At 8 o'clock the next morning Elsie took Mr Snowdrop his morning tea; a silver tray arranged with the best Crown Derby. Downstairs Win heard a loud scream and a crash of expensive crockery and rushed upstairs to find Elsie staring at Snowdrop, who was crouching on the bed that had not been made up, blue with cold. He had spent the night with just a silk spread over him. When Elsie demanded to know why he had not used the other bed, his reply was at least open to misinterpretation: he said he thought it was Win's. Elsie, who must have recognised the scent of sexual adventure after all those years with Sawley, thought that meant he had expected that Win would be sleeping in it. She nearly fainted. Win helped her down the stairs.

After this, Snowdrop's stay might have been difficult but he seems to have hit it off with Elsie with a combination of charm and forthrightness. When the question of Win visiting him in Spitsbergen was raised, she offered no objection especially since Win was expected to travel from Norway to the island by coal steamer rather than on *Perula*. So Mr Snowdrop left as a friend of the family (although there is no record of Sawley's views) for a night in Birmingham and then on to Newcastle and the ferry home the following day.

DUFFERS

Duffers on the Deep appeared in May and early reviews were good. It remains an entertaining read but one which captures much of the excitement of yacht cruising. Some of the experiences are horrifying given the level of experience they had, particularly since they were out of communication much of the time and far from rescue. You never quite forget that they were "duffers" because of the honest and direct writing (she followed Davies' advice and wrote as if to a friend) about their problems. But equally reminders of the remoteness of their adventure are always there. Even when she is reliving the warm and good times they had in distant and isolated communities, these are just episodes punctuating a long and quite dangerous journey. As an advert for the book in the *Observer* newspaper put it:

> The famous airwoman's first sailing adventures make absorbing and at times hilarious reading
>
> "An even stiffer test of endurance and nerve than winning the King's Cup Race. Extremely readable." *Sunday Times*[3]

Quite how much time and inclination Win had to enjoy her new fame as an author (perhaps still impending at this point) we cannot know. Sailing matters were once more afoot. They were going to Norway again.

NORWAY AGAIN

They left Menai on 16 June 1939 and made their way north via Douglas (where they stayed for three nights) and were in Loch Ewe by the 21st, anchored between the Isle of Ewe and the mainland, sheltered from the strong northerly winds They stayed here while the winds blew around the high pressure systems established over Greenland and Iceland, northerly moderate to strong. Then, on the 26th they weighed anchor and left for Lerwick, passing north of the Orkneys. They arrived at Lerwick on the following evening after logging around 600 miles from Menai.[4]

It was the herring season and Lerwick was full of fishing boats belching black smoke. There were also warships (or "battle-waggons" as Win called them) in large numbers.

WINIFRED BROWN

INTERNATIONAL SITUATION

They had set out on the voyage at a time of extraordinary international tension. After the Munich Agreement that allowed Germany
to occupy the Sudetenland of Czechoslovakia without conflict in
September 1938, there seemed to some the prospect of a Germany
satisfied with this and its earlier recovery of the Rhineland. Others
saw the avoidance of conflict in 1938 as an opportunity to prepare
for an inevitable future war while to some appeasement was a
shameful moral and political failure that made war, if anything,
more likely. Notably the crisis exposed the lack of readiness for war,
particularly war from the air, and Sir John Anderson was put in
charge of Air Raid Precautions because it was thought that any declaration of war would be followed promptly by intensive and prolonged bombing from the air. A significant step diplomatically was
the statement on 6 February 1939 by Neville Chamberlain, the British Prime Minister, that Britain would respond to any attack by Germany on France. The French offered a reciprocal guarantee.

In March Germany took control of the remainder of
Czechoslovakia and began to make threats against Poland and
Lithuania. At the end of the month Britain and France guaranteed
Polish independence.

The Navy was already more than a match, it was thought, for the
German fleet and aircraft production had tripled since the Munich
Agreement was made, mainly as a result of earlier plans. In February
a commitment was made for a large increase in the Army. On 27
April 1939 the Military Training Act was passed requiring men of
20–21 years of age to do six months military training. Just after that
Hitler renounced the Anglo-German Naval Agreement that limited
warship construction (he had disregarded it for some time) and the
German-Polish Non-aggression Pact.

The atmosphere was reflected in the newspapers of the week before they left Menai.

Air raid precautions were prominent with news of how "glow-
worm" road signs would be used in the blackout to be imposed on
the outbreak of war. Some were concerned about the costs of air

raid shelters for flat dwellers. Business leaders visited the Chancellor of the Exchequer to express their concerns about war risks to property; the Association of Health and Pleasure Resorts were worried that the evacuation camps that the Government proposed to set up might be used as holiday centres and steal some of their business. 650,000 steel air raid shelters had been distributed (with another two million to come) and 350 million sandbags were on order, half of them from India. Arrangements for evacuation of hospitals were discussed as was the creation of a national blood transfusion service for air raid casualties. There were calls for the building of deep air raid shelters in London — calls resisted by the Government because they would foster the wrong attitudes to defence. The first 20,000 of 90,000 Territorials were about to be trained in the use of anti-aircraft guns and searchlights on an air defence system that was reckoned to be about complete. The Civil Defence Bill passed through Parliament.

There were reports of the Tientsin incident when, on 14 June, Japan had blockaded the port of Tientsin in northern China.[5] The affront to Britain's imperial power caused outrage in Britain and contributed to the notion that the empire was threatened by foreigners. There was a significant impact on the financial markets (although oddly interest rates for war-risks for shipping were reduced).

Finally there were reports of the talks between Britain, France and Russia about a possible three-power defence pact that were, supposedly going smoothly and entering their concluding phase.

So, as they set off, Britain and much of the world were preoccupied with a coming war which many, by June, thought inevitable. There were still hopes. Thomas Cook was still advertising holidays abroad to Le Touquet in France, Ostende in Belgium ("The Queen of Seaside Resorts"), the Nordic countries and Switzerland. But to many it would not seem to be the moment to set out on a lonely adventure in a small boat across a sea around which great powers were arranging themselves for battle.

WINIFRED BROWN

NOTORIETY

The weather kept them in Lerwick until 11 July. Ron potted seagulls with a catapult — they were usually just stunned — but it attracted the attention of the Royal Navy warship nearby. They were for the time being engaged in similar pastimes and extended an invitation to their Wardroom. Catapults and gin kept them more or less amused until at just after 14:00 on the 11th *Perula* motored out of the north entrance of the harbour and set a course for Ålesund. They sighted the Norwegian coast just 24 hours later and after another 24 they were tied up in Ålesund to their "usual buoy". It had been remarkably uneventful. The next day or two were not.

They were welcomed once more as friends but there was something different about the atmosphere, crystallised perhaps by a man she had just been introduced to asking if she would care to sleep with him that night. At the sailing club, on the small island where it still is, there were giggles and she realised she was causing them. She caught someone disparaging Sverdrup and sharply corrected them. Everyone nearby laughed. "So it's true!" howled someone.

The following morning someone showed her a Norwegian newspaper. On its front page was a photograph of Win and Sverdrup with a caption that read, in translation, something like "She had come to Norway to find love." The article that went with the photograph explained that the famous English aviatrix and yachtswoman was returning to Spitsbergen to visit Sverdrup for romantic reasons. He was sending a special coal steamer to collect her; he found her too entertaining to allow her to risk her life in her little boat. Win was not worried for herself (she says) but for Sverdrup ("Think of his position!" she wrote) and for the wife she knew he had. At least, she may have reflected, they don't know about Aberdeen. And then she may have wondered if, in Ålesund, she was thought of as a loose woman, encouraging men to invite her into their beds. It would explain the earlier invitation and indeed what happened next.

That evening she had a party thrown in her honour by a man she had never met before. When she did meet him he turned out to be a

German, Karl, who fairly quickly suggested she abandon her plan to go to Spitsbergen and go to Finland with him; he was very wealthy he said. Win declined rather politely but accepted another drink. And then another.

She woke up with him in a small bedroom in the morning. She had earlier confided to the readers of *No Distress Signals* that she could count comfortably on the fingers of one hand her lapses from the straight and narrow. Now she said she needed both hands. She had also said that her code of honour meant she was permitted only one love at a time; she was wretchedly in breach of that. She blamed it on the drink — it wasn't genuine Scotch but some adulterated local hooch. After all Ron had drunk the same stuff and was unconscious in another room. He would never have been felled by real Scotch; he had been born in Inverness.[6]

She left Ron insensate surrounded by the debris of the party and was taken to catch the coastal ferry by the German. She gave him a necklace strung with monkeys' teeth, a good luck charm from the Amazon. He may have reflected that he had already got lucky once in the last twenty-four hours without its help; Win later rather regretted giving it to him. The ferry carried her to wherever she picked up the coal steamer and this took her on to Longyearbyen and Sverdrup.

SNOWDROP AT HOME

She first saw Sverdrup through binoculars. He was walking down the hill towards the ferry berth. He took her to his house and she straight away realised that things would not be as they were in Scotland and England. She would stay in the house; he was booked into the Club. For decorum's sake it seemed. "There has been talk enough," he said.

They quarrelled continuously after that. It started when he refused to entertain the coal steamer captain and his wife to dinner, something Win had arranged and had to cancel. He could not socialise with his inferiors. Not here in Norway.

They visited the mine and were enveloped in swirling black dust from a roof fall in a disused working. When she called out for him there was no answer and she stood there crying for a while until he returned. He had been checking on what had happened and simply left her. He seemed to care more for the mines than her.

So when the Sysselmann invited her to visit another part of the island with him, she accepted.

NY ALESUND

The Sysselmann, Mr Marlow, took her north on the *Maiblomsten*, a whaler he had chartered for the summer, to Kongfjorden at the northern tip of King Charles Foreland.[7] The journey of close to 100 miles and two days took her over some of the sea they had struggled through when they missed Isfjord the previous year. This time they turned into the Kongfjorden and made for a place called London on the north shore about 10 miles up the fjord, the site of a deserted and long-disused marble quarry. Here they searched among the abandoned houses looking for one that could house the Sysselmann's chickens; scavenging like this was not uncommon because of the shortage of wood on Spitsbergen. Having found something that would do, they packed it up and motored south across the fjord to Ny Alesund and civilisation.

Civilisation was the "Nordpol hotellet", the most northerly hotel in the world, which had opened in 1936. Its cocktail bar offered a Polar Bear Special or an Eskimo Lady and Win chose the Polar Bear Special. Outside there was not much: disused coal mine workings littered with rusting junk, an old railway engine and some wooden huts set on the path to dereliction. There were too the remains of an airship hangar and a mooring mast that told of a past and why a harbour nearby is to this day called Zeppelinhamna and a mountain is named Zeppelinfjellet.

She had her photograph taken beside the Amundsen memorial, a vertical slab of brick and concrete embedded in a crumbling concrete base. It commemorated his attempt in 1925 to get to the North Pole in two Dornier flying boats with five companions. The expedition was unsuccessful. The flying boats took off on 21 May but were forced to land some 250 kilometres short of the pole. The party then spent 30 days on the ice and cleared a runway for one of the planes (the other had been damaged). On 15 June they all climbed aboard and just managed to take off and return to safety.

The skeleton of the airship hangar can be seen in the background of the photograph. This had been built to accommodate the *Norge* the 100 metre-long airship that Amundsen set off in on 21 May 1926 (exactly one year after the flying boat attempt) to reach the North Pole. Accompanied by several of the people who had been with him on the previous attempt, including the American Lincoln Ellsworth, this time he was successful and the team landed in Alaska two days later. They are usually credited with being the first at the pole, where they dropped flags. The Italian flag dropped by the airship's designer Umberto Nobile, who led a small group of Italians, proved to be larger than those of Norway and the USA, to Amundsen's evident annoyance. The airship hangar was constructed of canvas and wood and disappeared in the course of the Second World War, possibly scavenged for the wood. The base remains as does the 35 metre-high pylon built to tether the airship to.

As they savoured their cocktails they were joined by a French lady in a negligee, a Pole in purple pyjamas, a fat Swede and (somewhat surprisingly) Karl, the German who had invited her to Finland. Win and Karl took a walk on which he quizzed her about what she was doing and why she had come to Spitsbergen twice. He seemed to think that she might be some kind of spy (she always seemed to be writing, sketching or taking photographs after all) or at least know something about the mines. If only he knew, she thought.

ADIEU NORWAY

The next day they went back to Longyearbyen and Win reports that they "again captured the bliss of Aberdeen." It was a quickly-curtailed bliss: after breakfast the next day Sverdrup told her to go. He had entertained her for two weeks he said. In a fury she said she

195

would take the next ship south and he said (probably already having checked the steamer schedule you feel) there would be one the day after next. There was a farewell party but it was a chilly, inexplicable departure. They shook hands. She says in *No Distress Signals* that she saw hopeless misery in his eyes as she left.

Exactly when she arrived back in Ålesund and to Ron is not clear but they moved the boat back from Bjørnøya to Ålesund on 18 August. In Ålesund she met Karl, the German, once more and with friends they went on "a drunken orgy of the fjords" that lasted from 22 August to the 24th. They did not go far. On the first night they anchored at Sykklven and were surprised when a seaplane made a forced landing and tied up to them for the night. They invited the pilot and his passenger aboard for the night and they all drank into the early hours and at about 3 am put on a firework display for the locals with all the emergency flares. When they got back to Ålesund, war suddenly seemed much closer, imminent even.

WAR PREPARATIONS

The situation had dramatically worsened while they were away. The negotiations that had been going on between Britain, France and Russia to secure a three-power defence pact came to an abrupt end when it was announced (a "bombshell" said Chamberlain) that Russia had signed a non-aggression pact with Germany on 23 August. It was deduced in London and Paris that this meant that Russia would not intercede if Germany invaded Poland and indeed that Poland might be divided between the two countries if they did. Hitler had already been demanding the return to Germany of the free port of Danzig and the corridor of Polish territory that gave the Poles access to it (and separated East Prussia from the rest of Germany). Now these demands were becoming reality: there was German agitation in Danzig and German troops were massing at the Polish borders. German planes flew over Polish territory and were shot at; German troops sporadically attacked Polish border installations. The Poles called up reservists. British people were advised by the

Foreign Office to leave Germany and France and on the 25 August Britain signed a mutual assistance treaty with Poland.

In Brussels the neutrals, including Norway, met to discuss their options and concluded they should stay neutral — this was a matter for the Great Powers. The Pope appealed for calm. A planned strike in Britain was cancelled. Some ten million men were under arms, gazing across borders and grey seas.

BACK TO WALES

Their friends begged them to stay, at least to leave *Perula* and find a safer mode of transport home. The North Sea was already closed; there would be U-boats and mines. But Win was determined and on the evening of the 26th they said goodbye to Norway, the only concession a Norwegian flag over the stern instead of the British Blue Ensign they had proudly flown so far. However, they soon took that down and put up the Blue Ensign again and celebrated with a couple of double gins. Then, a little British ship once more, they set a south-westerly course and motored towards Lerwick.

The 27th passed without incident except the odd groan from Ron who was listening to the radio, absorbing the latest war news. At 08:15 on the 28th they ran into thick fog and had to slow down. At 10:05 they passed a small unidentifiable island close to starboard. At 11:00 a dark shape on the port bow resolved itself into a trawler and Win hailed a man on deck to ask if they were on the right course for Lerwick. The reply was not encouraging: the man said he had been looking for the place for two days himself. Soon after that they identified Green Holm and found themselves motoring down Bressay Sound. By 12:30 they were anchored in Lerwick, which was deserted.

All the warships were elsewhere. Patrolling, hiding in Scapa Flow or even milling about in the thick fog shouting occasionally at a desperately lost trawler (after the encounter he had set off in a direction that would have taken him away from land) for guidance. Wherever they were, it was a sign that things had changed. As was the harbourmaster's instruction that they must wait for a convoy.

They obeyed the instruction for the rest of that day and the whole of the following one. Then, on the 30th, they crept off at 04:50 in the morning fog. Nothing much happened until just after midnight when they were west of the Orkneys, about level with Scapa Flow. Then a pipe burst on the engine cooling system sending water spraying round the engine room. They stopped the engine and drifted around hopelessly under sail for a while. They briefly contemplated sending up distress signals expecting that the Navy would come to their rescue (*Perula* would probably be interned for the duration) but quickly realised that they had blown all their pyrotechnics at the seaplane party a few days before.

Fortunately Ron managed a temporary repair and they headed at half speed to round Cape Wrath. This they did at 10:30 but the leak became worse and they decided to put into Loch Inchard which, the sailing directions told them had three villages, three post offices and an prominent hotel and surely therefore enough resources to mend a broken engine cooling pipe. They anchored at the top of the loch at Rhiconich off the prominent hotel — which had been converted into a police station.

This proved to be a stroke of luck. They found the policeman in his garden and after careful inspection of the broken pipe he suggested that his friend Jamie, a blacksmith, might be able to help. The only problem was that he lived in Durness, nearly thirty kilometres away. So the policeman flagged down the post bus and they set off with the mail, newspaper, milk, chickens, a few ducks and a goat, and Ron clutching the pipe. The bus delivered and picked up at farms on the way, off-loaded the goat with some relief (it had chewed Win's clothes). They had a drink or two at a pub and the bus finally dropped them in Durness where they found Jamie who repaired the pipe. Somehow they returned to *Perula* in the early hours and the following morning Ron replaced the pipe and they set off again. But not before they heard on the radio that Germany had invaded Poland early that morning (Win recorded it in the logbook at 10:30).

They motored 54 miles that day and anchored to the north of Longa island in Gairloch where they spent several hours trying to cover the portholes and skylights with cardboard. The following day they covered a determined 82 miles to anchor off Tobermory at 23:00 that night. As were passing Eigg the water pipe had started to leak again so that they had to slow down. The next morning, the 3rd, they set off early.

As they motored, a lone boat, through the calm sea just off the two whale-backs of Dubh Sgein in the Sound of Jura at 11:15 on a most beautiful morning, they listened to Neville Chamberlain on the radio announcing that Britain was at war with Germany. The Prime Minister's sad voice strengthened as he moved from explanation to conviction. The statement ended with the words:

> Now may God bless you all. May He defend the right. It is the evil things that we shall be fighting against — brute force, bad faith, injustice, oppression and persecution — and against them I am certain that the right will prevail.

It was followed immediately by Government announcements and instructions that Chamberlain had said they should give their closest attention. They did and found they covered almost all situations that people might find themselves in. Except there was nothing for two people on a small boat, its dicky engine chugging and carrying them, not in a convoy, down an empty sound off the west coast of Scotland. They must have been discussing what to do when Nature made their minds up for them.

A violent storm swept in about 16:00 with lightning flashing across a black sky until it was all blotted out by torrential hissing rain that made it almost impossible to see. So, proper navigation out of the question, they felt their way into West Loch Tarbert and anchored for the night.

To the west, the U-boat U-30 was stalking what he thought was a warship but was actually the *SS Athenia*, a 13,000 ton Donaldson liner out of Liverpool heading for Montreal with 1400 people on board, many of them Americans escaping the imminent war (they had left Liverpool on 2 September, before war was declared). As she zigzagged without lights, the U-boat fired its torpedoes at 19:40 and one struck a fatal blow. The *Athenia* began to sink by the stern. Mercifully she stayed afloat until the following morning and all but 112 people were rescued. But she had the tragic distinction of being the first vessel sunk in the conflict.[8]

At 10:00, just as the *Athenia* was sliding below the waves, Win and Ron heard the news of the torpedoing on the radio. They were already three hours into their passage to Menai and approaching the Mull of Kintyre; Win decided to pass to the east of the Isle of Man rather than the west. It was a jittery passage. At 18:11 they passed floating wreckage. After that they pasted newspaper on the navigation lights to dim them for the night. When the night came so did ships. They seemed to be dashing everywhere, looming up in the dark, with or without lights, some close by, many signalling. One monster, speeding through the dark with no lights, swept towards them veering off only at the last moment to pass astern. Small wonder Win reported a flaming wreck that turned out to be the moon rising.

They arrived back at Menai at 14:10 that afternoon, Tuesday 5 September 1939 and tied up alongside another boat temporarily. So the last entry in the log for the voyage was "15:30 Changed moorings." In fact it remained the last entry in the logbook for almost twelve years. Win must have glanced at the book from time to time over the following decade and when she looked at those two words she may well have thought "How true, how true." Everything was to change for her too.

WAR WORK

Ron and Win lived aboard *Perula* after they arrived back, through the period of rather forced gaiety as people faced the prospect of war while nothing at all actually happened. There were no bombs and no planes, not just in North Wales but anywhere. In the nervous atmosphere people crowded the pubs and clubs and drank. Between bouts of this the two looked for something useful to do beyond just filling in all the forms that were required to live on the boat. Nobody seemed to have any idea how to use them: they had a boat but neither had any qualifications and, worse, Win was a woman.

FISHING

It was Win who came up with the idea of fishing: it was useful, they had a boat and they had enough experience to actually do it. There were a few hurdles. First *Perula* had to be registered as a fishing boat with the Fishery Board again and became FD61. Then a Permit to Fish had to be obtained from the Port Fishery Captain and then a Permit to Trawl with an Engine had to come from the Lancashire and Western Sea Fisheries Committee. (Later she found she was registered as a wet and dry fishmonger and was provided with a form to record births and deaths on the boat.) Second she needed a proper crew and not just Ron. Quite how she looked for one we do not know but she seems to have had a flood of applicants. From it she choose Will (a fish and chip shop owner who was formerly a seafarer), Dunny Walker (a dapper and well-heeled retired cotton broker) and a young man (un-named) who wanted to get into the Navy and was able put some money into the enterprise.

Dunny, Dunstan Massey Joseph Walker, was not your average crew of a fishing boat. Born in 1885 in Birkenhead, the fifth son of a family of eight, he was educated at Ampleforth College in North

Yorkshire, the leading Benedictine Roman Catholic school. He joined the 1st Volunteer Battalion of the Cheshire regiment in 1907 and was appointed to the 4th Battalion proper in April 1908 as a Second Lieutenant, where his brother Victor Joseph was a Captain. For some reason he resigned his commission in July 1910. Perhaps it was linked somehow to his marriage to Marguerite. When war was declared in August 1914 he was quick to enlist and joined the Liverpool Regiment and then the Royal Engineers. At that point he listed his occupation as Salesman but, at the end of the war, he and two of his brothers set themselves up as cotton merchants in Liverpool. He was successful and soon led the partnership "Dunstan Walker & Co". He and Marguerite lived first at Heswall on the Wirral and then in Cefn Mawr Hall near Mold in Wales. By the early thirties he seems to have made enough money to retire and moved to the bungalow he had built overlooking the Menai Straits and the small island he owned — Ynys-y-Big.

Win's fishing plans were held up for a while by the lack of a net, because the one that had been ordered was sent in error to the Bangor in Ireland not the one in Wales, but, on 6 December 1939, they had a net and set off to trawl. It was a relaxed experiment with little real hope of catching any fish but they went through the whole business under the guidance of Will, while consuming chocolate cake, a few doughnuts and a couple of drinks. It started to go wrong as they hauled in the nets with sunset imminent: they were much heavier than they expected and it was a struggle to get them up. The problem was that they had caught some fish. There were starfish, jellyfish, crabs and plenty of seaweed but mixed in were some skate and flat fish. With dusk falling and a bank of fog creeping towards them Win took to the wheelhouse and left the men to sort out the catch.

Much of it was returned directly to the sea but the actual fish were kept. The really unpleasant task was cutting the wings from the still-living skate and dumping what remained of them over the side. This was done by Dunny and it required alcohol in some quantity and a hammer. The alcohol was used as a mild anaesthetic for

Dunny and the hammer served a similar purpose, although stronger and more permanent, for the skate.

Win took the catch to Bangor where she received £6; £2 for *Per-ula* and £1 each for the crew. Encouraging though this might seem from a first and rather relaxed effort, two of the crew defected almost immediately. Will went back to his core business of fish frying while the young man with no name lost his enthusiasm and was seen only very sporadically after this.

Will was replaced by Dan and they carried on fishing. Prices were so low that professionals were throwing their catches away — but what else was there to do?

SAWLEY

It was during the early days of fishing that she heard that Sawley was ill. The news was in a letter from Sweetie Pie, his girl-friend. Not only was he seriously ill but he was not being properly looked after. The letter ended with the words "Please come at once or it may be too late." So she rang Elsie who told her, as she raged about Sweetie Pie, that Sawley was to be taken to the Castle[1] at Ruthin, North Wales the next day. Then she slammed down the phone.

Win went to visit her father at the Castle which is about 80 kilo-metres from Bangor. It had opened in 1923 as "a private hospital for the investigation and treatment of obscure diseases" and treated patients for conditions some, one might have thought, not so obscure: diabetes, obesity, gastric and duodenal ulcers and gallstones.

Sawley's illness was obscure though. When she saw him he seemed not much more than slightly depressed and rather listless with no appetite; afterwards the doctor was rather vague, suggesting that they might "tap his liver". The condition was more mental than physical, he said , and she should come as often as she could. So she visited him, taking fresh fish to tempt his appetite, and they talked of the sea and boats in his small white room looking out over the gardens. He seemed better when she was there but the depression returned when she left.

One day a doctor took her aside and gave her Sawley's cheque book to look after. He had been tormenting himself scribbling on cheques and then tearing them out. It is here that Win excels herself in obliqueness because she tells us that she could read a half-obliterated name on some of the cheques — but she does not tell us what it was. We can guess it was Sweetie Pie's but we cannot be sure.

He improved over the days that followed and on one visit asked Win to find him a seaside cottage to end his days in looking over the water and being close to her and *Perula*. The following day he had a relapse; he had been found after he wandered into another patient's room. When she saw him later that day he was sitting up in bed but everything else had changed. He swore at her, said he did not know her and talked of death and funerals. She was firmly led out of the room by the doctor who suggested that she go and see her mother, to comfort her. There was not much comfort to be given or had. Indeed she was deeply shocked when Elsie told her that Sawley had tried to gas himself before he was sent off to Wales.

The following morning, 24 January 1940, she had a phone call telling her that Sawley had died peacefully in the early hours.

When his will was read a few days later at Lodore it was discovered that he had left everything (£16042 3s 1d) to Winifred. But that was much less than they had expected. Elsie was furious because she had been left nothing and threatened to tell Win what had happened to the baby at St Anne's — and to herself. To tell her exactly what Sawley had done. Win said she already knew.

Horrified, presumably that Win had remained close to Sawley even though she knew what an evil man he was, Elsie threw her out. The passage in *Under Six Planets* is dramatically written but does not tell us what we want to know: what actually happened in St Anne's. Whatever it was though, it had clearly been traumatic enough to bring up all these years later at another moment of family crisis.

The family and some friends gathered in the snow for Sawley's funeral on 26 January at the Manchester Crematorium without Elsie — who had stayed behind to play dance music on the radio. There was relief that Sweetie Pie did not show up as had been feared and Kendals, the funeral directors, had weeded out her wreath, if one had been sent. The only hitch was caused by Sawley who turned up late, the hearse delayed by the snow on the trip from North Wales. Afterwards, Winifred and friends went to the "Manchester Limited", the venerable and smart business restaurant under the Royal Exchange as she had often done with Sawley and they drank him a silent toast in champagne. He would have liked it, in his better days.

BEAUMARIS

Sometime in the next few weeks Lodore was sold and Winifred took 5 Green Edge, a three-storey terraced cottage overlooking the Green and the Menai Straits in Beaumaris but, for some reason, she and Ron continued to live on *Perula*. Elsie came and lived nearby.

As Win says in NDS: "If war hit Beaumaris, it was a glancing blow." But the next few months were not without incident.

First Win describes the Home Guard invasion exercise that could have formed a whole episode of the television series *Dad's Army*. The tragic star is the Councillor "a nice little man, small with ruddy complexion" charged with blowing the whistle, warning of an impending air raid.

> In a small place like Beaumaris, untouched by real war, the mock invasion was an event of tremendous importance. There had been weeks of preparation and on the great day the 'corpses and injured' were carefully labelled and laid out in the car-park behind the White Lion, ready for the ladies of the Red Cross to deal with. The ladies of the Red Cross, led by a local doctor's wife, were a highly efficient body of women. Every Monday and Thursday they made bandages, and as they trooped in, they donned white gowns and white tennis shoes. Even Miss Editha, who was deaf, had to have a special white cover for her ear-trumpet. Cigarettes were, of course, taboo, so several of the ladies abandoned the Sewing

Bee to serve in the Red Cross White Elephant Shop, where the smell of smoke was more apt to disinfect the atmosphere than pollute it.

So, on the night of the Invasion, two ladies of the Red Cross, one a smoker and the other a non-smoker, arrived at the car-park behind the White Lion to deal with the injured.

"Send for the Ambulance!" said Mrs Non-Smoker to Mrs Smoker, with authority.

"Ridiculous!" snorted Mrs S., consulting the label on the body.

"This man is as good as dead — we will pass on to the next."

"Oh, no we won't" all-but spat Mrs N.S. "While there is life there is hope — send for the Ambulance."

"I will do no such thing!" shrieked Mrs S. "This man is dead — our duty is to the living."

After a painful ten minutes it was decided to consult the doctor for a ruling on the matter. It was while the ladies had gone to the doctor's house that the Councillor came out of the White Lion. It had been cosy in "the snug", and he was beautifully warm, both inside and out. Being a compassionate man, his heart bled for the bodies lying on the cold ground of the car park.

"Wot ye lying there for, ye daft so-and-so's! Get up and b —off home!"

The bodies needed no further encouragement, and when the ladies of the Red Cross arrived with their Medical Officer —·the cupboard was bare!

Fired by the success of his humanitarian action, the Councillor then arrested the Umpire [presumably appointed to oversee the Exercise], locked him up in the gaol and lost the key. So until this day nobody knows who won the Battle of Beaumaris. In the commotion that followed, the Councillor was relieved of his duties, and took the matter so much to heart that he took to his bed and died. [2]

The second event, in March, was a Spitfire crashing onto Mrs Parry's house. No-one was seriously hurt even though Mrs P was hanging her bedroom curtains at the time. The plane's pilot dangled in a nearby tree, snagged by his parachute and un-noticed while a comic search took place for the town's ambulance driver so that Mrs Parry could be taken to hospital. Improvised use of a car was considered but dismissed; the town had an ambulance so it was proper that it should be used. The driver was eventually spotted gazing at the fire that had developed at the crash site and, once Mrs Parry was on her way to hospital, the pilot was cut down by some children.

The third event of note was that, in the summer, Win and Ron were married, a surprise for their friends and a shock for Elsie. Win was pregnant.

About this time, she had a letter from Sverdrup. It offered an explanation for his cold even cruel behaviour that ended her visit to Spitsbergen the previous summer. It seems he had known war was imminent and wanted her to escape before it came. If he had told her, she would have wanted to stay. The only way to make her leave quickly, he thought, was to drive her away. It explained his apparent cruelty and also his dejection as they parted.

THE CABIN BOY

They carried on living on *Perula* and trawling for as long as they could but in November 1940 they gave up as birth became imminent and moved into Green Edge. On 11 December she went to a cocktail party then went home and ate two helpings of steak and chips. The indigestion that followed quickly turned to labour and this quickly produced the "Cabin Boy" as the bump had been called. He was named Anthony Sawley Adams. Later in life he was usually called Tony (and that is what has been done here) but Win always called him Anthony.

She stayed in bed until Christmas under doctor's instructions; this "lying-in" was normal practice at the time. On Christmas morning the doctor found her in bed right enough but sharing the room with about thirty others, drinking champagne. When everyone had gone she topped up her glass and raised it to her absent lover. "Skål!" she whispered.

A PROPER JOB

Nineteen forty one started badly. Win was told that *Perula* was to be requisitioned by the Admiralty and she was inconsolable (although thoughts of Sverdrup might have had something to do with that). She was saved by an unexpected meeting with Harry Broadsmith whom she had last seen in Australia on the hockey tour: he had lent her an aircraft. Harry, having been thwarted in trying to create an Australian aircraft industry, had returned to England in 1938 and was a director of Saunders-Roe. He was in North Wales because part of the company was being moved to Anglesey from Cowes on the Isle of Wight, where it was subject to continuous bombing. Soon enough "Broadie" moved there with his deputy Les Ash, the Chief Test Pilot.

They had bought the Burton estate at Fryar's Bay a mile or so north of Beaumaris and were building a factory there to fit radar and other equipment to the Catalina flying boats being brought from the USA. Win, Broadie decided, was just the sort of person he was looking for; she knew about flying, the sea and the local waters. He decided that he needed *Perula* too. So it was settled. When the Admiralty turned up with their requisition order, Win could point out that *Perula* had been chartered the previous day by the Ministry of Aircraft Production.

At first Win had no specific role but soon enough she had her first command; a small launch in which she ferried workmen to the Catalinas. When a bigger launch came she found that command of that went to Dunny and she became Chief Engineer of the vessel. Dan, the fishing companion, joined the crew too. Together they ferried Catalina crews backwards and forwards from the planes' moorings and towed the planes to the slipway. Ron was appointed Marine Superintendent and was therefore (technically she would have said) Win's boss.

Beaumaris seems a quiet place these days, looking out across the Green and the Menai Straits to Great Orme Head and the mountains of Snowdonia. A moated castle, a pleasant seaside promenade and an elegant terrace or two suggest a dignified past but it soon strikes you that there are quite a few pubs and hotels and the Royal Anglesey Yacht Club nestles beside the green. They hint at a livelier past. And, during the war, a livelier past there was.

The arrival of Saunders-Roe transformed the place. Workers and managers flooded in to service the Catalinas and all manner of people serviced them. There was more money around and more people spending it. The town had always been a favourite of yachts-men — especially at regatta time — but now there were people working hard and playing hard year-round. The pubs were usually full and the cocktail crowd thrived, centred on the Royal Anglesey with that careless wartime freedom and rather desperate gaiety.

And then there were the Americans who flew the Catalinas in, exotic and heroic creatures, bringing chocolate and nylons to win over the locals. All together, it made it boom-time in Beaumaris.

In September, *Perula* was brought in to inspect the many buoys that had been laid (at times tethered Catalinas stretched all the way from the Gazelle to Fryars Bay) but this was hardly started before news came that might involve Sverdrup.

SVALBARD & GAUNTLET

Germany invaded Norway in April 1940 and on 10 June the Norwegian forces laid down their arms. After this the Norwegian and Soviet mines on Spitsbergen continued to supply coal to northern Norway with the consent of the Norwegian government-in-exile and the British (mainly through concern for the northern Norwegian population). In April 1941 the Germans were reported to have taken control of the Norwegian-owned mines but the island and its resources were not considered major strategic issues. After Operation Barbarossa, the German invasion of Russia, started on 22 June 1941 Allied policy changed and it was decided to progressively evacuate the Norwegian and Russian populations of Spitsbergen.

All the national newspapers on 9 September 1941 reported on the Gauntlet expedition to Spitsbergen. In this Canadian, Norwegian and British troops had landed at Longyearbyen on the 25 August to prevent the Germans taking full control of the coal mines. The landing was unopposed and the mineworkers and their families danced in the street (such as it was) and showered the troops with gifts. Everyone on the island was evacuated by ship and the troops then set fire to the coal dumps and buildings, made the mines unusable and blew up radio masts. The columns of smoke could be seen from 25 miles away. The evacuees, about 1000 people, were landed at an unnamed British port; many of the men were expected to join the free Norwegian forces.

It was Dunny who showed Win a newspaper report of the events and her first thought was to find out what had happened to Sverdrup. She approached a newspaper editor who had printed some of her work and he quickly found out that Sverdrup was in Brixton Prison. So she wrote to him and "offered him my money, my home, everything I possessed."

He eventually replied explaining that there was nothing she could do; his own Government was trying to have him released and he would then join the free Norwegian forces.

CATALINAS

The Catalina was a remarkable aircraft. Designed in the mid-1930s as a patrol bomber with the range to seek out and destroy enemy shipping in the Pacific, it found a variety of uses when war actually came. With its cruising speed of 200 km/h it could carry a payload of some two tons over a distance of 4000 kilometres. In its maritime patrol role its most celebrated achievement in the Atlantic was perhaps finding the battleship *Bismarck* after she had eluded the forces hunting her in May 1941. A painting of this event hung in the canteen of the Beaumaris works. The plane's function as the Navy's eyes was also vital at the crucial Battle of Midway in the Pacific.

It was very suited for search and rescue and the hopes of many distressed sailors and ditched airmen were raised by the sight of a

Catalina overhead. Some later models even had a rescue dinghy that could be dropped.

For its anti-submarine role it was equipped with Air Surface Vessel radar (ASV) allowing it to find and bomb U-boats travelling on the surface. Since the submarines had to spend several hours on the surface running their diesel engines to charge the batteries that powered them under water, the possible presence of aircraft could be a serious operational restriction. In the initial years of the war the submarine was relatively safe on the surface at night or in bad visibility but developments in centimetric radar made this even more hazardous than being there during the day. A radar-equipped aircraft could find the submarine and approach it undetected until, at the last moment, an extremely bright searchlight, a Leigh Light, in a nacelle under one of the wings was turned on to illuminate the target. This blinding light was the last thing that many German deck crew saw.

From this point on no U-boat crew could feel safe on the surface at night or in bad weather whether to charge the boat's batteries or in preparation for an attack on a convoy. The Catalina (and other planes like it) thus played a part in turning the tide of the Battle of the Atlantic: by mid-1943 the Allies were building ships faster than U-boats could sink them and U-boats were being lost at an unsustainable rate.[3] And most of the U-boats were being sunk by aircraft.

In all, 4000 Catalinas and variants were made during the war and almost 400 of them passed through Beaumaris where they were fitted with armament, radar, and, as required, the Leigh Light.

The majority of the aircraft were supplied under the Lend-Lease Agreement between the USA and Britain signed in December 1940 and started to arrive in Britain in the early months of 1941.

From November 1941 the Catalinas started to come into Menai directly after a 30 hour non-stop flight across the Atlantic and they were brought by a crew of seven or eight, generally American civilians but with a sprinkling of airmen from Canadian, Australian and British air forces. The weather could be appalling and they had no defence if attacked so the crews were often a rather wild and hard-drinking bunch.

NEWS OF SNOWDROP

About now Win was receiving letters from Sverdrup. He had been released from Brixton Prison and was living in a flat in London. In one letter he wrote desperately that he had to see her so a date was fixed, food was bought and the house was cleaned. Sadly he failed to arrive. The explanation came a few days later: he had been sent to Scotland. He had been to Edinburgh and sat at the table they had sat at in the North British Hotel. He had been to Aberdeen and planned to stay in the room where they had their night of passion but, alas, the hotel had gone. His memories had been taken, he said.

Then, probably in April or early May 1942 , she had a phone call from him insisting that she came to London. She said she could not; he should come to Beaumaris because her job was more important than his. He pleaded, saying he could not talk about it on the phone but that he needed to see her. When she refused to go again, he swore and slammed the phone down with the words "I didn't start this bloody war."

By chance at this time there were a few Norwegian crews around trying out a new version of the Catalina (the PBY-5A) which had retractable landing gear so could operate from land as well as water. One of the pilots, "Yogie" a Lt Commander in the Norwegian Navy, even remembered seeing *Perula* in Norway when he flew for the postal service. Win, it turned out had a photograph of his plane landing. They became friends and one night she told him about Sverdrup. That night she had a dream that Sverdrup was with her, in her room.

It was a surprise when Yogie turned up a few weeks later for no apparent reason. She met him at the railway station and he explained first that he had come on holiday and then later, as they drove, he told her that Sverdrup was dead. He had been shot in Spitsbergen. Or maybe his ship had been blown up in Scotland. He seemed unsure.

She remembered Sverdrup's imploring phone call; how he had wanted to see her so much, so unreasonably. He must have known he was about to do something dangerous and desperately wanted to see her for, perhaps, a last time. But surely she would, have known if he was dead. She remembered his presence in the vivid dream of a few weeks before and decided not to lose hope.

BROADCAST

Sometime shortly after this she appeared on radio. The BBC was running a series called *My Working Day* about the war work that women were doing. This particular episode was about the launch *Saro I*. Dunny was the skipper, Win the Chief Engineer and Dan the crew. Dan refused to take part because of his distaste for publicity, Dunny's trousers were ruined in the process of making one of the sound effects (they had to splash heavy ropes around in the sea to simulate the sound of casting off a tow rope) and he could be clearly heard moaning about the BBC. When it came to the actual recording in Manchester, only Win was involved; the other parts were played by the BBC Repertory Company.

The broadcast (there does not seem to be any record of it) did have one surprising result. It was heard by "Mr H", an old friend of Sawley's, who was in the rubber business. He was Managing Director of the Balloon Division of a famous (but un-named) rubber company and wanted to try our a new design of rubber dinghy that could be sailed.

Bombers often carried rubber dinghies as compact survival craft but the only motive power they had were paddles. If a plane ditched a long way from land these were of little use and all the survivors could do was drift around waiting for rescue. How much better, it was thought, if they could put up a sail and head for land. At least, the theory was, it would keep their spirits up. The two trial dinghies Mr H sent to Menai in November 1942 were yellow and about 3 metres long with side tubes inflated by a carbon dioxide canister. The mast was telescopic, expanding from half a metre to four metres, and it slotted into a fin beneath the hull that served as a centre-board, essential for controlled sailing since otherwise the dinghy would usually simply be blown sideways. The boom (and this was a key innovation no doubt) was inflatable using a bicycle pump. With the addition of a rudder (which folded for storage) it made a compact and navigable little vessel. It did though need to be tested.

Two dinghies, the Oxford man from the Royal Aircraft Establishment who had invented them and a small, pale man who was Mr H's human guinea pig came on Win's birthday. The understood arrangement with Mr H had been that Win and her team (Dunny and Dan) would take one of the dinghies with the two men out to sea and set them adrift. This proved to be slightly wrong. Paleface did take to the dinghy but it was Win and Dan who climbed in with him.

They managed to un-telescope the mast (which showed a preference and even enthusiasm for the alternative telescoped condition throughout) but got no further because someone had forgotten to bring the bicycle pump to blow up the boom. With a flaccid boom there was little to do but return to *Perula* and get it. After that they did manage to sail, admittedly the dinghy filled up with water and, at one point, collapsed and nearly sank because of an air leak and Paleface was sick thirteen times and everyone was frozen — but they sailed. When they warmed up later in the Gazelle they agreed that the little vessel had done well; they had covered at least five miles.

A race between the two trial models the following day proved inconclusive. One of them developed an air leak and nearly sank while the other had a water leak and filled to the brim with sea water. Paleface and the Oxford man left the next day, presumably to make the minor improvements necessary to keep the dinghies afloat for more than a few minutes at a time (an important factor given their intended purpose). But they were soon back with a larger dinghy.

By now the perils of the exercise were well-known and the only guinea pigs they could find were cadets from the training ship HMS *Conway*. This time the dinghy seems to have performed well but all but one of the trainees were prostrate with sea-sickness and they had to be taken ashore to recover.

The test ended badly. The Oxford man wanted to see how the dinghy would ride to a sea-anchor in a gale. The gale duly appeared but while Paleface and the Oxford man were releasing the ready-inflated dinghy from its retaining straps (which lashed it to the veranda of the Royal Mersey Yacht Club) it was caught by the wind, flew through the air and landed in some rose bushes where it hissed itself into a crumpled mass of rubber. The two visitors, deflated too, must have gathered it up and left because they disappear from the narrative.

THE ADMIRAL

Also in November Admiral Sommerville[4] came to see the moorings on the Straits and to visit HMS *Conway*. They had smartened themselves and the launch up for the occasion but Win's bluntness seemed to have let them down when she told him that a new mooring system for the flying boats (called the Mouse Trap) was "bloody awful". Things did not go so well after that because when they arrived at *Conway* the Admiral was not expected, the letter confirming his visit having been lost in the post. Unphased by this (an Admiral is not an Admiral for nothing) he invited Dunny for sherry at his hotel later and asked him to bring the lady along. The Admiral later wrote Win a little note, presumably having learned of her nautical pedigree:

> Dear Lady,
> If I had only realised what an expert was displeased with 'mouse-trap' buoys, I would have told Weblin [the Commander who had accompanied him] at once to replace them with 'rat-traps' or even 'lobster-pots' !
> Sommerville

WINIFRED BROWN

HOPE FOR SNOWDROP

It was about this time that Ron revealed that he had talked to a
Norwegian pilot who had flown in from Spitsbergen. The pilot told
him that he had taken Sverdrup out there, in the uniform of a Captain in the Norwegian Army, some time before. Unfortunately Ron
had not asked when this was so it did nothing to resolve what had
happened and the agony lingered on. Sverdrup might still be alive.

FALLING OUT

December 1942 brought a gale and fallings out. Just before the gale
struck the Straits a Sunderland flying boat appeared overhead and
landed. A basic crew was left on board and through the gale, as the
aircraft was thrown about violently and relentlessly on its mooring
buoy, it was impossible to get them off. To ease the strain on the
mooring they even started the outside engines. After a false alarm
when somehow the Navy was called to come and rescue the crew
there was a real emergency when one of the planes wing-floats started to leak. To counter this Win, Dunny and Dan had to go out
with sand bags to balance the water that had entered, to prevent a
capsize. On the return they scrunched aground just off the Beaumaris pier. Everyone got wet and afterwards Dunny and Dan were
found to be covered in oil from the engines that had been run.

The next morning they set off in the launch *Saro I* to take the
Sunderland crew out but they had not got far when its engine cut
out. Win, Chief Engineer, fixed it (it was caused by water in the fuel
tank) but later Dunny criticised the engine, saying it had never been
right. Winifred took this to be a criticism of herself as the engine's
custodian, made a scathing remark about his bottom (we are sadly
not told the details) and Dunny's response was to stride off and
resign. Apologies from Win were dismissed when they met shopping in Beaumaris. Dunny was holding a pork pie she had just
bought when she told him she would never speak to him again if he
did not relent. Dunny then uttered the immortal phrase:

"Goodbye for ever and — take your pork pie."

As a result of this upset Win was given command of *Saro I* by Ron (who emphasised that it was not a permanent appointment). She had hardly a moment to appreciate this hard-won and deserved post. As she sat in the saloon of her launch, Dan came in and congratulated her — and then resigned. He had never taken an order from a woman in his life and did not plan to start now. So Win had a command but no crew.

The replacement, Albert, lasted for a while but was transferred to shore duty because of poor time-keeping. Eric Evans joined (or rather formed) the crew of *Saro I* after that and stayed with Win until the end of the war. Albert meanwhile rejoined the Merchant Navy and did rather well; Win later saw him covered in gold braid, a rather magnificent figure.

NEW BOATS

In early 1943 they were promised a new boat, a seaplane tender with an enclosed wheelhouse, saloon, galley and even a toilet. Win had been instrumental in getting it and expected to be given the command — although Ron did not actually promise it. One day they were told that a large vessel was awaiting them outside the Police Station in Bangor. Win thought this must be the new tender and set off to take charge of it. The large vessel proved to be an ugly 14 metre-long refuelling vessel on a huge lorry stopped and blocking the road. The driver refused to take it any further because further meant crossing the Menai bridge which was clearly too narrow.

It fell to Win (someone spotted her yachting cap) to sort it out. She had it moved temporarily to the yard at Dickies and then organised for it to be lifted off the lorry on jacks. Ron was so impressed with her performance that he gave her the command of the tanker there and then so she had it lowered to the ground the following day and put in the water. The chugging ungainly hulk was not what she had in mind as her command.

We can only reflect that Ron must have enjoyed himself in this episode because when the seaplane tender arrived three other slightly more modest, less racy, vessels came too and Win was given the seaplane tender and moreover put in charge of a little fleet of six vessels (which included *Perula*). But is seemed as if it was to be quickly snatched away.

She was told by Les Ash, second-in-command of the Saunders-Roe operation at Beaumaris, that the RAF had got wind that the tenders for the flying boats were being run by civilians. This was, they claimed, an affront to the Service and so Win and her team were to be replaced by twelve servicemen.

Time passed and nothing happened. On the day the RAF men were expected they did not arrive. When Win tackled Les he revealed that he had surreptitiously given them away to Air Sea Rescue. Best keep quiet about it he said. It could cost them all their jobs. Les seems to have been a smooth operator.

SPITSBERGEN

In September 1943 there was more news from Spitsbergen. On the 10th British newspapers carried reports that warships of the German Navy had attacked the island. A battle group led by the battleships *Tirpitz* and *Scharnhorst* had bombarded Longyearbyen on 8 September in a very brief sortie from Altafjord. It was claimed by the Germans that extensive military installations had been destroyed and coal mines made unusable; troops had landed and taken many prisoners. In Britain it was taken to have been a raid made for training and propaganda purposes: there was little left since the British raid of September 1941. What the Germans claimed were military installations were actually meteorological observation posts.

Whatever the facts, Win derived some tantalizing comfort. There were Norwegians on Spitsbergen so, Sverdrup being Sverdrup, he might well be there with them.

ADAMS

It seems to have been about this time, late in 1943, that the relationship with Ron began to break down. As he returned home from work and relaxed, Win was out drinking at pubs and, afterwards, bringing people home to carry on the merriment. Ron retreated to the attic.

MAID AND NURSE

Win had a maid, Let Pritchard, and a nurse, Nurse Gladwyn, for Tony. They were both young and it was inevitable that they would be "called up" for more warlike work. This happened first to Nurse Gladwyn. She used all her professional skills (and it seems most of her feminine ones) to persuade the doctor who examined her for fitness that she was not medically suited to anything more demanding than looking after Tony (see below) and she escaped with a Grade 3 rating.

Excused war-work, she developed a life-threatening illness (we are not told what) shortly afterwards and had to leave Win's employ. So Let had to look after Tony as well as do all the cleaning and shopping.

To all appearances Tony was a sweet even angelic child, tumbling golden locks and large brown eyes, but wilful; today he would no doubt be diagnosed with some syndrome or disorder but, in those far-off days, he was simply naughty. He would scream across the Green and dive, fully-clothed in his Sunday-best, into the water. He presented an old lady with a present beginning with "D" he said, which turned out to be not the expected daisy but a handful of dung.

When Gladwyn left, Elsie came to help care for Tony. This involved feeding him with sweets and food that was generally bad for him, presumably keen to get him up to Win's childhood 95 kilograms as quickly as possible. She also objected to Tony using the grown-up lavatory — it meant a walk down a cold and draughty passage — so bought him a commode. This Tony enjoyed immensely, peeing in it as often as he could manage and encouraging his toy panda and the cat to do the same. It came to a painful end when the heavy lid fell as he was relieving himself trapping his "whatnot" (Win's term) and leaving it bruised and swollen. The doctor was called and he advised that if Tony could "spend a penny" everything would be alright. So Tony tried, his golden curls matted and his big brown eyes full of tears, and it still worked. So there was no long-term damage and indeed some good came of the episode: Elsie stopped interfering for a while.

Let, the maid, received her call-up papers to go and work for Saunders-Roe; the Labour Exchange advised that Win could give up her job and look after Tony. The only way of avoiding Let's call-up was persuading a Tribunal that it was not in the national interest. So Win, Let and Tony set off, in a car thoughtfully provided by the Ministry of Aircraft Production and with a letter from them in support, to make the case.

Tony threw an inkwell at the Tribunal's Chairman and managed to intimidate the rest of the panel so much that they all recognised that this charming little fiend needed expert and determined care. Win could keep Let after all.

THE SECRET BUS

The Royal Navy owned a secret bus. To be precise it owned a bus with a secret purpose. Converted from a London double-decker it roamed the country performing its secret tasks, packed with secret equipment. One day it was dispatched to Holyhead on Anglesey and it was then that it was discovered that it could not get across the Menai Bridge because the arches were too small (or, it might be argued that, since the Bridge had been there over 100 years, the bus was too big). Whatever, the Navy had a solution: the bus could be ferried across with the help of those people at Fryars Bay who handled flying boats.

On 15 November 1944 the bus turned up perched on a boat, a Landing Craft Tanks (LCT505 to be precise) and this was eventually persuaded to moor between Bangor and the Menai Bridge for the night. When Win boarded the large and clumsy vessel she found four sober men (a Lieutenant Commander, two Lieutenants and a Trinity House Pilot) in the Wardroom eating bread and jam (rather than juicy chops, after a substantial intake of pink gins, as Win expected of the Navy). If they wanted to go ashore (one of them wanted to telephone Holyhead), she told them, they had better get a move on.

This wisely they did and, after a rather tentative trip in the pitch-dark they arrived at Dunny's jetty on Ynys-y-Big and walked up to his house, to use his phone, only to discover that there was a party in progress. So, Win being Win and the Navy being the Navy, they joined in. It went so well that, when time came to leave, everyone was too inebriated to contemplate a boat ride back to the LCT so Win invited them to stay at Green Edge. The journey in her Austin Seven was interrupted by a visit to the Gazelle but at Green Edge they had a meal prepared by a drunken Lieutenant Commander while Ron stayed in the attic and tried to get some sleep. The Commander did a ballet in Win's roll-on undergarment and then collapsed asleep in her blue silk dressing gown. One of the Lieutenants woke to find himself wearing a mauve angora sweater.

The next morning, after they had changed into more usual clothing, the bus was unloaded, there were congratulations all round and the Navy throbbed off in LCT505. The bus trundled off on its secret mission and the following day Win was promoted to Chief Coxswain by Les. She had been calling herself that for some time, he said, so he thought he might as well make it official.

The bus was probably one of those used to train naval personnel in the anti-submarine use of radar called Attack Teachers. They were packed with the necessary equipment and used at smaller training centres around the country.

TONY TO SCHOOL

In mid-1944, aged 3½ Tony went to school in Beaumaris; the Hermitage. His curls cut off and instructed to mind his language, he set off in his new school uniform with a giant satchel, promising to be good. He tried but:

> After about an hour at school something went wrong and Anthony, remembering his promise remarked: "Ooo-DASH!"

The head looked sternly over the top of her spectacles. "No dash in school, Anthony, please."

The boy looked puzzled. "Oo damn, then ?" he questioned politely, seeking knowledge.

"Good gracious! NO! Certainly not!"

Tears came into Anthony's eyes: he had said the wrong thing and let Win down, and after he had promised!

"Oo B———! I should have said Oo dear!"[5]

PEACE

Peace came with VE Day on 8 May 1945 and things began to wind down. Saunders-Roe started to move back most of their operations to the Isle of Wight (part of the company stayed behind and moved on to bus manufacture). Win's boats were returned and, in September, Win herself was paid off.

Les Ash made his last test flight of a Catalina on 9 August and wrote on the safety documentation:

> Last test flight at Beaumaris
> Last test flight in my career
> Last flight I ever made
> Completed 10,000 hours experience & over 100 types[1]

Win and Ron parted. Ron was to carry on visiting Win and Tony every Friday for several years. He carried the pay packets for the workers at the quarry he was now managing — and a revolver. One of Tony's pleasures was, most weeks, being allowed to fire it.

They were amicably divorced in early 1947 and in June of that year Ron married Pat Heeley, a lady who had moved up from Birmingham and become his secretary. They lived in a house near the Gazelle.

OPERATION FRITHAM

Win wrote to Norway as soon as she could to find out what had happened to Sverdrup and the news was bad. In early 1942 the Norwegians were very keen to return to Spitsbergen but to comply with the terms of the treaty between Norway and Germany and avoid if possible the wrath of the enemy, it was important to limit the number of people who took part. Then it could be passed off as miners returning.

So, on 30 April, a force of 85 from the Scottish Brigade of the Norwegian Army, set off from the Clyde under the command of Lt Commander Sverdrup in the Norwegian icebreaker *Isbjorn* and the sealer *Selis*. They were mainly former Spitsbergen miners, with some military training, but there were also a few British advisors. After a stop in Iceland to replenish fuel and stores they arrived at Isfjord on 13 May. Crucially, through a failure of communication, they were unaware that Catalinas had seen enemy activity in the area and indeed had attacked an enemy aircraft seen on the ground.

The jetty where it had been planned to unload was surrounded by ice and Sverdup ordered the icebreaker to clear a path. While this was going on a German Ju88 aircraft flew over and must have called up Fokke Wolf Condors because, in the evening of the 14 May 1942, four of these long-range aircraft came and bombed the ships. The icebreaker was sunk and the sealer badly damaged; thirteen men were killed, including Sverdrup.

The survivors managed to struggle ashore without most of the stores they had brought (which were at the bottom of the fjord). They survived in the remnants of the buildings, supplied by air drops by Catalinas, reinforced by more Norwegians and supplied in Operation Gearbox, until the end of the war.

Win kept a photograph of Einar, in a silver frame, close to her for the rest of her life; not generally on display, it was tucked away somewhere safe.

THE YACHT BUSINESS

The war at an end Win spotted a business opportunity. She approached the RAF and bought two of the launches *Saro I* and *Fryars I*. They were to be based at Dunny's dock and they would use them to service yachts on the Straits. She broke the news to Dunny, who was to be her partner in the enterprise, waking him from a doze over a newspaper in his bungalow, quite unaware of this exciting turn in his fortunes. They had already, she told an astonished Dunny, been appointed local agents for the Royal Air Force — who expected to be flying seaplanes from Beaumaris for years to come. And so Yacht Services Afloat came into being.

THE MOORINGS

It was in this period of elation that she bought "The Moorings", a large house overlooking the Menai Straits not too far from where Dunny was living. An impressive carriage drive led through an arch of trees and it looked out across the Straits towards the mountains of the mainland. Elsie moved in with them for a while and as usual took command of the running of the house and alienated a series of servants, who left. Poor Let was the first one to go: she survived just a week. Elsie herself seemed to sense that sharing was not going to work and moved out. Win settled down with an indoor staff of three and a gardener.

It soon became clear that the lifestyle was unsustainable. Win had only a small private income (which she points out was heavily taxed), there were no wages coming in after the departure of Saunders-Roe (and Ron) and the yacht business does not seem to have thrived.

She decided that The Moorings would be turned into a residential club for yachtsmen. This promised a relaxed idyll of civilised drinking with well-heeled patrons, perhaps with the odd diversion of some light flower arranging. But of course it did not work out like that at all. There was help from friends like Rodney Jones but she found herself making beds, cooking and cleaning.

She sometimes had as many as 40 people staying, particularly during the August Menai Regatta Week

ELSIE

Apart from the brief period at The Moorings, Elsie seems to have spent most of her time staying in lodgings in the area usually, one gets the impression, from choice. She lived this lonely life around Anglesey and North Wales (moving on as she fell out with the landlady). She was in Colwyn Bay for several years (Win sent her food parcels) and, during this period, she absented herself from her digs and booked herself into a private hospital and had a major operation without telling anyone.

Win took Tony the 50 kilometres to see her every week she could and Elsie as always devoted her time to stuffing him with potted shrimps, cakes, chocolate and sweets. Afterwards they would go to the funfair and Tony would be topped up with ice-cream.

On the morning of 8 August 1949[2] Win had a message to contact the police in Colwyn Bay about Elsie and she drove over to see what had happened. When she arrived she was told quite bluntly that her mother had dropped dead in Greenfield Road that morning — and that she was in the mortuary. It seems to have been a quick death and one that caused the minimum of fuss and inconvenience, something Elsie would have liked. On the other hand, collapsing in the street while shopping was perhaps not quite the respectable end that she might have hoped for.

ADIEU MOORINGS

Elsie died during Regatta week and Win struggled through with her full complement of guests — who showed great sympathy. It was afterwards when Stefan, the Polish cook, said something rather ill-judged that she cracked — as did the plate she threw at him. Then another and then another until the air was filled with flying crockery. When this was exhausted she cast wildly around for more missiles and her eyes fell upon a magnificent Queen's Pudding, glowing with golden meringue. She reached for it and Stefan cowered when Tony's small voice called out: "Not the pudding, Win — please not the pudding." She paused and reached for some handy tableware and threw that instead.

She was distracted by a young man-friend who sat through the china storm without flinching and remarked languidly that his ex-wife had thrown dressing-tables, so what were a few plates. Taking advantage of the moment, Stefan made a dash for the garden and a porcelain-free environment. Pursuing him, she threw a soda-siphon which missed but shattered impressively on the rock-garden. This explosion somehow brought closure and she stalked back into the bar and and accepted a large brandy with dry ginger from the young man-friend. She announced that she would be selling The Moorings as soon as possible.

A frightening experience the next day convinced her that she needed to do something like that. She dived into the water from *Perula*, as she had often done, and when she surfaced found she could not swim. She did flail about with Tony screaming at her from the shore and somehow managed to reach dry land. But it was a sign. The doctor said she must escape from the stress of the The Moorings immediately. *Perula* was the only refuge so she and Tony moved in straight away with Dasher, the black Labrador, and three cats as companions.[3]

That night they ate cold bully beef by the light of a candle as rain seeped in through the neglected deck and dripped on them crouching in the saloon. Tony confessed that he preferred it to The Moorings — which was sold quite quickly for £3500. Win spent the winter on *Perula*, swimming each day, at first tentatively and then with her old confidence.

Tony was away at school during the week and Win found herself alone for much of the time — apart from Dasher and the one cat that had survived the rigours of the first few months of ship-board life. She found herself enjoying this and recognised that as a warning sign. She was retreating from life itself. So first she took a small flat in Beaumaris, more sociable than living on an isolated boat. But this, she soon realised, was not enough — and there was Tony's future to consider. Her two friends Mrs Welling and Mrs Richmond were already pulling his leg and saying that, if he was unqualified, he would be sent to forced labour in the nearby pits and quarries. He was only nine but he looked at the workings all around him in despair. So when Win came up with a possible career path, he was relieved as much as excited by the exotic prospect of becoming an actor.

The idea came as, one day that spring of 1950, she listened to Ruth Conti talking on the radio about her stage school in London.

WINIFRED BROWN

She remembered how much she had enjoyed her own flirtation with the stage in the 1930s and, particularly how welcoming and generous the professionals had been, seemingly not at all resentful of this girl pilot topping the bill. With Tony's agreement, she wrote to the school and soon enough they were invited to an audition. It was decided that they would combine the visit to London with a holiday.

SOUTH

They travelled down to London that spring and made their way to the School in Archer Street, just behind the famous Windmill Theatre in the West End, where the audition was conducted by Miss Hillary. After the preliminaries, Tony was given a poem to read:

> Anthony though not unkind
> Had a disbelieving mind
> At a pantomime or play
> Anthony would yawn and say
> Let's go home for I believe
> That this is merely make believe

He read it, but reading from the unfamiliar written word was not a strong suit, perhaps reflecting the fact that for much of his childhood he had spoken Welsh. Miss Hillary was hardly impressed and Win suggested that he might recite something he knew by heart — such as his favourite poem. Tony was unsure but, urged on by Win, he did recite it.

> There was a little bird
> That flew away to Spain
> But found it was too hot there
> So flew back home again
> On the homeward journey
> He met a bleeding auk
> Who plucked his bloody feathers out
> And said, now you bugger walk

He delivered it faultlessly and was immediately accepted for the school. He and Win then went straight on to their three-week holiday which, strangely enough, was in Spain.

SPAIN

Win and Tony went to Alicante, flying from Northolt, London to Madrid by the Spanish airline Iberia (which turned out to be an unexpectedly splendid experience) to stay with a family she had taken in for a while at The Moorings.

It started badly. They managed to get from Madrid airport to the railway station by showing the rail tickets to a taxi driver. At the station Tony wanted a a drink and something to eat. So an orange juice was ordered — something that generally led to him wanting the toilet quickly afterwards — and some food. Win decided upon some white fish in a cream sauce from the menu. Whatever she actually asked for — she spoke no Spanish so it was something of a lottery — Tony was served with an oily fried egg balanced on a heap of even oilier rice. He peered at it in disgust.

The lavatory reflex was then triggered by the juice and Tony was quickly wailing for relief. As Win tried to explain what was needed, at first through what Spanish she could conjure up and then through increasingly embarrassing mime, the waiter called the station master, who called the police. Confused or alarmed by this strong and strident woman gesturing wildly and provocatively (who knows exactly what was going on by now) the police called the military and Win and Tony were ushered into a spare room at the station and locked in until midnight when they were released to catch the midnight train to Alicante.

After the overnight journey from Madrid they found that the family could not accommodate them so stayed in a cheap and gruesome boarding house that cost 7/6d (about 40p) a day, all in. Win was constantly pestered: a woman who travelled alone on trains and smoked was clearly a prostitute. She was, of course, not alone; young Tony was with her. But this just made it worse: she was a careless, unsuccessful prostitute. They were short of money and

Tony sang for drinks in bars. Win downed amontillados and ate almonds.

ADIEU WALES

Soon after they got back to Wales, they packed up her Austin Seven with some belongings and set off for London and a small basement flat in Paddington at 54B Westbourne Terrace, an avenue of grand, four-storey terraced houses with modest but columned porticoes. A whole fresh adventure was starting. A life without Elsie, and (with regret) without Ron, and without Menai. They were to visit Wales seeing Ron and his wife, Pat, and their other friends. Win kept in touch with Dunny. Yacht Services Afloat was wound up in 1952 and Dunny and wife Marguerite moved to the large house at Pen-y-Parc above Gallows Point near Beaumaris and then, for unknown reasons, to its gatehouse. Sometime about 1950 they moved to Victoria Terrace in Beaumaris, the spectacular (and now Grade I Listed) building designed by John Hansom that looks out across the Green and the Straits to the Welsh mountains.

WESTBOURNE TERRACE

Win had rented 54B at £3 10s 6d a week, unfurnished. It was quite large (Tony remembers it as cavernous). A gate in the railings in front of the house led to steps down from the street, past the barred window of the front bedroom, to the entrance. Inside, a hallway paved with flagstones stretched back, curving to the right, when the floor became concrete and was painted a dull red. To the right a window rather oddly looked into the living room and then there was a bathroom and further on a kitchen, with nothing at all in it, lit by daylight from a large glass dome in the ceiling. Windows in the kitchen and living room gave views of two small yards. A blocked staircase off the hall showed where the servants, who would have lived in the basement, fetched and carried for those living upstairs and there was a door to a boiler room which kept the flat warm. Empty, it must have looked bleak indeed and, until furniture was obtained, they went to live with Connie Nixon and her husband Ben in nearby Craven Terrace.

Connie was Tony's god-mother and Ben, who was French, had been a pilot but now, injured in a crash, he was not in full possession of his wits. Something of a hero to Tony, his seemingly cruel treatment by his wife (probably from necessity) rather upset the young boy and he came to referring to Connie, behind her back, as his "hell-mother". Unfortunately Connie came across a letter he had written to a friend back in Wales, Rodney Jones, in which he used the word. She was furious and, of course, Win was equally annoyed that Connie seemed to have been rummaging around in their belongings to find it. They stormed out and went to live at 54B, ready or not.

An expensive *Vi-Spring* bed arrived, rather mysteriously from Tony's viewpoint, from Wales, the only furniture that ever did. Over time Win bought some more from "Junk Joyce" in Paddington and it came hauled on a barrow by the man himself but, after leaving the Nixon's, they camped out with very little in the bedroom and cooked on the fire in there. Slowly the flat filled with furniture from Joyce. A milestone was the arrival of the second-hand Eureka Series One gas stove, a mottled grey enamel. Welcome as it was, it was always difficult to light: Tony made a small heap of paper on top of it, lit it, turned on the gas and retreated before a fiery whooomf said it was alight.

They were, it struck Tony later, very poor. To save electricity they often sat in the front bedroom, where the natural light was good during the day and a street lamp outside gave illumination at night; they crept to the bathroom after dark with a torch. At the beginning it was less comfortable than it had been on *Perula*. When it rained the great dome in the kitchen leaked and at night cockroaches swarmed over the kitchen floor, Tony stabbing at them with a bayonet from the little armoury he had brought from Wales. Their numbers were reduced when men came and sprinkled green powder but they were never eliminated.

Quite where the money had gone is a mystery. Most likely the yacht services business with Dunny had not brought in much and may have been financed by loans; there may have been a mortgage to pay off from The Moorings. There was now enough to pay Tony's school fees and the rent but not much more.

THE CONTI

The first few trips to Archer Street were by tube but Tony never liked the noise and the crowds. It was much better when he was al-lowed to go on his own, on the bus. So most days he walked across to Praed Street and caught the No. 15 bus from outside St Mary's Hospital with 2/6d in his pocket for lunch in the Harmony Inn just across the road from the school. As grim as its name was soothing, he had the same thing to eat there every day: fish and chips. After dark it was a place where musicians gathered and later, in the early hours (it never closed), spivs and even gangsters (Mick the Hammer and Jack Comer — better known as Jack Spot) were patrons — so who knows what went on. On special days he went to the more ex-pensive Stage Door Grill (three courses for 7/6d rather than the 2/6d at the Harmony) and chose chicken vol au vent. Nearby, in this seedy by day and racy by night area, barbers did a furtive trade in condoms, there was a sweet shop, and, on Mondays, musicians gathered on the street to collect their pay for the previous weekend, in hope of work to come. Just up the street were the stage doors of the Lyric and Apollo theatres and at most times of day showgirls from the Windmill Theatre, famous for its nude tableaux, spilled out of its back entrance, just across the street from the Conti. They and the male performers in the shows drifted around the market, cafes and shops in full stage make-up.

Tony was to stay there for five years. There was a break for a few months when Win became concerned that academic standards were too low and sent him to Arts Educational until he asked to be taken away. The school refunded his fees, pleased to see the disruptive lad depart. But he learned his trade and was soon practising it. His mat-ron, the sturdy Mrs Vayne, took him for his first job to Elstree Studios in the summer of 1951 where the film *Magic Box* was being made as part of the Festival of Britain celebrations of that year. The film was crammed with stars, celebrating British cinema in a story of William Friese-Greene, the supposed British inventor of the cine camera. Tony's contribution was lost on the cutting room floor but he did have lunch with the actor playing Friese-Greene, Robert Donat ("a man with a name like a cake" as he later told Win). Before he left the Conti he had many actual appearances to his name.

WIN

Win stayed in Westbourne Terrace, the flat filling with furniture as Mr Joyce trundled pieces round on his hand cart, rather eagerly as he seems to have taken a shine to her. She cooked for Tony and the results were passable but mainly she wrote a book about her war: *No Distress Signals*. Encouraged once more by Peter Davies, she worked while Tony was at school and at night when he would often get up for a pee to find her scribbling away in the lounge in her well-formed longhand, writing on whatever paper came to hand. The manuscript was typed up by a lady called Nellie Kidd; she had a strange smell and was, somehow, "knitted" Tony thought. They enjoyed Nellie's many errors (in fairness she was typing things about a strange world). A favourite was a sentence which described how Win once sailed with her bargee upside down on the mast. It should have been "burgee" of course — but then Nellie may have read enough of Win's writings to know that a bargee up there was just about a possibility.

Quite how long it took to write we do not know but it was published late in 1952 by Peter Davies. An advertisement by the publisher in the *Observer* included a good review:

A vastly entertaining true account of the author's wartime adventures and misadventures on the sea and in the air.

> "Through it there shines the personality of a very remarkable woman. She is a real character, a 'card' if ever there was one." - *Manchester Evening News*[1]

The prolific sailing writer John Scott Hughes was not as generous in the *Observer* just before Christmas:

> It is not properly a seafaring story, but a longish gossipy
> book as much about people as about the land, sea — and air
> (Miss Brown has won the King's Cup Air Race). But once
> begun it will hold any reader who does not readily tire of a
> diffuse, slangy and, here and there rather vulgar, narrative
> style.[2]

LONDON

Britain was still suffering the effects of war. In much of the city
there were still bomb-sites, gaps where buildings had been ripped
apart by high explosives or crumbled by fire. They were now being
colonised by plants, so they were often splashes of green, sometimes with flowers, in the drab city. There was also still rationing of
food and other goods. It came as a shock after Wales where they
had chickens and eggs and, no doubt, some other meaty unregu-
lated luxuries.

That summer though there was the Festival of Britain, a great
event designed to celebrate Britain, its people and its achievements
in design, science and the arts. As a centrepiece, an area on the
south bank of the Thames, partly cleared by the Luftwaffe, was
smartened up and exhibition halls were constructed. The Dome of
Discovery (the largest construction of its kind in the world at the
time) held exhibits on geography, science and technology and the
Skylon, a shiny vertical steel cigar 70 metres long suspended on
cables, from a distance, seemed to hover. The Royal Festival Hall
was built for the arts and, not too far away in Battersea, the Festival
Pleasure Gardens offered relaxation and entertainment.

Win and Tony went several times that summer. Tony was briefly
awed but worn down by the crowds and the queues and perhaps
sensed the essentially earnest intent to cheer up the nation, so had
no lasting memories. Except, that is, an impression that Win spent a
lot of time in the beer tent.

PERULA GOES SOUTH

In July 1951 Win and Tony went back to Menai to collect *Perula*. Win had put together an unusual crew for the passage: her hairdresser Ted Goodman and Dennis Hull Brown, a distant relation who had been a banana planter in the French Cameroons. Dennis was rather expecting servants who passed him tumblers of whisky on a luxury motor yacht (perhaps with baths) so washing by kettles in a sink and having limited headroom came as a surprise. Both of them seemed to settle down though.

Ron Adams had already prepared the little-used engine for them by giving it a top overhaul. It performed faultlessly but gratitude for this act of kindness was limited by the fact that he had painted it with an oil-based paint rather than with one designed for engines. The clouds of smoke produced when the engine warmed to its task lasted for just a few hours but the fumes and the burning smell lingered through the voyage.

They found *Perula* in reasonable condition, certainly watertight, and took her across to Dickies where new seals were fitted on the portholes and the glass that had been cracked as the old seals hardened was replaced. New sea-cocks were fitted and she was given a coat of anti-fouling paint. After that, at 09:00 on 1 August 1951, they set off through the Swellies and into a moderate southwesterly wind. By 16:00 they were abeam of Bardsey light and soon after that the wind freshened. In the early hours of the 2nd, they tied up to a buoy in Fishguard Harbour in South Wales having motored about 80 miles.

They stayed until the 4th and were joined by Robin, a close friend of Ted's. He met them while they were playing billiards in a hotel and on the way back to the boat, as he tried to get into the dinghy, he fell in. Ted saved him and afterwards there were jokes about the kiss of of life. They seemed that close.

They left on the Sunday morning and coasted around the tip of the Pembroke peninsula but picked up a forecast of strong westerly or south-westerly winds and made for the shelter of the eastern side of Lundy island, in the middle of the Bristol Channel, where they anchored for the night, tucked well in on the south east corner (they had considered anchoring there in 1936 but the easterly wind had made it unsuitable). The following morning, they went ashore early to get a weather forecast from the lighthouse but were made extremely unwelcome, as if they had landed on a foreign shore. What they did not seem to know was that the owner of the island since 1925, Martin Coles Harman, regarded it as just that. He was prosecuted in 1930 for, contrary to Section 5 of the Coinage Act 1870, issuing coins (called "Puffins") with his head on one side and a puffin (the island's symbol) on the other and fined £5.00. A colourful (he was prosecuted for fraud too) City financier, he insisted that Lundy was a "vest-pocket sized self-governing Dominion" not subject to the laws and taxes of the UK. A phone call to his agent on the island told them that they had to pay a landing fee either at the hotel or the tavern (Marisco's). Win opted for the tavern and they were all astonished to find it in full swing at seven in the morning, taking advantage of the absence of local licensing laws. After paying and no doubt having a few drinks, they walked back to the anchorage and looked down to see *Perula* surrounded by rocks as the tide slipped away; Win had anchored a little too close in. So, with the tide falling and a forecast that suggested a change in wind direction that would leave them exposed, they lifted the anchor at noon, carefully edged out between the rocks and set course to round Land's End.

Rumbling along at a steady five knots or so they passed Trevose Head near Padstow before midnight and by 04:00 they were off Pendeen. Soon after that they must have been able to turn to the south to leave the Longships light and Land's End to port. They rounded the Lizard at midday and headed for Falmouth where they anchored at 16:00.

They stayed in Falmouth, which had been the southern limit of their cruise in 1936, for a week and set off again, without Ted and Robin, calling at Plymouth and Torquay. After a few days anchored in the outer harbour at Torquay, they motored across Lyme Bay with a plan to anchor or moor in Portland Harbour, the enormous naval facility tucked into the eastern side of the peninsula. Win entered by the eastern entrance and found the area crackling with gunfire and even rockets whooshing around. Practice it may have been but they beat a rapid retreat out of the northern entrance and headed for Weymouth.

Here they tied up on the east side of the harbour. They enjoyed the stay of 10 days in spite of the need to keep adjusting the mooring warps as the tide came and went and to clamber up and down steep and slippery ladders for the shopping. But the town was vibrant with cheap restaurants and good pubs, so they enjoyed themselves. Then at the end of the month they cast off and went to West Cowes and quickly on to Southwick where *Perula* was to spend the next five years in the locked basin of the canal here without moving much at all.

The first berth was at Mrs Sweet's (what is known now as Riverside Yard) some way up the north side of the Canal, beyond the Sussex Yacht Club. It was not the smartest of locations and, right from the start, Tony looked at the fine, shining yachts — like *Vagabondia*, reputedly owned by an oil millionaire — at Lady Bee's Marina, settled here after summers in the Med and other exotic locations. Mrs Sweet's had its compensations though. One was Sammy Youles. Sammy was rich, owned a Brighton company and was an ex-flier. He had made his name by inventing (some said co-inventing) the Pinta Pilot, an early and rather reliable autohelm, based on George, the famous airborne autopilot. It was now installed in many yachts and one was to be fitted to *Perula*. He was, somehow inevitably, eccentric as evidenced by his car: a Citroen 2CV, the most basic of French cars. To protect it from rust he coated it, completely and liberally, in engine oil. So, as he drove, it gathered dust and dirt and sometimes, and in some lights, it looked a little like a small dune or a sandcastle; in others it, rather ironically, looked as if it was covered in rust. They became good friends and when he married his partner Joyce after living with her for 27 years, Win sent a telegram congratulating them but wondering if they weren't rather rushing into things they might rather regret when they got to know one another better.

Mrs Sweet herself (nicknamed "Pussy" because her real name was Mrs Catt) was a strong and forceful woman — a law unto herself — and, perhaps surprisingly, she and Win got on very well. Her husband, Mr Catt, had been the harbour-master some years before and was rather famous for, through incompetence, ill fortune or neglect, having allowed the canal to drain away into the sea, leaving yachts and ships high and dry. It was called "Catt's Folly".

Over the next few years they used *Perula* as a weekend cottage year-round, driving down on a Friday evening in the Austin Seven and then following the same routine of climbing aboard, starting the engine, and hanging the bedding in the engine room to dry and mask the faint, cold smell of mildew and other boaty aromas with warm if rather oily ones. In winter they lit the fire. Then, leaving the boat to become a little more hospitable, they would go ashore to the Nab Cruising Club in Albion Street to have a meal and let Tony watch *I Love Lucy* on the television.

Later they would move *Perula*. First to the Sussex Yacht Club moorings and then, Tony's ambition achieved, to Lady Bee's. The harbour was the usual mixture of serious sailors, who came and went quickly, those who whiled away the summer weekends pottering around on their boats and quite a few live-aboards, at turns slightly mysterious and rather alarming.

Once a year they would take *Perula* out through the lock gates and allow her to dry out so she could be anti-fouled. The water of the Canal, warmed by the power station that stood on its edge, was subject to serious infestations by teredo and other worms brought from warmer climes by the steamers. Tony had to replace part of the keel at one point, it was so badly damaged. But, this annual anti-fouling apart, for five years *Perula* never tasted the open sea.

FRIENDS

Win made a few friends and saw some old ones in these early years in the capital. She and Tony continued to meet Marjorie Cussons, often at her suite at the Savoy Hotel. Marjorie would sit, always it seemed dressed in black, and they would talk. She would from time

239

to time take a cigarette from the "Craven A" tin that always seemed at hand. Win would reach for the "Julian Empire" tin that carried her smoking equipment and roll a cigarette for herself. They both seemed comfortable in this environment. Once when Win found she had no Rizla cigarette papers left, a waiter was sent out for supplies, to return with them (one hopes) on a silver salver.

In another incident, this time in the Savoy Grill, Win was rummaging in her handbag for something and produced a white rat. She put the rat on the table and resumed delving. She was quickly surrounded by waiters. Marjorie said "Put that back!". So she did. Why she had the creature and what happened to it after its brief exposure to opulence we can only guess.[3]

Marjorie was rather down-to-earth about wealth. She later sent her children to work in Boots the Chemist to learn a bit about business from the bottom up. At one time, in the 1950s, she complained to Win that she was running short of money and seemed depressed enough about the fact to make Win write to Marjorie's brother. He replied that, when she got down to her last half-million, there might be something to be concerned about.

Marjorie also continued to fuss about the Cussons' workers, touring the factory in carpet slippers checking on their welfare. She travelled to Africa, where she took an interest in the welfare of lions. Later she would become President of the company.

They met for the last time in 1982 when Win, now 82, went north to Marjorie's 80th birthday celebrations. A Cussons chauffeur, George, was sent down to collect her from Brighton and convey her in some style. Some way into the journey he thought the white-haired, elderly lady might like a break and suggested that Madam might care to stop for a cup of tea. "Bugger that!" was the response. "Find a bloody pub!" Over the next few hours they seem to have found several.

Win was smuggled into the celebrations as a surprise for Marjorie. She stayed with the family for three days — all waking hours were spent talking and laughing with Marjorie. It seems to have been the last time they met.

She kept in touch with her old friend from hockey days Margery Walsh — who, with her husband Knowles Pearce and daughter Jean, had often visited in Anglesey and was, of course, the seagull feeder who had visited *Perula* in the early days. She became Jean's god-mother.

There were some new friends in London. Eric Marshall their so-licitor and Rear Commodore of the Royal Thames Yacht Club used to invite them to his house on the Thames at Twickenham. He was a member of the Red Duster Syndicate, funding a British challenger for the Americas Cup. Win also liked Pat Baird who lived in the flat above and sometimes went out with Grace MacPherson from the BBC. And sometimes there were visitors, like Mol and Bulge.

Mol and Bulge were friends Win had met while she ran The Moorings. The kept a pub near Chepstow in Wales ("The Cherry Tree") and Win seemed to like Moll for her straight talking. She was very small and slight with hardly any neck; Bulge was bigger and quite why he had acquired the name is a mystery. There were no ob-vious bulges but there was something strange about his appearance. He seemed, Tony recalls, "ruptured or somehow bandaged". Whatever, he said very little; a background figure generally hum-ming or "bumm, bumm, bumming ..." rather vacantly as the women talked. They came a few times to Westbourne Terrace, sleeping somewhere else, staying until Chepstow drew them back.

While at Westbourne Terrace Win struck up a relationship with Aage Thaarup, the Queen's milliner.

Danish, Thaarup came to London in 1932 and set up shop in London where he soon acquired prestigious clients like Mrs Simpson, the consort of Edward, Prince of Wales. He also then and throughout his career made hats for the royal family with perhaps his most famous being the bearskin tricorne worn by the Queen for the Trooping the Colour ceremony — although he contributed carefully matched hats to many of her outfits. Business flourished in Mayfair. There was a hiccup in 1942 when he took Hulton Press to court.

The *Times* reported that:

> Mr. Thaarup complained of the publication of his photo-
> graph in the issue of *Lilliput* for August,1942, showing him
> in his capacity as model hat designer, with an woman's hat
> trimmed with snowdrops on a model head, before him. On
> the opposite page was a picture of a Home Guard in a
> garden holding a gardening fork in a minatory attitude with
> the words printed below it: "Keep out of my garden." The
> caption below the plaintiff's photograph was: "I only
> wanted a few pansies."[4]

Mr Thaarup complained that the words and the photographs taken
together implied that he "was a degenerate who should be shunned
by all right-thinking members of society." This now seems a reasonable concern given that the magazine was famous for its use of
paired photographs (known as doubles) with captions that linked
them. The original judge found in favour of Hulton Press, the publishers, but, on appeal, a re-trial was ordered. Hopefully, Thaarup
won a victory over small-minded, sleazy bigotry.

He overcame this and business continued to thrive, under a variety of company names, until 1955 when he was judged bankrupt
having given too much money to friends and extended too much
credit to seemingly well-heeled clients. He recovered — retaining
royal patronage — and rebuilt his business. His photographs show
him as a rather polished Stan Laurel figure with his signature bow-
tie at a ten-to-four angle giving his "cheerful disposition" (as the
Times said in his obituary) a certain camp quality (which the Times
did not say). He died in 1982 when the obituary concluded with the
perhaps coded words of the time that "He never married."

Win went out with him while they were at Westbourne Terrace
between 1951 and 1954, presumably while he was struggling with
his business problems. They may have met because Thaarup's studio was for a while over the Cussons offices in Brook Street. They
dined together; Tony remembers Thaarup calling for Win and coming into the bedroom to say goodnight to him as they left. Where
they went, what they did and what they talked about no-one knows

but hats must have come up because he gave Win a rather striking yellow cowboy-style one with pom-poms on it and a broad brown band round the crown. She looked, all agreed, rather good in it with her strong features. They must have been a striking if enigmatic couple whatever they did.

TONY'S CAREER

In 1952 Tony appeared in the film *Father's Doing Fine* and, at Christmas *Peter Pan* with the comic actor Kenneth Williams — someone who lived near them and was to become a regular visitor. Then in spring 1953 he was invited to join the Royal Shakespeare Company and he and Win moved to Stratford for nine months, staying with Bert and Ettie Shakespeare in their beautiful house, "The Old Ferry House", looking over the river Avon, where the ferry plied back and forth through the day. Win was by now his official chaperone and taught him tennis on the lawns of the house. She mingled with the aristocrats of the British theatre, like the Redgraves, as an equal rather than as Tony's attendant. She was well-known in her own right; a colourful and engaging character who, indeed, had her own unique experience of the theatre — or at least the music halls. In October the Stratford season ended and they transferred to the Princes Theatre, London to give *Anthony and Cleopatra* for six weeks.

That Christmas Tony made his first appearance in *Where The Rainbow Ends* at the Royal Festival Hall. This was a jingoistic stage fantasy from a children's story in which two middle-class children set out (with two young friends and a lion cub) on a magic carpet to rescue their parents missing-presumed-dead while returning from a stint in India. An evil aunt and uncle and a Dragon King try to stop them but the aunt and uncle meet tragic ends while the Dragon King is killed by St George who is acquired as protector by the children earlier in the story. They find the parents alive and well but shipwrecked in a tale replete with imperialist imagery and messages about integrity and fortitude. At the end, right having triumphed, St George appeals to the young audience: "Rise, Youth of England, let your voices ring/For God, for Britain, and for Britain's King." The epic was first staged in 1911 and was performed for several weeks to packed houses each winter with most of the cast coming from the Conti school. Tony played Crispian — one of the supposed orphans — while the director, Anton Dolin, took the role of St George. Dolin — everyone called him Pat — was Artistic Director of the Royal Festival Ballet at the time. He was gay and Tony was told that he liked little boys. Confused (didn't everyone?) he asked Win about it but all she could say was that he was a "pansy". Which left him more confused still.

109 DEVONSHIRE MEWS

In the spring of 1954 Tony came into some money left to him by Elsie. It meant that, if Win borrowed some from the bank, they could afford to buy rather than rent. They looked at a mews in Paddington but Tony was adamant that he could sense Elsie's presence and it was rejected. However, one day he went with Win to Portland Place to audition for the part of the young Jesus in a radio play. The part went to another aspiring lad but as they walked away they stumbled on a mews flat for sale at 109 Devonshire Mews South. Once viewed, they both loved it and bought it for £4500.

So late that spring they moved from 54B into the freshly-decorated 109. After an initial plumbing malfunction (when they flushed the toilet the bath plug-hole brought up liquid) was fixed, they could enjoy their new home — now back above stairs rather than below.

Originally the stables to 109 Harley Street, the ground floor was two garages, a double and single that they could let out (the Austin Seven was left outside), and the front door opened onto a flight of stairs that led up to the accommodation. A small kitchen was lit by a skylight and a high window (but no great leaking dome), Win's bedroom looked out onto the Mews while Tony's had a high window opened by a pull-cord, there was a neat bathroom and the living room gave them views onto the Mews.

This was and is a trendy location and they saw all sorts of people come and go over the years. Ralph Richardson, the distinguished actor would roar up on his motorbike, all goggles and leather, to spend time painting in the conservatory of the mews flat a few doors down. There were also comings and goings of celebrities slipping into the back entrance surgery of a well-known cancer specialist ("Magic Mac") at the top end of the mews to avoid the press: they saw the Duke of Windsor and David Niven. It was a well-heeled neighbourhood and Tony made some money, between engagements, valeting Rolls Royces and other luxury cars.

Later, for a while he was chauffeur to Sir David Webster, the chief executive of the Royal Opera House, Covent Garden. A successful Liverpool business man, Webster had, since the end of the war, established Covent Garden as a world-class centre of opera and ballet with two respected permanent companies. A generous employer, he often invited Tony to functions as a guest — an actor — rather than as an employee. The only time he asked him to wear a uniform was when he was to drive Maria Callas, the extraordinarily talented and colourful Greek soprano.

A notable resident, living opposite them for a while, was Stephen Ward, a fashionable osteopath and artist. Tony got to know him quite well and visited for coffee in the mornings; Ward encouraged him to draw. Win and Tony both found him a charming man who always seemed to have a beautiful girl on his arm. Ward invited them to stay any time at his cottage at Cliveden on the estate of Lord Astor. Alas for the narrative, they never took him up on the offer — activities at Cliveden were to feature large in the biggest scandal of the nineteen-sixties.

Tony was present at Ward's Devonshire Mews flat when Christine Keeler, one of his girl-friends, made a subsequently notorious remark. Stephen was talking on the phone to a friend and called out to her: "He wants to know what you'd like for Christmas". She replied, jokingly, "An abortion!" It was later used in court as evidence that Ward was an abortionist.

In July 1961, while living at nearby 17 Wimpole Mews, Ward introduced Christine to John Profumo, the Secretary of State for War and they had a brief affair, meeting at Ward's flat. He ended it, on advice, on the 9 August. And that could have been the end of the story but for Johnny Edgecombe. Miss Keeler's life had been colourful and sexually inclusive. Edgecombe was a former lover who had attacked another Keeler beau because, she told him, he had assaulted her and held her hostage. He did him (Aloysius "Lucky" Gordon) enough damage with a knife (17 stitches) to invite prosecution and was unhappy when he learned that Keeler was planning to give evidence against him. On 14 December he turned up at Wimpole Mews with a gun looking for her and, when access was refused, he fired several shots at the door. When his trial arising from the shooting started in March 1963, Miss Keeler, called as a witness for the prosecution, failed to turn up and it seemed she was not being pursued. Questions were asked in the Commons about the relationship between Profumo and the missing witness. Profumo denied everything in the House of Commons in March but the press now had the opportunity to investigate and report the whole sorry business.

It then turned out that Keeler had been simultaneously (well nearly) having sex with Profumo and Edgecombe and, as if more spice was needed, a relationship with a military attaché at the Soviet Embassy, Yevgeni Ivanov. Profumo then admitted everything and resigned in June to sink from the limelight and do good works.

Ward meanwhile was prosecuted for procuring women and living on immoral earnings and was briefly imprisoned in Brixton gaol. His trial started on 22 July 1963 and the stories of sexual intercourse (as it was then known), two-way mirrors, whippings and drugs recounted by Keeler, another of Stephen's friends Mandy Rice-Davies and others entertained and outraged the country for over a week. On 1 August he was found guilty of living on immoral earnings but he had already taken an overdose at a friend's flat. After being in a coma for several days, he died on 3 August.

Win wrote to him while he was in Brixton Prison. Ever after she thought him a charming, perhaps a trifle racy, man who had been wronged by the press, politicians and the Establishment. Like many, she saw him as a scapegoat and Tony thought much the same: Ward was not a sexual man but enjoyed the company of beautiful girls.

Win mixed with Tony's friends and acquaintances, rolling cigarettes and chipping in from time to time, a colourful older lady. She always seemed to attract gay men. Anton Dolin certainly took to her and was a regular visitor for several years; he liked the way Win cooked chicken and was sure to eat with them whenever he came to London. The young Tony detected the warmth between Dolin and Win and hoped they might marry; he adored Dolin and thought he would make a wonderful father. Not much later he came to see that it might not have worked.

For some reason Win decided that the Shakespearean actor Robert Harris, who turned up with his friend Norman, could not possibly really be homosexual and challenged him that she could prove it. She dragged the gloriously pompous thespian, stunned, into the bedroom. Screaming and shouting followed, cries of pain and ecstasy filling the small flat while Tony and Norman sat in the lounge, drinking and unavoidably listening. Norman just laughed and Win and Robert returned, grinning and grimacing in equal measure. Tony later saw footprints on the bedroom wall where (presumably) they had struggled to take their shoes off. Was the seduction real? You can never quite be sure.

UNDER SIX PLANETS

Win worked away through 1954 and early 1955 on *Under Six Planets* and it was published soon after.

It was, no doubt, intended as the story of her life up to the move south and it works rather well as a story. One notable oddity is the character Duncan who dominates the early years as her fiancé on the Australia trip, accompanies her in her flying exploits and goes with her and Elsie up the Amazon. This is of course Ron Adams. Ron makes his first appearance in *Under Six Planets* as her sailing companion after she bought *Perula*. It seems that Ron became "Duncan" (a name chosen to reflect his Scottish origins perhaps) in those early adventures at the insistence of Ron's wife Pat, presumably as an attempt to hide the fact that the relationship had been a long-standing one and rather more than as companions. We know that Peter Davies, her publisher, was incredulous about the device but went along with it. A photograph of Ron and Win holding the King's Cup and the Siddeley Trophy, no doubt intended for the book, has written on the back the words:

> Note for Peter (my publisher) A good picture but it would have to be WIN & DUNCAN (not Ron) & Ron might object as he wishes his name changed to Duncan.

It never made it to the book.

The association with Davies ended tragically. He benefited little when his benefactor J M Barrie died and some suspect that this started him drinking seriously. He also had a mystery illness, suffering from severe shortness of breath and fainting episodes. It became so severe that, not long after *Under Six Planets* was published, he stopped working. He was living in the Royal Court Hotel, Chelsea, when, on 5 April 1960, he walked out of the bar and jumped under a train in nearby Sloane Square station. The inquest concluded (having heard about the illness) that it was suicide while in a state of depression brought on by an apparently incapacitating illness. After his death Win never thought seriously about writing more books. It may be that the *Yellow Waters* manuscript, describing the Amazon adventure, was abandoned because Davies lost interest.

PERULA WANDERS AGAIN

Win seemed happy enough with *Perula* at Southwick. She spent long hours varnishing, mending and maintaining. Tony, though he enjoyed the trips down to the boat most weekends, began to feel that she ought to go somewhere. She was a boat (indeed, a famous boat) that had made two impressive voyages and an outstanding one before he was born, and he knew her stem to stern; he could overhaul her engine in his sleep. They had come south of course but since then *Perula* had been corralled in the dead waters of the Southwick Canal; the engine had been run for hardly more than drying bedding. It was time for more adventure, waves to lift her bow and stern and for the engine to push her beyond the horizon. So after five static years, on Saturday 4 August 1956, they left, crawling west past Worthing Pier and, taking the Looe Channel, through the treacherous Owers rocks and shoals off Selsey Bill. Then across Bracklesham Bay, with the entrances to Chichester and Langstone harbours hardly visible on the featureless coast, until they passed between the forts that guarded the eastern entrance to the Solent. Or did they sneak through the narrow gap in the submerged wall that stretches from Horse Sand Fort to the shore at Southsea? After the night of the 4th in Cowes, they motored across the Solent, up Southampton Water and then turned into the Hamble River. By lunchtime they were tied up at Solent Ship Yards at Bursledon where they were to get a new mainmast. They left *Perula* to have the new mast fitted and she was there altogether ten days.

When the work was done they took her on a short Solent day cruise. First to the beautiful Beaulieu River a few miles to the west, back to Hamble village and then across to Cowes where *Perula* seems to have spent the winter in a mud berth just past the chain ferry on the west side. Here they both worked on her. Tony re-caulked the decks with pitch — and nearly set fire to the boat in the process. Cowes was to be *Perula*'s home for the next ten years, much of the time in a mud berth at Groves and Gutteridge, the famous yard just inside the harbour entrance.

TO CHERBOURG

The following year they had a short trip down the Solent to Yarmouth but on 28 August they set off for farther seas. First stop was Weymouth where they moored up to the buoys in the river to avoid the endless fiddling with mooring warps that seemed necessary last time they were there. Even so they became caught up in pyrotechnics as they had in nearby Portland Harbour six years before — but this time it was a firework display rather than armaments.

Tony had decided that they needed a foreign adventure and suggested a crossing to Cherbourg. The weather forecast was beautiful with a promise of variable light winds and a slight sea. Win was against it because she had doubts about the engine; it needed, she insisted, a top overhaul before embarking on such a trip. It is something like 70 miles of open sea after all; she had really done nothing like it since 1939.

Somehow she was persuaded and at 05:30 on the 29th they cast off, went out of the harbour, set the foresail and mizzen to steady them and headed towards Cherbourg. The tide would, for a few hours, sweep them westwards and then at about 09:00 it would turn and carry them east for about six hours. As they approached Cherbourg it would turn again and, since the tide runs strongly round the tip of the Cotentin peninsula, if they ended up down-tide it could be a long haul clawing their way against it to the entrance. However they made the right allowances in setting their course, sighted the French coast at midday and arrived at the entrance to the Grande Rade, the gigantic outer harbour, at 16:00. It was just before that that things started to go wrong.

The engine coughed and one of the four cylinders cut out; a little later another did. So they chugged in on the two left with just a little help from the sails and managed to get into the Petite Rade and drop anchor. The engine had spewed out soot as it back-fired its last gasps and Tony, who had been tending it as best he could, looked like a chimney-sweep. He wished he had not put on his best and whitest kit, for an impressively smart arrival, just before the problems started.

It was then that the stately 23 metre motor yacht *Cordelia* motored smoothly past, her twin Gardner engines pulsing quietly and the Royal Anglesey ensign fluttering at her stern, heading for the inner harbour. This was just where they wanted to go, so they hailed her for a tow. They were not seen or, more likely, ignored.

It was getting dark by now so, if they wanted to reach the sanctuary and facilities of the inner harbour (now called Port Chantereyne), there was nothing for it but to put up the foresail and try the engine. It started but still struggled with just the two cylinders. However, with its help they struggled in, belching thick black smoke, an old lady puffing a fag at the wheel and, it seemed, a chimney-sweep holding a warp. The only place to tie up was against the pristine *Cordelia* (which was secured to a buoy in the middle of the harbour) and this they were doing, with the help of her crew, when the owner appeared and told the crew to drop their warps. He did not want this foul vessel against his immaculate yacht.

Win, as you might expect, put him straight on the fellowship of the sea and the responsibilities seafarers had to others in trouble, quite probably with rich colourful language. The owner slipped away, leaving matters to his paid skipper and crew, and the situation was rescued by the appearance of another motor-yacht, equally grand, that was looking to tie up alongside *Cordelia*. *Perula* was moved so that this could be done and she then went alongside the newcomer, *Musette*.

Tony set about fixing the engine problem. Unfortunately, as he was working, a vital brass washer from a cooling water pump slipped from his fingers and skipped away to fall into the ballast under the engine. The following morning *Cordelia*'s skipper came aboard for a drink, apologised for the owner's behaviour and explained that he was so unreasonable that the whole crew was thinking of jumping ship. He asked if Win could take them back to England if they did.

When they explained about the washer *Cordelia*'s skipper offered a deal: you take us back to England and we will take out the ballast to recover the missing bit. So the ballast was moved, the washer was retrieved and the pump was refitted. Tony overhauled the cylinder head, carefully regrinding the seats of the valves and cleaning out the ducts that carried the cooling water around the engine so that, by the evening, they were ready to go.

However, everything changed when the unpleasant owner invited the couple aboard for a drink. It seemed that he had been told exactly who he had been rude to; she was not some cranky old bird helpless in a sooty boat with a filthy deckhand but a celebrated flier and distinguished yachtswoman. Soon, millionaire Cedric (Tony knew him as Rex) Pochin had two new friends. Win told Rex about the mutinous crew and he took her and Tony, with his guests, to dinner. Later that night, *Cordelia*'s engines were started and she motored out of the harbour. They were to see her again.

CHERBOURG

They tied up to one of the buoys in the harbour. A dozen boats could be fitted onto each one, with a fender at the bow to prevent damage. There being a pressing need for toilet rolls they went ashore and walked the short distance up to the town. Here they encountered, unexpectedly it seems, the French phenomenon of pâtisserie. The francs that had been put aside for paper were invested in food; allocated from output requirements to input desires. Or as Win put it; "Bugger the toilet rolls, let's get some cakes." This seems to have been their big and memorable treat. Not for them the pavement cafe watching the world go by, or eating out in expensive restaurants. Instead, they enjoyed the cakes and Win stocked up with booze from the warehouse, even then close by the marina offices. And then, at 07:50 on 8 September, they untied themselves from the mooring and motored off out through the Grande Rade and set a course to take them back to Weymouth. The engine ran smoothly throughout and, unusually, they put up the mainsail. By 1920 they were tied up in Weymouth again where they lingered for a week (both of them still liked the town) before returning to their berth at Cowes.

COWES-BASED

From 1958 they were based at Cowes for nearly ten years and the sailing was generally restricted to the Solent. Indeed in 1958 *Perula* had got no further than Beaulieu.

There were several friends.

Win had known Uffa Fox, the sailor and boat designer, for some time. Certainly since the years in Menai. Quite how they met is uncertain but they were both published by Peter Davies so that may be the connection. Whatever, both enthusiastic drinkers, they shared some raucous evenings. On one in the Menai years, perhaps on a whim, they poured brandy over the curtains in the Bulkeley Arms in Beaumaris and set fire to them. The were probably thrown out and later, certainly, Win's knickers fluttered from the hotel's flagpole, presumably in protest at a punishment that seems, in retrospect, better than proportionate. A much larger than life figure in Cowes, Fox achieved fame as a boat designer and then as the man who crewed for and taught the Duke of Edinburgh to sail in his boat *Bluebottle,* one of the Dragon class that Fox had designed.

Some measure of the man comes from his driving behaviour that led to a summons to the magistrates court in Newport, Isle of Wight in January 1960. The bus driver involved explained, as reported in the *Times* , that he had stopped at a halt sign opposite a parked car and a queue had developed behind him, waiting for him to move. At this point:

> ..a large black car driven by Fox pulled out, crashed into the parked car, bounced off and on to the bus, and then reversed into another vehicle. When the bus driver asked Fox for his name and address he replied: "I am Uffa Fox of Cowes. I have a boat to catch. Move this ———— bus."[5]

Fox pleaded Not Guilty but was fined £30 and had his licence endorsed in his absence. Outraged, he appealed to the Isle of Wight Quarter Sessions but the appeal was rejected. He refused to pay the fine several times and was as a consequence dragged before the County Court in December where he complained that justice had not been done. The judge interrupted the tirade to tell him that his Court was not one of appeal and then Fox said " Do you want a cheque or notes?"

The judge replied that "Notes would be preferable." Fox then handed over an envelope containing notes saying: "You had better count it."

Afterwards Fox explained to reporters that he was acting on behalf of all motorists and had already written to the Queen (one imagines her showing it disdainfully to the Prince with some comment about his friends), the Prime Minister and the House of Lords.

Tony recalls that, in spite of the long friendship, he never met Fox; even during the Cowes years Fox seemed to disappear when Tony appeared. But, with Clare Lallow (the owner of the celebrated eponymous shipyard) and others, they drank away plenty of evenings in the Island Sailing Club.

It was probably in one of these sessions that the No F***ing Yacht Club was formed. It was intended as a home for people who had little time for conventional yacht clubs, people like Win and Fox. Meetings usually took place in an upstairs room of the Fountain Inn in Cowes with acceptance for membership depending on a willingness to pee out of the first floor window over the front door into the street (Win was not required to do this).

Win had other friends. The harbour staff dropped in for tea most days and there was always a cheery word with Chubby Williams, the man who swept the streets. She knew the Bekens, so famous for their yachting photographs, the Red Duster syndicate and many of the prominent yachtsmen who came to Cowes. As always, she took people for what they were, not for who they were.

TORQUAY

In 1959 Tony signed up for a season at Babbacombe in the revue *Gay Time* and they decided that they could take the boat to Torquay and use it as their home. So on 2 May they left Cowes, and after a few days in Weymouth (always a favourite) they arrived in Torquay on the 5th. They berthed at the "cab rank", where the bow was moored to the quay and the stern to a buoy. The summer passed, Win enjoyed the town being so close and no doubt became something of a quayside character. One unexpected visitor was *Cordelia* with Cedric Pochin aboard.

Win cooked for him and, while they were there, the encounter of the previous year developed in to firm friendship. So close that when he died in 1980 *Cordelia* was offered to Tony, a gesture that Tony had to decline because he already then had a boat of his own.

When the season finished in early October they went back to Cowes.

COWES & SHOREHAM

For the next seven years *Perula* was based in the Solent, much of the time in Cowes, sometimes on a Groves and Gutteridge buoy and at others in one of their mud-berths. The log records just "Local cruising" in 1961 and voyage to Poole, 30 or so miles away, in 1965.

They returned to Southwick in July 1967 (it may just possibly have been 1968) and there then is no record of any trips until 1970.

HIGH KICKS

Over the years they did return to Anglesey a few times to see old friends. They went for Tony's 21st birthday in the winter of 1961 when they saw old friends and celebrated in the Gazelle. Win, now 62, showed that the spark was still strong by dancing on the bar and repeating her old trick of high-kicking the rafters.

BELGIUM

In May 1970 they had two short excursions on the boat. First to Newhaven on the 22nd (probably to anti-foul since they arrived a few hours before low water and left at the following high water just after midnight to arrive back at Southwick in the early hours). The following week they went to Cowes for two nights. Tony began to feel once more a need for something a little more adventurous (the force that had sent them to Cherbourg more than a decade before) and between them they decided on a voyage to Belgium and Holland. Perhaps one attraction was the idea of returning to Ostende, retracing by sea the flight with Ron in VZ in 1928, forty two years before.

They left Southwick early on 29 July and motored to Dover on a pleasant summer day, a little cool for the time of year but with sunny spells and none of the forecast rain. The moderate westerly wind encouraged the engine, pushing them steadily through the rather slight seas. They tied up in Wellington Dock and stayed there the following day, given the forecast of moderate to fresh winds as a small depression swept across the northern UK. But then on the 31

July they set out just before ten o'clock in the morning and just 3½ hours later, with help from the tide sweeping them up the Dover Straits, they were moored up in Calais, waiting for the lock to open. When it did, at 10 o'clock that night, they went through to the yacht basin where they stayed for five days.

On 5 August they motored to Dunkirk in the afternoon, against a modest north-easterly wind and through a slight sea. It was here they found a large schooner-rigged yacht with a problem. *Zeehund* was an elegant yacht with a long bowsprit but flat batteries. Tony managed to charge them using the portable generator they were carrying and as a thank you they were taken for a sail by her French owner, M Nagelaterre, outside the harbour in the strong winds that had picked up; the schooner, beautifully built in steel, creamed through the rising waves untroubled. Tony dwelt on the contrast with the sturdy chugging *Perula* but was not sorry when the exhilaration ended and they returned to Dunkirk (the wind had risen to force 7).

The following morning they had a further thank you. There was thick fog so they followed *Zeehund,* which was equipped with radar, towards Ostende ticking off the buoys that slid past in the gloom, to be sure. Although it looks featureless the sea bed is rutted by the tides with sandbanks that run parallel to the coast and the buoys mark the safe channels through them. They hugged the coast, seldom much more than a mile offshore, and the buoys marked their passing: E9, E12, Trapegeer, Weststroombank and Zuidstroombank. It was a relief to find Ostende. Although only 20 miles or so, the poor visibility had made it hard work.

They stayed for a few days and then on the 10th set off for Middelburg. As so often seems to happen in sailing, after several quiet and even sunny days, the wind got up and as they passed Zeebrugge it had reached force 5 or 6; the foresail came adrift, flapping wildly about until tamed, and the were forced to reef the mainsail. Soon after that it started to rain heavily. But by 13:45 they had found the W10 buoy which meant they could turn and head up the estuary for Flushing. Here, just a half hour on, they turned into the harbour and entered the lock. They took the Walcheren Canal the four miles up to Middelburg, noting in the log that the three bridges were slow in opening. But by 16:45 they were tied up alongside the quay.

This was the farthest extent of their cruise and they may have expected to stay for a while but there proved to be little of interest in Middelburg and after just one full day they were off again. On the 12th they went back down the Canal and the following day out through the locks and back to Belgium. They must have looked back at Holland thinking that they had probably not seen the best of it but they enjoyed the passage back to Ostende. Once they were snug in the yacht basin Win wrote in the log: "A pleasant passage in good weather."

Ostende was a different prospect from Middelburg and Flushing: a lively town with endless inexpensive food and inviting (if sometimes intimidating) bars lining the dockside. They enjoyed the place and stayed for ten days — maybe Win took Tony to some of the places she and Ron had visited forty two years and a devastating war ago. Whatever, they left on the 22nd for Dunkirk and then, after a night there, they returned to Calais and, in the afternoon, they locked into the yacht basin, where they stayed for a few days.

On the 26th, with an almost perfect forecast of light easterly winds and a slight sea (a region of high pressure had settled over Scotland), they left for Newhaven at 7 o'clock in the morning. This was just about high water at Dover and the tide was still streaming up the Channel so, for the first two hours they had to allow for that as they first clung to the French coast and then struck out across the Channel. The tide would help them for a while in the early afternoon but, after that, it would be against them but fairly weak. The route was actually fairly direct and took them north of Le Colbart and south of the Varne, two undersea ridges in the middle of the Channel that are almost shallow enough to stand on at low tide. They saw the low lying headland of Dungeness at 12:30 and then made their way across Rye Bay to pass Hastings and find their way through the Royal Sovereign shoals. They rounded Beachy Head at 18:15 and by 20:00 they were in Newhaven. The crossing of something over 70 miles had taken almost exactly 13 hours; an average of just over 5 knots. The following day they completed the passage back to Southwick.

GREAT YARMOUTH

In 1971 Tony had a summer season at the Britannia Pier in Great Yarmouth with Ronnie Corbett, the diminutive comedian, as Corbett's stooge and as principal dancer and singer. The town has a harbour and it seemed obvious that they should move *Perula* there for the summer. So they set off on 9 May, spent a few days at Newhaven cleaning and anti-fouling the hull and then pressed on to Dover, Ramsgate, Lowestoft (where they were helped in by the Commodore of the yacht club and there was the luxury of baths in the club) and arrived at Great Yarmouth on the 19th. Here they tied up to the quay on the east side of the river for the summer, perhaps a little close to what seemed to be a sewage outlet, where the crab pots stood in a great tumbled web. Tony went off most days to *The Ronnie Corbett Show* (sometimes twice daily); Win pottered happily around the boat, no doubt chatting to passers-by. She was probably known to some as the mother of one of the stars of a summer show but very few would have known about Winifred Brown's past. To many she was just a friendly (probably dotty given that she lived on a wooden boat) white-haired old lady.

There were occasional visitors. A good-looking young man who cruised up and down in a speedboat nearly every day, none too adept at boat handling, proved to be the comedian Freddie Starr. He was just making it big after an appearance on the TV show *Opportunity Knocks* and was starring in a summer show, *Holiday Startime*, with Norman Wisdom at the ABC. He came aboard regularly and chatted to Win. Generally zany on and off stage he was later to be famous for a headline in the *Sun* tabloid newspaper in 1986: "Freddie Starr Ate My Hamster." He denied the accusation — that one night in Manchester he had been refused a sandwich at a friend's house and had, in retaliation, put their live pet between two slices of bread and eaten it. Tony and Win liked him. Ronnie Corbett came often too, with his family.

Win listened to the radio as she had always done: *Book at Bedtime* and *Any Questions* were favourites. She rather lamented the demise of *Mrs Dale's Diary* (latterly *The Dales*) in 1969; they had stopped the engine on passages on *Perula* to catch the 16:15 broadcast on the Light Programme, or its repeat at 11:15 the next day. But sometimes, when there was nothing to listen to and no one about, they would get out Tony's ball-bearing gun and pot objects floating past in the river.

And so the summer passed and, on 12 September, after the season finished, they went home to Southwick, retracing their steps except for a stop at Harwich rather than Lowestoft. After this adventure *Perula* would be confined to the south coast: the log shows she went no further east than Newhaven and no further west than Poole.

In September 1972 she went from Southwick to Cowes, Lymington, Portsmouth and back to Southwick over a period of a week. In July 1973 she went to Newhaven for a few days (maybe to anti-foul) and then to Cowes and back — for how long the log fails to tell us but they were back at Southwick on 27 August.

After this the log becomes fragmentary with few dates but they seem to have returned later in 1973 to Cowes and spent the winter there. Win lived much of the time on the boat; Tony travelled down between his appearances in *General Hospital*, taking the train and the Red Funnel ferry from Southampton to join her. He had won the part of Dr Neville Bywater in ATV's soap opera, a British version of a successful US series.

HUGHIE GREEN

During one period at Lymington there was a remarkable coincidence that brought the war years back. They were on Berthon Marina on Christmas Eve 1973 when Tony spotted a beautiful boat he had seen before and coveted, *Enalios,* looking for a berth. *Enalios* (the name is an anagram of sealion) was owned by the TV personality

Hughie Green, who presided over a long-running talent show, *Opportunity Knocks*. With a TV persona inescapably that of the used car salesman, the seemingly-false American accent that went with it and a contradictory catchphrase "And I mean that most sincerely folks", he was a big star. Tony directed the elegant silver boat into the berth next to *Perula's*, giving the impression he was one of the marina staff. He struck up a conversation with Green, who was with his girlfriend of the time June Thorburn and the legendary and aged Mrs Carr, his housekeeper who accompanied him everywhere. He asked him if he might be prepared to sell *Enalios* and it started a conversation which concluded with an invitation to come aboard *Perula* for drinks later.

When Green arrived he was fascinated by the engine, quizzing Tony, and was then introduced to Win and given a gin and tonic. He sat in the saloon quietly and a little distracted for a while and then, rather suddenly, said: "I'd like to tell you all a story."

He then recounted how he had been a Catalina pilot, ferrying the planes across the Atlantic. It was a hazardous business: the planes were unarmed and crammed with spare fuel tanks that meant they could not fly high enough to avoid trouble. He had been flying to Wick in Scotland but was diverted, because of bad weather, to somewhere he had never heard of, the Menai Straits. When they reached the Straits just after midnight it was pitch black and they could make out very little but the radio operator picked up landing instructions in Morse code from a seaplane tender and Green duly landed. The tender came and towed them to a mooring buoy. It then came alongside to take the crew off and the effing and blinding from the crew that normally accompanied these operations, releasing the stress of the long and dangerous flight, abruptly stopped. "What the fuck is going on?" shouted Green down the aeroplane. The reply came back: "Hughie, the launch-man is a woman! And she's in a dress." Green soon saw the woman, dressed in a long black evening gown with a fox fur wrap, who had single-handedly managed the whole tricky mooring operation, for himself.

He paused for a moment at the end of the narrative and then turned to Win to say, in an appropriately dramatic tone: "I believe that woman was you" And, of course, he was right. It was all so extraordinary that he invited Win onto his TV show to repeat the story.

There were trips to Poole and Cowes and several times to the Beaulieu River. On 18 May 1974 they returned to Newhaven and the following day Win made the last entry in *Perula*'s log: "Engine seized — full of water". It seems to have been the end of the line and the association with the boat seems to have ended in Newhaven — one of their least favourite ports.

SEAWAY

It was about now that Tony fell for a new boat of his own. With the prospect of a steady income from *General Hospital* for a while, something more comfortable than *Perula* could be found.

Seaway was a motor yacht with a funnel and she lay in London Marina. There was plenty wrong with her but, after some negotiation, a price was agreed and she was Tony's. He knew the funnel was false (it proved useful as a shower room later) but there was quite a lot to be done before they could be comfortable with her. For a start the saloon was pink.

But Win was outraged: it all appeared to have been done behind her back, she had not been consulted, it was a motor boat and, perhaps unspoken, Tony was rather obviously becoming independent. However, the deed was done and she came to terms with it so, as soon as they could, she, Tony and Gladys (not her real name but Tony's girlfriend of the time) took *Seaway* down the Thames and round into the English Channel. At some point Tony felt the need for a drink and. never one to drink and drive, he asked Win where they were. She knew exactly: "Three fag papers off Ramsgate." Whatever this unconventional metric meant (she apparently used it quite a lot), it was enough for an enthusiastic turn to starboard for a drink in Ramsgate, a drink that turned into a six-week refit.

WINIFRED BROWN

It was while this was going on that *Perula* was sold to Ray Hamilton: the broker had taken him to see her (wherever she was) and he fell for her cream deck and new tan sails. Tony never thought she was the right boat for Ray but he already had two others and he was rich.

After the refit *Seaway* looked splendid. Seventeen metres long with a beam of four metres she had been built by Dickies of Tarbert, teak on grown-oak frames. Her Gleniffer engines were in a proper engine room towards the front of the boat, driving the two propellers through long shafts. She motored like a dream, the engines humming quietly with, because of the underwater exhausts, not even a hint of fumes at the stern. She could cruise at a pleasant 8 knots if the sea was not too rough and Tony could get 9½ if he really tried.

The wheelhouse led down to a large saloon with comfortable seating around a large table; a separate galley was off to port. Tony's cabin was reached by a passage down the port side, past the engine room, in the fore peak where there was a shower. At the stern there were cabins (one was Win's) on either side and a toilet and then, right at the stern, the aft cabin.

After *Perula* it was luxury. There was more space because the boat was longer and, although her beam was about the same, while *Perula* pinched in at the stem and stern, *Seaway* carried her full width for most of her length. Everywhere the teak and mahogany shone. The King's Cup was kept in the aft cabin and, since the door to that was usually open, it confronted anyone who went aft of the saloon, sparkling (on a good day) in front of a mirror. To the onlooker, from boat or quayside, the teak topsides were complemented beautifully by the extravagant cream faux-funnel behind the wheelhouse and the cream boot topping that crisply marked the waterline, the red anti-foul paint below.

They went to Southwick for a few days and then on to Lymington at Win's request: she liked the town and the welcome at the boatyard. They stayed here until Win began to complain about the nearby marshes and they moved to Brighton Marina for a year or two until Win began to pine for Lymington. So they relocated again until once more the marsh fever struck and they went back to Brighton. This was now the late 1970s and this time they stayed put, moored opposite the marina office, hemmed in by the massive concrete walls that protect against the English Channel that beats upon them.

LIVING ON SEAWAY

They had sold the Mews in 1976 and, after that, Win lived permanently on *Seaway*. She had started to experience balance problems in 1974 and now she was clearly not as mobile as before.

It was during the last stay at Lymington that she began to need someone to keep an eye on her and help her while Tony was away. The first carer had to go when she caught him doing something tasteless in the saloon (let's just say it was nothing to do with food and leave it at that). The second was a girl friend of Tony's who lived in Lymington and visited at least once every day to check on her. That seemed to work fine.

In Brighton Win sat by the wheelhouse door, often in her pyjamas, so that she could take the sun and speak to people who walked past. They were often invited aboard and she would tell them stories from her life — latterly including one that she had taken *Seaway* up the Amazon. She drank rather a lot and some of the visitors took advantage; things were stolen from the boat.

Tony had joined the cast of the extraordinarily popular soap *Crossroads* in 1978 as the racy heart-throb Adam Chance and was spending the week in Birmingham where the series was made. He went down to Brighton most weekends and was increasingly worried about his mother. There had been a series of paid carers but none of them stayed long. Win had become increasingly confused and often got up in the early hours, frequently making herself a vodka martini thinking it was evening. It was becoming difficult to find people to look after her.

It was on one of his weekend visits that Tony was invited to go out with the lifeboat (he was allowed to drive) on a publicity exercise. When they returned to the Marina he invited the crew aboard *Seaway* for a drink and it was while this was going on that he saw one of the lifeboatmen speaking to a mystery man.

Anyone who has spent time on a boat in a marina knows about mystery men (these characters are seldom women): they appear from time to time strolling along quays and pontoons, seeming to arrive from nowhere and belong to nowhere. Some prove to be recluses living on boats but some just are just rubberneckers. Mr X was a regular visitor who studiously avoided eye contact and never spoke as he walked past. It rather annoyed Tony so, when he saw him talking, he invited him aboard.

It was about then that Win appeared from below in her pyjamas and dressing gown asking in a rather confused way who all these people were and what was going on. Mr X, stranger that he was, insisted on looking after her.

When Tony escaped from chatting to the guests and having the various required photographs taken he realised that Win was not sitting in the wheelhouse as usual. He found her with Mr X, clutching the vodka martini he had made her and watching him frying her some fish fingers (which was pretty much her staple diet). Tony soon found that some lamb chops were being cooked for him too. The mystery man had been a male nurse and it was soon agreed that he would keep an eye on Win, visiting every day, and if necessary speak to Tony when he made his nightly call to check on his mother. There was much about Mr X that Tony did not know at this point and would find out later but for the moment he seemed the answer. He seemed a genuinely caring person and indeed he proved to be one over the next nine months, looking after Win and reassuring Tony.

ILLNESS

Everything changed in May 1984 when Win had two strokes on *Seaway* that left her partly paralysed. Tony raced down from Birmingham after a phone call from Mr X to find her in a poor distressed state. Treating her there was quite impractical — not least because the bunk-beds made access very difficult — and Tony was advised by his doctor that she should go into a nursing home. After some searching he found the Fairlight Nursing Home in Hove but was warned that she was unlikely to survive more than a few days — the shock of moving from familiar surroundings when she was so feeble could be fatal.

The ambulance came to the marina to collect her and quite a crowd gathered to watch her being lifted from the boat on a chair. When she reached the Home she was taken for a bath and suffered a third stroke. Tony had prepared himself for the worst when he went to see her and was surprised to find her sitting up in bed while a male nurse rolled her a cigarette. "Have you stayed at this hotel before?" she said. "Bloody good!"

She kept going at first on cigarettes (with, who knows, perhaps the odd vodka martini) but later on Brompton cocktails (a concoction of morphine, cocaine, alcohol and syrup). She increasingly wanted just to sleep. Never in pain, it was as if she was preparing herself for another voyage. Tony visited at the end of July and talked to her, although she was sleeping. He remembers saying that he would see her next weekend and then doing something unaccountable he had never done before. He said goodbye. The following day, 30 July 1984, he had the phone call that told him she had died quietly that morning. She was eighty-four.

The causes of death were given as pneumonia, arteriosclerosis and hypertension. The funeral was a quiet affair with no guests — just Tony and Mr X — no flowers and no music, as she wanted. The coffin was set down and, just before the curtains closed, a shaft of sunlight struck it and the brass handles glittered for a moment.

Win's ashes came in a casket about the size of a shoe box and Tony had decided that a burial at sea would reflect her wishes. So, one day soon after the cremation, he and Mr X set off for Lymington to take the ferry to Yarmouth on the Isle of Wight where *Seaway* was having some work done.

The work was not quite finished but they started the engine and motored out of the harbour. Then, some way east of the entrance,

Tony stopped the boat and, standing alone on the stern, music pouring from the wheelhouse, he dropped the treasured, silver-framed photograph of Einar Sverdrup over the side and watched it waver away down through the water. Then he poured the vodka martini he had made after it and then he took the casket and gently tipped his mother's remains into the Solent. The outcome was not quite what he expected. Rather than drifting away on the gentle breeze and settling on the sparkling waters, giving him moments to remember and reflect, the ashes simply plunged straight down and disappeared in an instant; single-minded to the very end. This over, he started the engines again and turned the boat back towards Yarmouth.

POST SCRIPT

The list of early female aviators is long and diverse. A few have been mentioned, notably: Harriet Quimby, Mary Elliott-Lynn, Princess Anne of Lowenstein-Wertheim-Freudenberg, the Hon Elsie MacKay, Winifred Spooner, Amy Johnson and Amelia Earhart. There were many more. Some were serious pilots, some intrepid passengers. Some flew great distances; some raced. Some came from a privileged upper-class background, some, like Win, from the working middle-classes. For many flying was an exciting and fashionable adjunct to the jazz age.

OTHER FEMALE SAILORS

No doubt there have been female sailors as long as there have been boats. Some notable pirates were of the gentler sex and many women accompanied their husbands on epic cruises as virtual passengers. The husbands were, it has to be said, virtual passengers too since many employed paid crew. There were also some prominent lady racing sailors.

But the number who cruised as skippers or took some really active part in the sailing as a crew member seems to have been small in the first half of the 20th century. Four women stand out because they have written about their experiences.

Dulcie Kennard (who wrote under the name of Peter Gerard) was born in 1900 the second child of a military family, taught herself to sail on the south coast in the 1920s and met the well-known sailor Maurice Griffith. They sailed together on the south coast and in the Thames Estuary and bought *Afrin* in 1927 after they married. It was always her dream to own a boat of her own — she was an enthusiastic and capable single-handed sailor — and when *Afrin* was sold they each bought a boat. Dulcie's was *Juanita*, a pretty 32 foot yawl. She separated from Griffith and the marriage was dissolved in

1933 and later that year she married the marine painter Charles Pears, twenty-nine years her senior.

Pears had the well-known yacht *Wanderer* which they cruised but Dulcie had set up a sailing school for women on *Juanita* and separately cruised the Thames Estuary and the Channel — to the Scilly Isles — training her "Cadets" in the engine-less yacht. The story, recounted in her book *Who Hath Desired the Sea*, ends in 1942 with *Juanita* ashore for the duration of the war on the Fal River in Cornwall.

Dulcie was a contrast to Win in many ways. A slight, boyish figure she seems to describe herself in masculine terms quite often. The man's name was probably adopted in the expectation of being taken more seriously than a woman would be in her magazine writings. Of course, her sailing was confined largely to British waters but these are not without enormous challenges to seamanship especially as she sailed everywhere, often alone, with no engine to fall back on. She was driven by the romance of the sea and a need to master the boat — that seemed to be the uncomfortable pleasure — rather than long-distance voyaging. She of course had the benefit of two particularly seaworthy partners in Griffith and Pears while Win had only the loyal and willing fellow duffer, Ron.

Ella K Maillart was Swiss and sailed on barges and yachts in the Mediterranean, the English Channel, the southern North Sea and on the Atlantic coast of France and northern Spain. A few years younger than Win, she was an excellent skier and, like Win, played hockey at national level as captain of the Swiss ladies team. But she was different in that she took up sailing early; she competed in the 1924 Paris Olympics in the single-handed Monotype class (based on the gunter-rigged Meulan dinghy) as the only woman among the 17 competitors.

She always seems to have had an interest in cruising and did cruise extensively in the 1920 and early 1930s — so before Win — but usually with others experienced sailors and always to relatively well-frequented spots. All seas are potentially harsh and dangerous in a small boat but Win's Norwegian voyages were through particularly hazardous ones. Maillart essentially gave up cruising in the 1930s and took to a life of travel and adventure, exploring the USSR and Asia, writing articles and books and taking photographs.

Her sailing adventures are described in *Gypsy Afloat* published in 1940. There are many other books describing her later exploits.

Marion Rice Hart was born in London in 1891 to an American lawyer, part of a rich and well-connected family. She attended the Massachusetts Institute of Technology and obtain the first degree in chemical engineering to be awarded there to a woman. Always restless, she later went on to a master's degree in geology. She took a cruise on a commercial yacht around the Greek islands but was unimpressed by the skipper, who failed to put the sails up at all, so bought a 30 metre steel ketch, *Vanora*, in Cowes. After hard work to get it in a state for sea, she employed a skipper and, in August 1936, set off round the world.

The skipper almost wrote off the boat in strong winds in the Channel and then collapsed below with sea-sickness, leaving Marion and the inexperienced crew to get into Brest. Here she sacked the skipper and, with a fresh one, set off once more. By the time the reached the Red Sea she had sacked this one — and soon after his replacement — and decided she could probably manage herself. So, with a half-dozen crew, she continued on calling at various places including New Zealand, the Dutch East Indies and Singapore.

She reached New York in July 1939, after a three-year voyage covering 30,000 miles and visiting 101 ports. The newspapers showed her, cigarette in mouth and two hands on the wheel, a spare lady with a steely gaze. She published her letters home for some of the voyage as *Who Called That Lady a Skipper?* in 1938.

She went on to write a book on celestial navigation which was a standard work for many years and also took up flying. She made her first transatlantic solo flight in 1951 at age 61 and her last, the seventh, when she was 83. She routinely flew alone around North America until she was 87 and died in 1990 aged 98.

Ann Davison had acquired a commercial pilot's licence in the 1930s and she and her husband Frank were involved in several business ventures that failed: an airfield on the Wirral in Cheshire, quarrying, and farming on small Scottish islands. They bought a large fishing ketch and converted it, over two years at Fleetwood, Lancashire, into what seemed a handsome vessel. The money ran out , they fell into debt and to avoid their creditors, in May 1949, they hurriedly set off for the West Indies. Almost immediately struck by bad weather they made it to the Western Approaches but were blown up the Channel by gales and, with the sails ripped to pieces and the engine useless, nineteen days out of Fleetwood, they were wrecked on Portland Bill. They took to the liferaft but were swept through the Portland Race, the raft capsizing many times in the rough seas. Frank died of exposure or drowning but Ann was swept ashore and climbed the cliffs to safety.

This would have been enough to encourage most people to never set foot on a boat again but, after a period of reflection, Davison became convinced that she should complete the journey she had started with Frank, this time alone. In her book *My Ship Is So Small* she tells how she found her boat *Felicity Ann* (already named when she found it). At seven metres she reckoned her rather on the small side but a good survey and extensive modifications made her ready and, on 18 May 1952, just under three years after the fatal shipwreck, she set off from Plymouth.

It was a slow voyage down to Portugal and North Africa and then across to the Canaries. She left the Canaries on the 1 December and arrived at Dominica on 24 January 1953 at an average speed of just over 2 knots. This was just a little faster than the crossing started just a few weeks before by Alain Bombard in a five metre Zodiac inflatable with a small sail. Bombard made the crossing to Barbados in 65 days living off the fish and plankton he caught and drinking sea-water.

After a prolonged stay in the Caribbean, Ann then worked her way to New York arriving on the 23 November 1953. Slow it may have been and uncomfortable much of it was but she became the first woman to cross the Atlantic single-handed.

She continued sailing *Felicity Ann* for a while and then turned to motor boating. She took a small cabin cruiser from Florida up the East Coast to the Great Lakes and down the Mississippi back to Florida and then explored Florida's offshore islands by speedboat with her third husband Bert (the second marriage was short-lived). Then she took up cat breeding in Florida, where she lived until her death in 1992.

Win, the butcher's daughter from Salford, fits in well with this diverse group of women. Some were more privileged than others, some had more opportunities and more guidance. Some seemed comfortable alone, even exhilarated, others needed companionship. Two qualities they almost certainly shared were single-mindedness and immense drive and that meant that they would have had little interest in whether they were first to do something. Others mattered little; they were too busy battling themselves to spend much time wondering whether they were pioneers.

WIN AS A WRITER

Win's three books were all published by Peter Davies and perhaps *Duffers on the Deep* is most successful not least because it has an audience among cruising sailors and the subject is well-suited to Win's direct, generally undecorated and journalistic style. It stands up extremely well against other similar accounts of epic voyages particularly because it so frankly admits to inexperience and to the mistakes that go with it and eschews the more romantic notions of the sea and ships. The relationship with Ron is an enigma for more reflective readers.

No Distress Signals seems slightly less successful partly because the audience is not quite as clear; too much about flying boats and the detailed goings on at Saunders-Roe for sailors and possibly not enough wartime context to make it really interesting for the general reader. Nonetheless it is a valuable record of her life covering the episodes associated with Sverdrup, the birth of Tony and some of the immediate post-war period.

Under Six Planets is an entertaining account of her life up to about 1950 and the move to London. If it has a deficiency as a biography it is a certain coyness about some events and people. The death of Elsie's baby seems to have been important in the family but it is left, for whatever reason, quite mysterious. Some of the names of people were withheld and some were evidently pseudonyms. Ron is referred to as Duncan in the early part — but it seems quite possible that Hubert and many others were not the real names of the people involved. There is hardly any mention of her female friends, notably Marjorie Cussons, and, from the point of view of a biographer, it is rather short on dates.

The part-manuscript of a book about her Amazon adventures exists and has been the basis of the account in this book. In much the same style as her later writings, it is a pity it was never finished and published. It is a lively description of a remarkable journey.

THE BOATS AND PLANES

After *Perula* was sold in 1974 she passed through several hands and, at one point, was converted to a gaff-rigger and for a while the topsides were painted yellow. Given that she had poor sailing characteristics and the sails were more for steadying her than propelling her, the modification could have been effective as well as pretty. She did still roam to the Netherlands and, at least once, to Brest in France for the veteran boat rally held there. She was based on the Medway for several years but the owner decided round about 2010 to go to Falmouth. On the way she developed problems while passing through Rye Bay on the south coast and was taken into Rye and put on a slip. She was there in 2012, the insides in the chaos that soon overtakes boats under restoration. She is registered as an Historic Vessel.

Tony sold *Seaway* and she was given a refit that removed the false funnel. A less impressive motor yacht as a result, she was last seen by Tony on the French Riviera about 2010.

G-EBLV, the plane Win learned to fly in, is now, much restored, owned by BAe Systems and kept in the Shuttleworth collection. Win's first plane G-EBVZ was crashed by a subsequent owner rather soon after he bought it and was a write-off. Her second plane, G-ABED, passed through several hands after she sold it and was stored, there being no civil aviation during the war, in a disused race-course grandstand at the airfield at Hooton in Cheshire. It was destroyed, along with eighteen other planes (which included Amy Johnson's G-ACAB), in a fire in August 1940.

RON

After the war Ron became North Wales Area Manager for Cawood Wharton Quarries. There were no more big adventures: he never went abroad again and never again flew in a small plane. He and Pat had a daughter, Hilary, in 1951. The house by the Gazelle was exchanged for a quieter, more remote one above Menai Bridge.

The relationship between Win and Ron remains an intriguing one. They were together for something like 20 years. In *Under Six Planets* Ron is referred to as "Duncan" until the sailing adventures when he appears as himself, a laconic and seemingly stolid partner in the expeditions. He was erased from earlier history by Pat who insisted that the phantom Duncan should be the person who went to Australia, up the Amazon and took to the air with Win.

He is referred to as Ron in the unpublished *Yellow Waters* manuscript but then Win was clearly considering an extensive revision of this. There are hand-written changes to the Preface indicating that she was thinking about writing the whole thing in the third person with herself as Erica Baines and Elsie as Mrs Baines. She appears to have given up on the task before addressing the question of what Ron was to be called in the revised version.

He seems to have been a perfect complement to Win over their 20 years together. Where she was impulsive, single-minded and determined in her adventures, Ron seems to have been more circumspect — although not lacking in enthusiasm. Without him she could not have achieved what she did and, of course, with Win, Ron experienced things beyond the dreams of most insurance brokers.

He always kept an eye on Tony's career (not least as a secret watcher of *General Hospital* and *Crossroads*) and managed to hear news of Win through a friend. It seems to have been a contented, quiet life as a happy family man and proud father and grandfather, never mentioning those early adventures. Sometimes, in later years, Hilary thought she saw a wistful look — perhaps he was streaking through the sky, paddling a canoe through a jungle or contemplating cold, gleaming mountains. He never said.

He died in 1979, a few years before Win. Two hundred people came to the funeral of this kind and remarkable man.

TONY

One of Ron's generous acts was to marry Win just before Tony was born. Generous because it seems to have been generally acknowledged that Ron was not Tony's father. Win told him sometime in the mid-1940s that he had been conceived in a boathouse on a coil of rope; his father, she insisted, was Dunny Walker.

The conception on the rope must have taken place sometime in March 1940, about the time of the Spitfire crash. Win and Ron were living on *Perula* at the time, quite possibly on or near Dunny's dock with a boathouse to hand. There was doubt about the story in some minds because Dunny had a childless Catholic marriage and the assumption had been that he was infertile.

Dunny never really acknowledged his parenthood during his lifetime but one day, when he and Marguerite lived at Victoria Terrace in the 1960s, Win and Tony visited. Just before they were to leave to return to London, Tony and Dunny were alone and Tony blurted out the words "Goodbye Father!" Dunny just stared at him, dumbstruck.

It was only later that there was some recognition: when Dunny died in 1967 he left £17,000 to Tony in his will. It was the money that bought *Seaway* — Tony's treasure and Win's final home.

SKETCH MAPS

King's Cup course 1930
The Amazon
The Irish Sea
The Menai Straits
UK, Norway and Svalbard
Svalbard and Bear Island

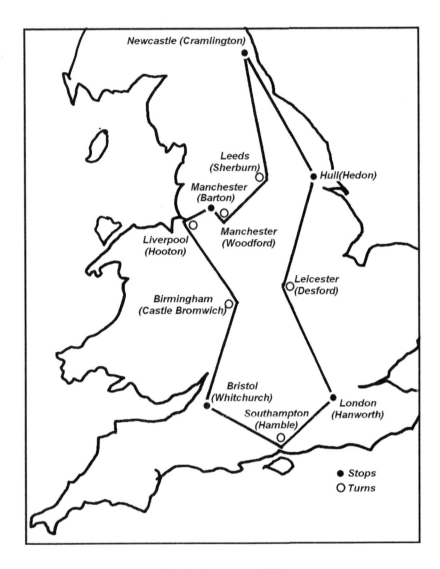

King's Cup course 1930

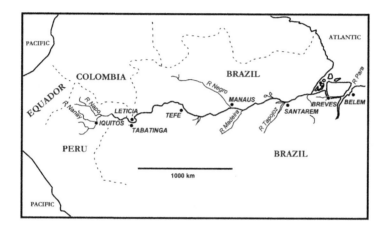

The Amazon

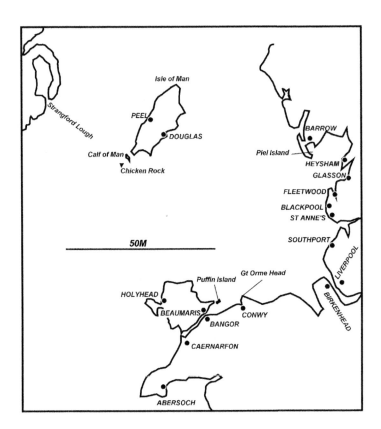

The Irish Sea

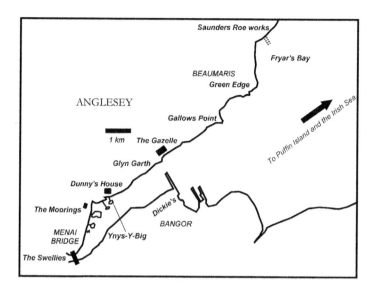

The Menai Straits

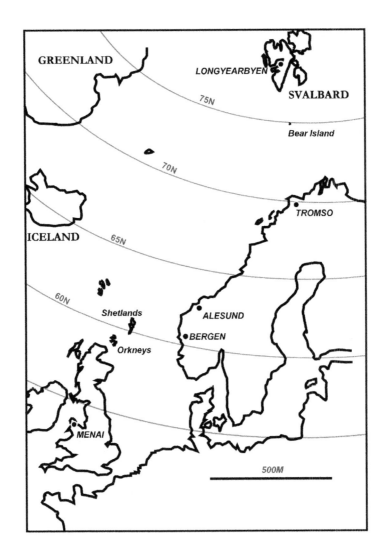

UK, Norway and Svalbard

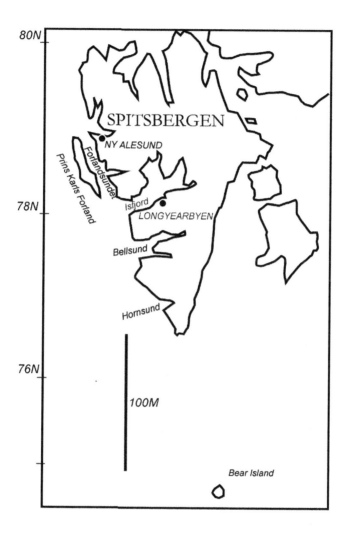

Svalbard and Bear Island

WINIFRED BROWN

PHOTOGRAPHS

Win and friends 1915

With the Lancia Lambda, Torquay

Sawley Brown

Elsie Brown

North Manchester Ladies Hockey picnic. Win in pads, Margery Walsh at the left of the basket looking down and Marjorie Cussons at the left of the second row.

The Touring Team of 1927 with Miss Thompson. Marjorie
Cussons on the left of the second row. Win third across

Win and Sammy Brown in G-EBVZ 9 February 1928

Ron with the King's Cup
and Win with the Siddeley
Trophy 1930

Ron in the canoe

Waiting for the fish. The poison fishing expedition

Perula being launched at Dickies; *Seaway* in the background

Perula in Ålesund

Ron, Sverdrup and Win at
Spitsbergen

Win and Dunny
Walker

Win and Tony at Green Edge

Win in the mid-50s. The
Frontispiece of *Under Six
Planets*

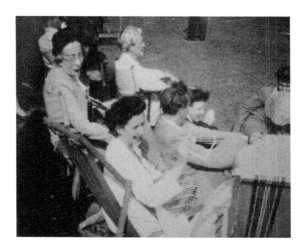

Win with Edith Evans, Peggy Ashcroft and
Michael Redgrave. Tony on the right

Ron in his garden at
Menai Bridge

PHOTOGRAPHS

Win and Tony about 1980

NOTES

PREFACE

1 *Duffers on the Deep*, Peter Davies: London, 1939: *No Distress Signals*, Peter Davies: London, 1952. *Under Six Planets*, Peter Davies: London, 1955.

THE YOUNG WIN

1 *Under Six Planets* (*USP*)

2 Slaters Directory 1905

3 *USP* p18

4 *USP* p18

5 *USP* p20 Edwards, a holder of the Distinguished Flying Cross, was a British comedian popular after the Second World War who grew a large "handlebar" moustache to cover the plastic surgery needed after crash-landing his Dakota at Arnhem in 1944. It became his trademark.

6 From Manchester Cruising Association records

7 The St Anne's house was disposed of before World War One (*USP*) and the pregnancy seems to have followed the purchase of Elwin in 1912.

8 *USP* p34

9 This has entered sociological literature (Housewifery in working class England, J Bourke, *Past and Present*, 147-197, 1994) as example of how working class wives withdrew favours from their husbands as a punishment. It is unlikely that Elsie would have been pleased to be regarded as a typical working class wife. After all, she had two tennis courts and a boat named after her.

10 Using the National Archives currency converter

11 Britain's Adventure Girl No. 1. *Manchester Evening Chronicle*, 5 Sept 1938

NEW LOVES

1 The fracas is recorded in *Under Six Planets*

2 *USP* p63

3 Light Aeroplane Flying Clubs, *Flight*, 14 August 1924 p513

4 Date based on her statement that the following week they went to the Yorkshire pageant *USP* p99

5 There were two volunteer instructors J C (Johnny) Cantrill and J J (Joe)Scholes. Since Joe Scholes instructed on LV while Cantrill used the other plane G-EBLR, it seems likely this was Joe. Three Score Years and Ten, Maher, P. ed., 1992., Manchester: Lancashire Aero Club.

6 Private Pilot's Licences were introduced by the Air Navigation Act 1920 as Class A Licences. Class B (Commercial) Licences allowed pilots to carry paying passengers. The Royal Aero Club introduced its Aviator's Certificates much earlier. The Private Pilot's Licence was in principle more demanding since it explicitly required a medical clearance and minimum flying experience but applicants for the Aviator's Certificate usually had these anyway.

GOALKEEPER

1 Negative by Lafayette in the National Portrait Gallery ref X69212 dated 19 April 1927

2 Lively boomerang. *The Advertiser(Adelaide.)*, 9 June 1927

3 *The Passing of the Aborigines* , Bates D M, 1938 Available at http://gutenberg.net.au/ebooks04/0400661.txt [Accessed March 20, 2011].

4 *USP* p117

5 At the Town Hall, *The Register(Adelaide)*, 6 June 1927

6   Women's Hockey Teams — Visitors Entertained, *The Argus(Melbourne)*, 13 June 1927. The mention of them leaving on the *Chitral* on 24 May is an error. This was the date of arrival in Australia.

7   Melbourne Talk, *Western Mail(Perth)*, 23 June 1927. Among other things the article mentions Win's Pilot's Licence and Marjorie Cussons's involvement with the family business.

8   Launched in 1913 on the Clyde the *Niagara* was known initially as the Titanic of the Pacific to reflect her style and luxury. There were around 200 first and 200 second class berths for her regular run between Sydney and Vancouver. Her image was somewhat tainted by the probably untrue story that she carried the great influenza epidemic to the antipodes in 1918. Her enduring fame came from her end. On 19 June 1940 she hit a mine laid by the German raider *Orion* off the coast near Auckland and sank, without loss of life, in 120 metres of water. The bulk of the eight tons of gold she was carrying was salvaged fairly quickly but enough remains there may be five bars to attract divers.

9   Originally the SS *Yugilbar*, 800 tons and built in Scotland in 1907 for the Australian coastal trade. She plied the Macleay River to Sydney route until sold to Burns Philp in 1925 and renamed. The Burns Philp fleet, with its distinctive back funnel with a wide horizontal white band containing a zig-zag black line, had numerous trading ships in the region. They traded until the 1970s although had disposed of much of their fleet well before that. The *Makatea* was scuttled off Beqa (or Mbenga) Island to the south of Fiji in 1933.

10   *USP* p133

11   The *Keewatin* crossed the lakes until 1966, always steam-powered and belching smoke. She is now a museum at Saugatuck-Douglas, Michigan. The *Assiniboia* was converted to oil-burning and her funnel cut off but she lasted just a year longer before being scrapped.

BACK IN THE AIR

1   Revue of pioneers. *Aerofrance*, November2010

2   Bill Lancaster - Love is in the air, Times Online, 2004, *Sunday Times*. Available at: http://www.timesonline.co.uk [Accessed April 19, 2011].

3   The company went on to produce many iconic aeroplanes: the Mosquito, the Vampire jet fighter and the Comet airliner. It produced the DH108 Swallow, in 1948 the first British plane to break the sound barrier, in the late forties. All three prototypes crashed killing their pilots, one of them was de Havilland's son. In 1960 the company was bought by Hawker Siddeley Aviation.

4   Manchester Woman Pilot,*Manchester Guardian,* 15 February 1928

5   Avro Heritage Centre Ref No 594/PO1886, 9 February 1928

6   The Afghan King at Croydon, *Manchester Guardian,* 22 March 1928

7   Air Accident at Dukinfield, *Manchester Guardian,* 26 March 1928

THE KING'S CUP AIR RACE

1   *USP* p169

2   Lancs Aero Club newsletter, *The Elevator* , December 1929

3   *USP* p185

4   The King's Cup air race, *Times,* 7 July 1930

5   Human bomb to plunge four miles, *Popular Science,* September 1932

CELEBRITY

1   From a local history internet forum. A Movietone News film held by the National Film Institute claims to be of the 1930 event.

2   *Daily Express,* 24 July 1930

3   Palace Varieties. *West Lancashire Evening Gazette,* 4 August 1930

4   Famous women at the Press Club, *Times,* 15 December 1930

OTHER LIVES

1   *Manchester Guardian,* 19 June 1931

2   There is something wrong here. In 1930 G-ABUG was allocated, presumably in a moment of civil service humour, to an aircraft that did indeed look like a bug: the Cierva autogyro. Elliott-Lynn's Avro Avian III was allocated G-EBUG much earlier, in 1927.

3 Win says in *USP* that the Isle of Man incident happened before the 1931 race. It seems clear from several sources that it happened just before the 1932 one.(For example, see the Isle of Man Airport website.

4 *Flight*, 13 October 1932

UP THE AMAZON

1 Distances relating to sea or river voyages are given in the main text in nautical miles. A nautical mile is equal to 1852 metres and is about 15% longer than a land (or statute) mile. It is not always clear which mile has been used in quotations — but it should not matter greatly. One knot is one nautical mile per hour.

2 The account of the Amazon adventure is based mainly from the unpublished and incomplete typescript written by Win around 1955 that was to form the basis for a book to be titled *Yellow Waters*. It has been supplemented with recollections of Tony Adams and some of the timings have been drawn from stamps in Ron Adams's passport. The evidence that the return was on the *Alban* comes from photographs in Hilary Date's collection.

3 *Yellow Waters* , Winifred Brown, Unpublished manuscript, about 1955 (referenced here as *YW*)

4 *Yellow Waters*(*YW*)

5 *YW*

6 *YW*

7 The visa in Ron's passport is dated 7 May so it seems that they received it two days later. The date of 10 May for the departure on the Belem comes from *YW*.

8 *YW*

9 *YW*

10 A small red insect that lives in the grass and, given a chance, burrows into the skin and causes massive irritation and sores. Win tried to deal with them by pouring disinfectant on her legs.

11 *YW*

12 *YW*

13 *YW*

14 Information from Tony Adams 2012

15 *USP* p239

LEARNING THE ROPES

1 *Duffers on the Deep*, Winifred Brown, Peter Davies, 1939 (referenced here as *DOD*)

TO NORWAY

1 *DOD* p76

2 Win made a pencil annotation later that changed the 13th to the 12th, the date she used in *DOD*. The following day is left as the 13 th. It is just possible that it was more dramatic to have been in Tafjord on Friday the 13 th.

3 Teddy cigarettes were introduced by Norwegian cigarette manufacturer J L Tiedemann and named after Theodore "Teddy" Roosevelt. At the time British and American companies were combining in an attempt to dominate the Norwegian market and Roosevelt was trying to fight such trust activity at home. He appeared, a smoking hero, on the packets of the unfiltered cigarettes to the 1970s. The brand was still in existence at the end of the century.

4 *DOD* p111

5 This is one of the few points where the outside world enters Win's writings to this point. The Spanish Civil War had been raging for just over a year, started by the rising of military garrisons against the republican government in July 1936. On 25 September 1936 the insurgents bombed Bilbao killing over 100 inhabitants, resulting in the murder of 60 of the many hostages held by the republicans in the city. A 500 pound bomb fell on one of the main street, the Alamada de Recalde, and it may be this that was in the photograph. Bilbao fell to the insurgents in June 1937 but the war raged on for almost two years, a bitter and murderous struggle, until the insurgents captured Madrid. How the man from Bilbao was involved we are not told.

TO SPITSBERGEN

1 The notes are appended in full to *DOD*.

2 *Norwegian Cruising Guide* , J Armitage and M Brackenbury, Adlard Coles Nautical: London, 1996 p95

3 Electricity in the home, *Manchester Guardian*, 29 January 1938

4 Ladies Northern Foursomes, *Times*, 8 April 1938

5 The entrance through Kirk Sound was the one used by the German submarine U-47 on the night of 13 October 1939 when, under the command of Lt Gunther Prien, she slipped through the blockships at high tide into Scapa Flow. She torpedoed the battleship Royal Oak at her moorings just three miles northwest of the entrance before leaving the way she had come. The Royal Oak sank with the loss of 833 lives. The eastern entrances were then blocked by causeways built by Italian POWs although they were hardly complete when the war ended.

6 *DOD* p169

7 Where they hoped to see Torghatten, the famous hat-shaped mountain with a large hole in it. Legend has it that a horseman, spurned by a maid, shot an arrow at her but the local king threw his hat just in time to intercept the missile. At this moment they were all, turned to stone, a perpetual risk at critical moments in those far-off heroic days of myth. Win has a different version of the myth not involving love but since the mountain was shrouded in cloud as they passed, we need not dwell.

8 *DOD* p184

9 *DOD* p194

10 Exactly 10 years before, on 18 June 1928, the Norwegian polar explorer Roald Amundsen had died when the seaplane he was travelling in to Spitsbergen, lost in fog, crashed into the sea. The last radio message from the plane was received at 1845 when it was probably just a few miles from where Win was anxiously looking for Bear Island. A few pieces of the seaplane have been washed up since the tragedy but an expedition in 2009 using a robot submarine failed to find any wreckage. Win seems to have been unaware of this anniversary.

11 *DOD* p226

12 *DOD* p231 Jeg har varet på besök ombord i Perula, hvor jeg fikk en udmerket aftens. Jeg har den störsto beundring for hvad Perula har utrettet, seilet fra England over til Norge og dufra til Spitsbergen.

13 *DOD* p240

14 It is a tradition for British yachts to dip their ensign by lowering it briefly and then raising it again as a form of salute on meeting warships of any nationality or Royal yachts at sea. It is also usual to salute the Commodore of a yacht club if you are flying the burgee of that club. There was no good reason for *Perula* to salute the *Cutty Sark*. She was probably flying the White Ensign, normally reserved for the Royal Navy, because Westminster was (surely) a member of the Royal Yacht Squadron.

15 "Heaving to" is a way of setting the sails and lashing the tiller so that the boat comes nearly to a stop and stays under control without human intervention. It usually results in a much less violent motion than ploughing through large waves.

16 Britain's adventure girl No. 1, *Manchester Evening Chronicle*, 5 September 1938.

SNOWDROP IN WINTER

1 *NDS* p20 He may actually have been Mr Tillemont-Thomason and thus possibly related to Frederick Ernest Tillemont-Thomason CE, FRSGS, prominent geographer and founder of the Empire Educational League. Frederick's daughters were christened Corawee de Courtheil Tillemont-Thomason and Victoire de Courtheil Tillemont-Thomason suggesting both exotic origins and a sense of style entirely compatible with Win's Mr Tilly. Frederick, one feels, would have known how to handle a silk-lined cape and a cane. A photograph of Frederick matches Win's description of her mentor very closely.

2 This seems to be the question in her mind on *NDS* p22

3 Winifred Brown: Duffers on the Deep, Advert, *Observer*, 4 June 1939

4   There is little detail of the passage in *NDS* and the account above comes from *Perula*'s log and newspaper weather forecasts. Win does say they had eleven gale warnings during the trip.

5   The area had been occupied by the Japanese in 1937 during the Sino-Japanese war but several concessions had been left under the control of foreign powers and one of them was to Britain. The Japanese believed (correctly as it happened) that four of the Chinese nationalists who had assassinated a Japanese bank official were hiding in Tientsin. The British arrested them and handed them over briefly to the Japanese who tortured them and extracted a confession before returning them. When the British refused to hand them over for punishment, the Japanese fleet blockaded the port. The crisis was resolved in August when the Chinese were handed over and executed.

6   On 20 July, according to the logbook, they took *Perula* to Bjørnøya a mile or two north of Ålesund and left her there until 18 August

7   Win may have been told that a fellow spirit had been on the boat just a few years before. Norwegian, Wanny Wolstad (1895-1959) had taken it from Tromsø, where she had been working as a taxi driver, to Spitsbergen in 1932. She spent five successive winters hunting and trapping animals including polar bears in the Hornsund area

8   The *Athenia* was sunk in contravention of the international convention and the Germany Navy's own instructions at the time. Both forbade the sinking of passenger vessels unless the ship was evacuated first. Germany denied that it had been responsible for the sinking (claiming the ship had hit a British mine) until, at the Nuremberg trials in 1946, it was admitted by Admiral Doenitz.

WAR WORK

1   Allison R S, Ruthin Castle: a private hospital for the investigation and treatment of obscure medical diseases (1923-1950), *Ulster Med J*, 46(1), 22–31,1977

2   *NDS* p65

3   In May 1943 Admiral Doenitz told Adolf Hitler that about one third of the submarines at sea had been lost in just one month.

4   This would have been Vice-Admiral Frederick Avenal Sommerville DSO. A veteran of the submarine service from the First World War he had retired in the mid-1930s. However he returned to the Royal Navy and became a volunteer Commodore of Atlantic convoys in 1941. He would thus certainly have had an interest in Catalinas.

5   *NDS* p271

PEACE

1   A Solent Flight , Ivor J Hilliker, Kingfisher, 1990 p111

2   As recorded in the probate record. She died, aged 76, on the public highway in Greenfield Road, Colwyn Bay close to where she was living. Probate was granted to Win and Olive Hudson, spinster, for £1067 16s 5d

3   Win's Wartime Identity Card records the move on 26 September 1949 but it could have taken place some time before.

SOUTH

1   *Observer*, 19 October 1952

2   Far voyaging, *Observer*, 21 December 1952

3   My thanks to Natalie Shrigley-Feigl for this story and the next one about the birthday celebrations.

4   *Times*, 23 July 194

5   *Times*, 12 January 1960

POSTSCRIPT

1...*Who Hath Desired the Sea*, Peter Gerard, Arthur Barker: London,1962. *Gypsy Afloat*, Ella K Maillart, Heinemann: London,1942. *Who Called that Lady a Skipper?*, Marion R Hart, Vanguard Press: New York, 1938. *My Ship is So Small*, Ann Davison, Peter Davies: London, 1956.

INDEX

Printed in Great Britain
by Amazon

17762795R00185